# NELSON
## NAVY & NATION

# NELSON
## NAVY & NATION

### THE ROYAL NAVY & THE BRITISH PEOPLE 1688-1815

EDITED BY

QUINTIN COLVILLE & JAMES DAVEY

INTRODUCTION BY N.A.M. RODGER

NATIONAL
MARITIME
MUSEUM

NAVAL INSTITUTE PRESS
Annapolis, Maryland

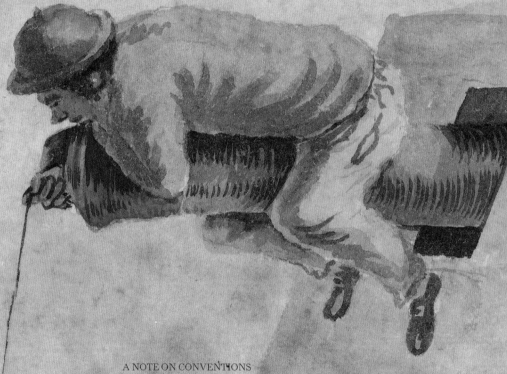

*A Sailor fishing off a gun Pallas*
*Jan.y 7s avrl 13*

This book is published to accompany a long-term gallery in the National Maritime Museum at Greenwich, entitled 'Nelson, Navy, Nation'.

© National Maritime Museum, 2013

First published in Great Britain in 2013 by Conway, a Division of Anova Books Ltd 10 Southcombe Street, London W14 0RA www.anovabooks.com www.conwaypublishing.com Twitter: @conwaybooks

Published and distributed in the United States of America and Canada by The Naval Institute Press, 291 Wood Road, Annapolis, Maryland 21402-5043 www.nip.org

Library of Congress Control Number: 2013940546

Published in association with Royal Museums Greenwich, the group name for the National Maritime Museum, Royal Observatory Greenwich, Queen's House and *Cutty Sark*. www.rmg.co.uk

All rights reserved. No part of this publication may be reproduced, stored in a retrieval system, or transmitted in any form or by any means electronic, mechanical, photocopying, recording or otherwise, without the prior written permission of the copyright owner.

ISBN 978-159114-6032
Printed by 1010 Printing International Ltd, China.

A NOTE ON CONVENTIONS

The information in this publication has been given as fully and accurately as possible but some areas of uncertainty inevitably exist. Captions for paintings and items on paper include titles, artists/makers, publishers, materials and techniques where known and relevant. For reasons of space, those for most other objects do not give materials, techniques and manufacturers. Dates of creation, where established, are given throughout. Relevant English inscriptions are given where they would otherwise be illegible. All the images and objects featured are from the National Maritime Museum or collections entrusted to its care. Reference numbers are given for every object, with full credit and collection information on p. 235.

Frontispiece (PREVIOUS PAGES): The Battle of Trafalgar, 21 October 1805, by J.M.W. Turner, oil on canvas, 1822–24 (BHC0565) This page: A Sailor fishing off a Gun [on the] *Pallas*, by Gabriel Bray, watercolour, 1775 (PAJ2016)

# CONTENTS

# DIRECTOR'S FOREWORD

To me, as director of Royal Museums Greenwich, the connections between Nelson, navy and nation seem obvious. Greenwich has been linked with the Royal Navy for half a millennium: Henry VIII founded two Royal Dockyards at Woolwich and Deptford, close to his birthplace and favoured retreat here. During the period covered by this book, the establishment of the Royal Hospital for Seamen at Greenwich, and the completion of its magnificent buildings, strengthened the local connection with the 'senior service'. In the 1820s, the Hospital's Painted Hall – itself a soaring monument to navy and nation, in which Nelson's body lay in state before his funeral – became the National Gallery of Naval Art, launching the modern role of Greenwich in presenting Britain's maritime heritage to the public. This display was soon enhanced by other relics and objects, many associated with Admiral Lord Nelson.

A century after the founding of this 'Naval Gallery', a successful campaign began to create a National Maritime Museum that would tell the story of Britain's eventful engagement with the sea from the viewpoint of both the Royal Navy and the merchant fleet. When the new Museum opened in 1937, it took over the privilege of caring for and interpreting the rich pre-existing Greenwich-based collections, as well as new ones added by major benefactors like Sir James Caird. Throughout all these developments, there was an unshakeable belief in, and understanding of, the importance of the Royal Navy to Britain's history, ongoing prosperity and very survival. The connections between Nelson, navy and nation were, therefore, still clear and present.

But times and perceptions change. Audiences visiting Greenwich today are more diverse than before and less imbued with (or impressed by) the certainties that once informed displays celebrating the age of Britain's seaborne empire. Now, Nelson is as likely to be followed by Mandela as preceded by Horatio. The Museum's new long-term gallery – 'Nelson, Navy, Nation' – reflects these shifts and presents anew the fascinating story of the Royal Navy and the British people in the 'long eighteenth century'. This book, which develops the gallery's themes, is illustrated from the Museum's world-class collections and underpinned by scholarship based on the unrivalled archival holdings of its Caird Library.

I thank the editors – our curators of naval history, Quintin Colville and James Davey – for their efforts in putting the volume together. They have assembled a range of distinguished contributors who represent the breadth of new scholarship on the subject. It is my belief that both the book and the associated gallery demonstrate the continued relevance of that enduring nexus of Nelson, navy and nation for twenty-first-century audiences.

Dr Kevin Fewster, AM FRSA

# EDITORS' PREFACE

In recent decades, naval history has been enriched by a wealth of new research from within and beyond the discipline. The Royal Navy has been used, for instance, to open fresh perspectives on questions of national identity and imperialism. Scholars of economics and the British state have explained its successes and failures in terms of finance, governance and administration. Others have re-examined the social realities of shipboard life, the nature of naval medicine and surgery or those resilient mythologies about maggot-ridden naval food and the workings of the press gang. Looking across this varied field, what seems most apparent is that there has been a shift from the study of the navy as a separate and separable institution, to an interest in the complex relationships between ship and shore, Britain and its empire, navy and nation.

This is, therefore, an exciting time to address this burgeoning subject. Capitalising on such vibrant scholarship, the chapters that follow focus on a period in which navy and nation went through remarkable changes. The years between William of Orange's arrival on English shores in 1688 and the defeat of Napoleon in 1815 were defined by intense competition and conflict with great European powers. This was also a time in which social, cultural and economic developments allowed more people than ever before to engage with national affairs through rising literacy rates, consumer practices and popular politics. Moreover, the political unions of 1707 and 1801 (with Scotland and then Ireland) saw the 'British' nation emerge as a territorial entity for the first time. It was within this crucible that the Royal Navy was transformed from an outnumbered and often isolated force into one that dominated the world's oceans.

Ranging across this chronology and many of its component themes, the book's contributors have placed the story in sharp relief. In so doing, they have created the context for understanding the career of a man who brought these worlds of navy and nation together as no other: Admiral Lord Nelson. The book locates him within this broader setting: the people and agendas that preceded him, the sophisticated and professional institution within which he served, and the civilian society that interpreted his achievements. It is only by these means that his life and dazzling celebrity can fully be appreciated. Finally, both the book and the gallery it accompanies demonstrate that the extraordinary collections of the National Maritime Museum not merely illustrate but also embody this multifaceted history.

QUINTIN COLVILLE AND JAMES DAVEY

# INTRODUCTION

## N.A.M. Rodger

The business of any museum, and the displays within its galleries, is to engage in a dialogue between history and memory. History is a record and an understanding of the past, as accurate as scholarship can make it, but memory is a dynamic force that constantly reinterprets the past to serve the present. Individuals continually reshape their memories as they look back on their past in the light of their present, and nations do the same. As individuals and as societies, our personalities are composed of our memories, for it is our experiences which have made us what we are. Our history is therefore inescapable; our choice is whether to learn from it and through it, or to ignore it and be imprisoned by the unacknowledged prejudices and assumptions we have inherited. The gallery that this volume accompanies deals with one of the key personalities and periods of British history. The extraordinary public interest in the bicentenary of Trafalgar in 2005 showed that the personality of Nelson and the dramas of his life have lost none of their power to arouse emotion and fascination. The navy, especially but not only of Nelson's time, remains to a greater extent than people realise a fundamental element of the British national identity.

It follows that both gallery and book have to present a dialogue between history and myth, which are not enemies like truth and falsehood, but rather kissing cousins. The 'myth of sea power in English history', as it has been called, is a strong and simple version of the truth, stripped of complexities and a good deal of context, highly coloured in parts and always tending to flatter the national self-esteem, but nevertheless derived from real events.[1] Its origins have been traced to the Elizabethan age, and specifically to the 1560s and 1570s, when English seamen with covert official encouragement joined the 'Calvinist International', the alliance of French, Dutch and Scottish Protestant seamen, to make their fortunes and advance the cause of true religion by a plundering war against Spanish and Portuguese shipping. The French Protestant seamen of La Rochelle, in particular, taught the English that true, national naval power was intimately associated with Protestantism, freedom, and private profit. In the national memory, the Elizabethan naval war against Spain was a naval triumph, but (1588 excepted) not a triumph of the Royal Navy. What people remembered was the private men-of-war which raided the Spanish Main and the Spanish convoys: Sir Francis Drake, not Lord Howard of Effingham. That part of the naval war which seized the national imagination was fought by private interests rather than by the crown, so that the prestige did not go to strengthen an image of royal power but one of national liberty. It made English sea power the ideal expression of the

A Union flag flown on the *Queen Charlotte* at the Battle of the 'Glorious First of June', 1794 (AAA0730)

nation in arms. At the core of the English political idea of sea power, as it was now established, lay a trinity of associations: religion, freedom, and money. True, natural and national English sea power was securely attached to these three, and the three belonged together as inseparable parts of a single system.

This idea of sea power was securely fixed in the English political imagination throughout the seventeenth and eighteenth centuries. Without it, it is difficult to imagine that parliament would have consistently supported the arduous and very expensive business of creating and sustaining a first-class navy. For governments, and especially monarchs, the navy was essential, but the naval myth was often an embarrassment. The political nation knew that the right kind of naval war

could not fail to be successful – meaning a war against Catholic rather than Protestant enemies, in support of the authority of parliament rather than the crown. Both Charles I and Charles II discovered to their cost that the Royal Navy was politically popular only in the right kind of war, which was not the kind they wanted or needed to fight. When William III seized the throne in 1688, and enlisted his new kingdoms of England and Scotland in wars against France, which lasted, off and on, for more than a century, he solved only part of the problem. The long-term consequence of 1688 (though certainly not William III's intention) was to create a governmental structure in which parliament controlled the navy, which became the darling of representative government and the symbol of Britain's balanced constitution. But

1688 also installed the first of a line of foreign monarchs, all of them generals with Continental possessions to defend, and committed to land campaigns on the Continent. As the leading Catholic powers, France and Spain were obviously the right enemies, but in the public eye this was still the wrong kind of war. Throughout the eighteenth century, therefore, a naval war was the easy, obvious and popular cry of the opposition (of any party, for the naval myth was common property). Naval power was intimately linked with popular radicalism, parliamentary and extra-parliamentary opposition to the crown. The navy never lacked for political friends, but there was a flavour of independence, if not subversion, about it. A naval hero like Admiral Edward Vernon found his natural political home in opposition, arousing popular excitement with his (quite spurious) charges that George II's ministers had neglected the navy and traitorously refused to fight Spain. A 'mad and vain nation...warmed and hardened by pride and prejudice', identified with the traditional, patriotic myths of national naval superiority, which dictated that a war against Spain must necessarily be easy, glorious and profitable.[2] Pious, virtuous and blessed by God, English sea power could not but be prosperous. Once again the naval virtues were evoked by references to Queen Elizabeth's reign. Thomson and Arne united to remind the opposition of Britannia's glories, and to conjure up a future golden age in which the traitor 'Don Roberto' (the prime minister Sir Robert Walpole)

Departure of William of Orange from Hellevoetsluis in 1688, style of Abraham Storck, oil on canvas, late seventeenth century (BHC0325)

ABOVE Dioramic model of the British victory at the Battle of the Saintes in 1782, after Richard Payton, c.1783 (MDL0011)
BELOW Halfpenny token, 1796 (MEC1732)

would be ejected from office, British sea power restored, and Britons nevermore be slaves. The navy, 'as essential to our Safety & Wealth as Parliament or Magna Charta', was the guarantor of freedom, virtue and conquest.[3] Admirals who failed to do their duty by the myths of sea power, like Mathews, Lestock or Byng, were condemned to public execration, if not execution. A generation later during the American War of Independence, Admiral Keppel briefly attained the status of Protestant hero, not for having won a victory, but for having diverted the navy from oppressing the Americans back to its proper role of fighting Catholics and defending English liberties.[4]

By the late eighteenth century, sea power had been an essential part of the patriotic English self-image for over two centuries, and patriotism had always been the first resort of the opposition. Governments might be obliged to take some account of inconvenient strategic facts, but oppositions could always triumph in the virtual reality of the English political imagination, in which sea power was ever-victorious, in the right kind of war, against the right kind of enemy. The navy was still, in the words of the *Gentleman's Magazine* in 1798, 'the sacred *palladium* of our laws, our religion, and our liberties, not to perish or be overthrown but with the downfall of Great Britain itself'.[5] Already, however, the moral and political value of sea power was changing. In the Seven Years War, the elder William Pitt (with a little help from Frederick the Great) made the national myth work for the government. In the American War of Independence, the spectacle of Whig peers openly rejoicing at British naval defeats, and Whig admirals refusing to fight the French, did a good deal to disgust public opinion and uncouple sea power from the opposition. After the war, still aided by the folly of its opponents, and later by the violence of the French revolutionaries, the younger William Pitt's government began to appropriate naval patriotism for itself. Anti-Catholicism, for so long an essential part of the English definition of liberty, began to wilt in the 1790s in the face of aggressive atheism. The navy now became the 'characteristic and constitutional defence' of the country, as Wellington called it, and its adoption as part of the political constitution of the state (as opposed to the moral constitution of the nation) marks a significant development.[6] The nationalisation of patriotism changed the symbolic value of the navy. To the consternation of the conservative, real seamen were allowed to walk in the 1797 procession organised by the government to give thanks for recent naval victories. Naval temples, in which to celebrate the new national cult, were proposed and in some cases built. Naval monuments to the fallen heroes were erected at public expense. Poets good and bad turned to the navy – 'the scene of our Triumphs, the source of our Wealth, and the safeguard of our Empire', in the words of the Poet Laureate Henry Pye – for inspiration.[7] William Pitt had caught the Whigs bathing and stolen their clothes.

Radical critics could no longer appeal to the easy certainties of the English naval myth, for the navy now belonged to the government as well as the people. Naval warfare still came naturally to them as the language of political rhetoric, but they had to invent new myths of sea power of their own. Thus, in the unpublished early version of his epic poem *Madoc*, finished in the same year as the naval procession of 1797, the young (and still

radical) Robert Southey enriched English literature with a lengthy description of the otherwise unrecorded naval battles between Prince Madoc of Gwynedd and the Aztecs. In this the brutally efficient Welsh stand as figures for the Royal Navy; while the freedom-loving Aztecs, their piety and domestic virtues marred only by the occasional human sacrifice, represent the French republicans.[8]

The navy of Nelson, therefore, was newly respectable, and even more central to national life and the national self-image than ever, but there were still things about it which were uncomfortable to the establishment. Its eclectic approach to recruiting officers, who received a thorough practical training alongside boys of

ABOVE Locket depicting Britannia, late eighteenth century (MNT0070) BELOW Earthenware bowl inscribed 'Success to the British Tars', late eighteenth century (AAA4438)

Nelson himself was by no means a gentleman born, and his ostentatious liaison with Emma Hamilton was exactly the sort of vulgar and embarrassing public misconduct that gentlemen would have instinctively avoided. It is clear that there were many among the common people and the lower deck who celebrated him partly for that reason, as a subversive, anti-establishment hero.

The navy of Nelson's day was a social pioneer, combining the traditional military ethos of honour and courage, which had always attached to the gentleman officer, with the thoroughly middle-class

LEFT Ceramic punchbowl, eighteenth century (AAA4425)
BELOW Rear Admiral Sir Horatio Nelson, by Leonardo Guzzardi, oil on canvas, 1798–99 (BHC2895)

no family or prospects, and were passed fit for a gentleman on the basis of a professional examination, stretched eighteenth-century conventions to the limit. By this means people of obscure birth were raised to the status of officers and gentlemen, without necessarily learning the manners and civility which were the badge of gentility. Commentators throughout the eighteenth century noted 'this roughness, which clings to the seaman's behaviour like tar to his trowsers, [and] makes him unfit for all civil and polite society'.[9] When George III visited his fleet after the Battle of the Dogger Bank in 1781, the captains were presented to him on the quarterdeck of the flagship, while the Prince of Wales and his friends sniggered at their clumsy bows:

*The manner, and awkward shyness of some
of these gallant men, unused to ceremonials
of this nature, might possibly at another time,
have occasioned somewhat of mirth, perhaps
of ridicule, but on an occasion like this, such
ill-timed levity was unpardonable. I hope it
was not so fully seen as I saw it – I was hurt
at the moment, & shall ever be so, when I
recall the circumstance.*[10]

# UNDRESS COAT (1795–1812 PATTERN) AND WAISTCOAT WORN BY VICE-ADMIRAL LORD NELSON AT THE BATTLE OF TRAFALGAR IN 1805
## (UNI0024, UNI0065)

The uniform coat Nelson was wearing when he was shot is deservedly one of the National Maritime Museum's most famous exhibits. Few artefacts have so much power after so long to arouse emotion as this garment, with the bullet-hole in the shoulder by which he met his end. The history of the coat is the history of Nelson's posthumous reputation in miniature. Initially preserved by Emma Hamilton as a private relic of her lost lover, it was given up by her to J.J. Smith in satisfaction of a debt shortly before she died, when her and Nelson's reputations were at their lowest. By 1845, Nelson the public scandal was gradually being replaced in the public mind by Nelson the fallen hero, and in that year Prince Albert bought the coat from Smith's widow and presented it to the Naval Gallery in the Painted Hall at Greenwich Hospital. There it became the essential Nelson relic, and passed into the care of the National Maritime Museum on its foundation.

In itself, the coat is in most respects a normal vice-admiral's undress (that is, everyday) uniform, with the notable distinction that Nelson possessed not less than four orders of chivalry: the Order of the Bath, the Order of the Crescent awarded by the Sultan of Turkey, the Order of St Ferdinand and of Merit awarded by Ferdinand IV of Naples, and the German Order of St Joachim.

It is sometimes suggested that wearing all four stars was a mark of vanity which attracted enemy fire, but it was no odder than a modern officer wearing his medal ribbons. Indeed, it is more noteworthy that Nelson was wearing a rather shabby undress uniform, with inconspicuous cloth replicas of his stars, and moreover he had forgotten to put on his sword. Many officers, for whom the day of battle was the summit of their professional lives, wore their full-dress uniforms in action, as Captain Hardy did. If the French musketeer who shot Nelson could see anyone distinctly through the smoke, he was probably aiming at the tall and flamboyant figure of the captain rather than the admiral. Nelson certainly was conscious of his public appearance; it was another way in which he betrayed that he was no gentleman, for a gentleman, and even more a nobleman born, knew himself to be superior and cared nothing for the opinion of lesser mortals. This self-consciousness, however, was also part of his greatness as an admiral. He possessed to a high degree the showman-like skill of many of the greatest commanders in history, who knew how to project their personalities with mannerisms and tricks of appearance so as to arouse the loyalty of masses of subordinates, few of whom could ever know them personally or even hear them speak. It showed in his use of the new Home Popham signals to make a one-sentence 'speech' to his fleet on the morning of Trafalgar – the signal 'England Expects That Every Man Will Do His Duty' – and it shows in his distinctive collection of orders and his empty sleeve, which allowed him to be instantly identified in a crowd ashore.

professional character of the seaman and navigator. 'Recollect that you must be a Seaman to be an Officer', Nelson advised a young protégé, 'and also that you cannot be a good Officer without being a Gentleman.'[11] The boy was a kinsman of Emma Hamilton, who was the daughter of a blacksmith, and he was certainly not a gentleman by birth: in effect Nelson and the navy were proposing a new gentility of behaviour rather than property or family. Among Nelson's contemporaries there were officers who had risen from very humble social origins, including a number who had been pressed into the navy, a mulatto captain who may have been born a slave, and a vice-admiral who was reputed to have been flogged around the fleet for desertion as a young man.[12]

In British society as a whole there seems to have been a gradual divergence between the public perceptions of the nobleman and the gentleman towards the end of the eighteenth century. The nobleman was tainted by association with immorality, irreligion, effeminacy and France, while the gentleman profited by connection with what had hitherto been middle-class virtues, as the middle classes themselves rose in public esteem. Sea officers were particularly well placed to benefit from this shift of ideas, because they had always adhered to the bourgeois standards of professional skill and devotion to duty, which were now coming to be regarded as national and patriotic qualities transcending birth. Since the seventeenth century the 'Wapping Tar' had been

Visit of George III to Admiral Lord Howe's flagship the *Queen Charlotte*, following the Battle of the 'Glorious First of June', 1794, by Henry Perronet Briggs, oil on canvas, 1828 (BHC0476)

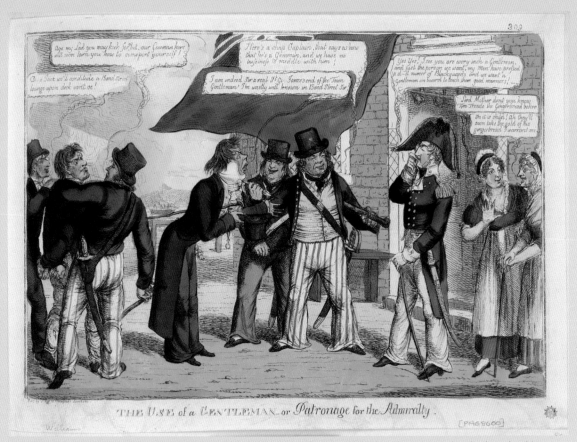

*The Use of a Gentleman – or Patronage for the Admiralty*, by Charles Williams, published by Thomas Tegg, hand-coloured etching, c.1810 (PAG8600)

a symbol of unaffected courage and patriotism, to be contrasted with the foppish effeminacy with which French manners corrupted the upper classes. Now sea officers and seamen were elevated from honest but somewhat comic figures of the stage, to the status of symbolic national heroes. Their plain, manly sincerity contrasted with the disloyal, Frenchified effeminacy of the Whig aristocracy, and the atheistic republicanism of the radicals. Indeed, the social characteristics of the nobility, for all its glamour and prestige, were acquiring further negative overtones. The aristocrats, who rejoiced in their country's defeats in the American War of Independence and supported the French Revolution; the 'macaronis', like Charles James Fox, who ostentatiously rejected religion and morality, only cemented a

contrast in the public mind between noblemen and patriots. By contrast the sea officer, regardless of his origins, had come to embody English virtues entirely compatible with gentility. As early as 1787, Nelson (to the astonishment of his Victorian editor) described his Portuguese-born boatswain as 'a most excellent gentleman'.[13] Outsiders still perceived the navy as less aristocratic than the army, but where formerly they had criticised its lack of polish, now they praised its patriotic virtue. Having seen both services in action in Corsica in the 1790s, the lawyer and statesman Sir Gilbert Elliot preferred the navy for his son: 'The character of the profession is infinitely more manly. They are full of life and action, while on shore it is all high lounge and still life.'[14]

Chatham dockyard, by Joseph Farington, oil on canvas, 1785–94 (BHC1782)

Changing attitudes towards class and authority, on both sides of the Channel, altered the conduct of war at sea. The French revolutionaries, affecting to despise the professional training in which the old aristocratic officer corps had taken pride (and unable to supply their skills), replaced the classical tactics of skilful manoeuvre and concentrated gunnery with a simple reliance on boarding. Just as attack in column had superseded the line ashore, so at sea the romantic ardour of the *peuple en masse* would sweep away the effete tactics of a discredited order. It did not work. Scientific gunnery proved decisively superior to political correctness, and in numerous actions French boarding parties suffered horrific casualties as they massed within close range of British

gunners. The French did, however, have an effect on British naval tactics. Since the French revolutionaries were indifferent to the useless sacrifice of life, and refused to surrender when their position was hopeless, British officers had to get into the habit of boarding the undefeated enemy. In an exceptional case, even a flag officer, Commodore Nelson at the Battle of Cape St Vincent in 1797, led a boarding party: nothing comparable had happened in the navy since the reign of Henry VIII. One result was to reinforce in the naval context the new classless, patriotic heroism, in which the officer led from the front, accepting the same dangers as his men, but even more of them. The new patriotic and ideological nature of war demanded no less.[15]

ABOVE *John Bull taking a Luncheon: – or – British Cooks, cramming Old Grumble-Gizzard, with Bonne-Chére*,
by James Gillray, published by Hannah Humphrey, hand-coloured etching, 24 October 1798 (PAF3941)
OPPOSITE Boardroom of the Admiralty (detail), by John Hill after Thomas Rowlandson and Augustus Charles Pugin,
published by Rudolph Ackermann, hand-coloured aquatint, 1 January 1808 (PAD1358)

The eighteenth-century navy participated in, exemplified and often led the transformations of society at many levels. Its administrative structure of offices, dockyards, stores, foundries and factories constituted the largest and most technologically advanced industrial system in the Western world (see pp. 18–19). The immense financial burden of prolonged war both required and encouraged the development of a fiscal and financial machine of unequalled depth and resilience. Both of these have been identified as key national strengths which raised Britain to the status of the world's leading trading power by the end of the century, and prepared the way for the Industrial Revolution. In the national myth of sea power, victory was won by heroism and skill, but in the real world it depended just as much on the administrative and commercial systems which built the ships and fed the men. These are examples of the real history which the gallery reinserts into the naval myth. This is a process which never ends, for scholarship continually advances. Only very recently, for example, it has been discovered that the proportion of men pressed into the navy during the French Revolutionary Wars was 16 per cent, a very much lower figure than has ever been suggested before.[16] In time this will force a complete reinterpretation of many traditional views of daily life and discipline in the navy. The new fact directly contradicts a cherished feature of the popular myth. Thus the dialogue of myth and history continues.

# 1

# INVASION AND THREAT

## Ted Vallance

Looking at the 'Glorious Revolution' of 1688–89 from the perspective of the role of sea power involves challenging three commonly held beliefs about English history. The first is the idea that, since the Norman Conquest, England has been secure from foreign invasion – providentially protected by its maritime 'moat' as George Savile, Earl of Halifax, described it in his *A Rough Draft of a New Model at Sea* (1694). God, Halifax said, had confined the English to their island, 'not as a Penalty, but a Grace, and one of the greatest that can be given to Mankind. Happy Confinement, that hath made us Free, Rich, and Quiet'. In fact, the revolution that brought William, Prince of Orange, the Dutch stadholder, to the English throne, was precipitated by a successful seaborne assault.[1] The second assumption is that the revolution of 1688–89 was 'glorious' because it was peaceful. Yet, the revolution led to England's involvement in William's lengthy, bloody and costly struggle with Louis XIV, a war that itself marked only the beginning of a century of conflict with France. Finally, it is often supposed that the revolution of 1688–89 secured English liberty and set the nation on the path towards parliamentary democracy, but in reality it was William's wars, not the revolution settlement, which transformed the English state.

Medals struck to commemorate the revolution depicted the Dutch armada that set sail in October 1688 as on a divinely ordained mercy mission to protect Protestantism and liberty (see pp. 24–25). The engravers at least got something right: the safe landing of William's fleet at Torbay on 5 November 1688 owed much to chance (or as Protestant contemporaries preferred to see it, providence). The armada had been raised on the basis of an invitation sent to William of Orange by seven English lords (the 'immortal seven') who called on the Dutch leader to intervene to defend the nation's church and constitution from the 'arbitrary' rule of the Catholic king, James II. After an initial 'honeymoon period', disquiet at James's policies in England had grown. The king's two declarations of indulgence offered toleration to both Catholics and nonconformists. However, to many Protestants, it seemed that the king's goal was not religious pluralism but to return England to the bosom of Rome. This prospect seemed all the more likely following James's imprisonment of seven of his Anglican bishops for refusing to read the second declaration from the pulpit. By the summer of 1688, the situation seemed dire. The government had expended considerable effort to ensure that James's next parliament would be packed with MPs who would approve the repeal of the Test and Corporation Acts – legislation

William of Orange landing at Brixham, Torbay, by Jan Wyck, oil on canvas, 1688 (BHC3095)

that barred Catholics from holding public office. Worse still, the ageing king, whose marriage to the Italian princess Mary of Modena had long been childless, had finally produced a legitimate male heir, with the birth of James Francis Edward Stuart on 10 June 1688. The hope that, following James's death, the crown would revert to his Protestant daughters from his first marriage to Anne Hyde was now dashed.

The problem for James's opponents was that the king's position remained relatively secure given the large army at his disposal (totalling some 40,000 men by November 1688) and the healthy state of the crown's finances. Insurrections in the form of the Monmouth and Argyll rebellions in 1685 had been easily crushed. External assistance was essential if an effective challenge to James was to be mounted. The Prince of Orange was the obvious candidate: he was a Protestant married to a Protestant (James's daughter Mary); he had well-established links with Whig politicians in England and he (or rather the States of Holland) had the financial and military resources necessary.

English Protestants clearly needed William to intervene on their behalf, but why did he and the Netherlands as a whole respond positively to this request? It was not, contrary to the claims of his propaganda, because of any deep concern for either England's liberty or its church. For William, the invitation from the seven peers represented an opportunity to do two things: firstly, to secure a parliament which would reverse James's pro-French foreign policy and instead move England into alliance with the Netherlands against Louis

XIV; and secondly, to protect his wife's inheritance, now threatened by the birth of the Prince of Wales. His motivations were dynastic and geopolitical, not confessional or ideological.

By September 1688, the Dutch had amassed an invasion army of 14,352 regular troops and 5,000 Huguenot, English and Scottish volunteers, with a full artillery train making a total force of over 21,000 men.[2] The fleet assembled to carry this force was four times the size of the Spanish Armada of 1588, with more than twice as many warships. The invasion force was assembled with incredible speed, the urgency driven by the military situation: with a land invasion of the Netherlands by the French seemingly imminent, William could not afford to wait for better weather in the spring. James, for his part, did not become unduly concerned by the military preparations being made across the North Sea until August, and even then seems to have thought that an invasion attempt in the autumn was unlikely given the adverse weather conditions. England, in any case, was not unprotected: James had a sizeable navy of his own, by the end of October 1688 numbering thirty-seven men-of-war and eleven fireships, and he instructed his admiral, Dartmouth, to move his ships further out than the Gunfleet 'for fear he should be surprised while there by sudden coming of the Dutch fleet, as being a place he cannot well get out to sea from, while the wind remains easterly'.[3] Significantly, Dartmouth

TOP Medal commemorating the embarkation of William of Orange at Hellevoetsluis, 1688 (MEC0105)
BOTTOM AND OPPOSITE Medals commemorating the landing of William of Orange at Torbay, 1688 (MEC0129, MEC1125)

ignored this royal direction, and James's own complacency was underscored by the fact that he did not question his admiral's decision.

Initially, it seemed as if James had been correct in his judgement that an invasion could not be undertaken at this time of year. As an experienced naval officer himself, James knew all about the difficulties posed by autumn gales. He had been appointed Lord High Admiral on Charles II's restoration to the throne and had taken part in the battles of Lowestoft (1665), a great military victory for James, and Southwold Bay (1672), the defeat which had ended his active naval career – Charles having finally lost patience with the heir to the throne repeatedly putting his life at risk.

The invasion fleet was forced to remain in harbour for a month in the face of adverse weather. At the first attempt to launch the armada on 19 October 1688, a fierce storm forced the fleet back to the Dutch coast with the loss of several ships and 500 horses. In the Netherlands, the press deliberately exaggerated the level of damage done in order to lull James into a false sense of security. Within a matter of days, however, the fleet was ready again and it set sail for England on 1 November.

It was at this point that the so-called 'Protestant wind' played the decisive role. Late on 2 November, William's armada turned away from the Norfolk coast to sail down the English Channel. Dartmouth's fleet, which had moved close enough for the admiral to see the Dutch outliers from his flagship, was now prevented from pursuing the invasion force by the direction of the wind, making navigating the Kentish Knock impossible. As the armada reached Dover, William ordered the fleet to stretch out in a line across the Channel so that, according to Gilbert Burnet, the prince's Scottish chaplain and later historian of the revolution, 'our Fleet reached within a league of each place [Dover and Calais]...This sight would have ravish'd the most curious Eyes of Europe. When our Fleet was in its greatest splendour, the Trumpets and Drums playing various Tunes to rejoice our hearts'.[4] The 'Protestant wind' blew the invasion force on towards the south-west coast, while at the same time forcing James's fleet to take shelter in the Downs.

William landed at Torbay on the auspicious date of 5 November 1688, the anniversary of England's last deliverance from the threat of popery. It took little more than a day for the news of his disembarkation to reach James in London. The atmosphere in the city was febrile, with violent assaults being made on the Catholic chapel in St James's on 11 November. The following day, four or five rioters were killed by the king's horse guards, evidence of the fact that even in England the revolution was not free from bloodshed. The strength of anti-Catholic feeling in the capital encouraged James not only to make preparations for his family to flee to the safety of France but also to head out and meet William's army before the political situation slipped completely beyond his control. During his reign, James had worked assiduously to increase his military capabilities, and the army that he assembled at Salisbury to fight the Dutch was larger than William's invasion force. However, most observers felt that the Prince of Orange's troops were better equipped and disciplined. Moreover, even before the king reached his army on 19 November, there had already been

# LANDING OF WILLIAM OF ORANGE AT TORBAY, 5 NOVEMBER 1688
## ENGLISH SCHOOL, LATE SEVENTEENTH CENTURY, OIL ON CANVAS (BHC0326)

This painting by an unknown artist brings home the magnitude of the Dutch invasion armada. This was a landing on a very different scale from that made by James Scott, Duke of Monmouth, the previous challenger to James II, at nearby Lyme Regis in June 1685. Monmouth's rebels had arrived on board just two small ships, with no cavalry and only four small cannons. The duke was wholly dependent on raising troops in the south-west, and the 'army' of cloth workers and farm labourers that he eventually assembled was barely deserving of the name: it certainly proved no match for the professional forces under the king's command.

William of Orange, in stark contrast, brought with him thousands of cavalry as well as regular troops, as the painting depicts. Aside from the military

force, the armada came fully equipped for a propaganda war, carrying tens of thousands of copies of the Prince's Declaration and portable printing presses to churn out even more. Indeed, although domestic rebellions against James's rule were raised in the north of England by the earls of Danby and Denbigh, William had little need (or desire) to gather English supporters – their involvement might only hamper his freedom of action and leave him with unwanted political debts to pay. When the invasion force arrived at Exeter on 9 November 1688, the army entered in full regalia, led by the Earl of Macclesfield and the rest of the English cavalry. But the cosmopolitan nature of

this force was made clear by the troops who followed – 200 of William of Orange's West African attendants, wearing 'Caps lined with Fur, and Plumes of white Feathers'. After them came another two hundred Finnish troops dressed in 'Bear Skins taken from the Wild Beasts they had slain…with black Armour, and broad Flaming Swords'. William himself rode in on a white horse, clad in armour, with forty-two footmen accompanying him. It was an awesome spectacle and one with barely disguised shades of a royal progress.

a number of significant defections among his officers to the Prince of Orange. James himself was laid low by a series of debilitating nosebleeds, which some thought (wrongly) were symptomatic of a brain tumour. On 23 November, the king's commander-in-chief, the Earl of Feversham, urged him to withdraw back to London. James, dispirited by the disloyalty of his officers and weakened by illness, agreed. The threat of another English civil war was over.

By this stage, James was almost certainly set on fleeing the country and on 11 December, accompanied by Sir Edward Hales, he took a small skiff down the Thames, throwing the Great Seal into the river on the way. This first attempt at escape was unsuccessful as James was apprehended by fishermen at Faversham in Kent, who mistook him for an absconding Jesuit priest. The king's flight nonetheless pushed power further into the Prince of Orange's hands: with James gone, William and his Dutch forces appeared to be the only body capable of restoring order to a country descending into anarchy. James's return to London was to be brief: on 18 December he left the city to take up residence in Rochester, and on the same day William entered London to a rapturous welcome.

Four days later, James, with considerable connivance from his effective captors, left Rochester, taking a ship to France on 23 December. There followed over a month of wrangling among English politicians as to whether James's second flight represented an abdication, and, if so, whether the throne could now be offered to William. Significantly, the Prince of Orange's own mind was made up: he had come to England to secure an anti-French parliament but he now had the prospect of holding the reins of power himself. He would not let the opportunity slip. William presented an ultimatum to the members of the Convention parliament that had been summoned to settle the kingdom: they could offer him the throne and his troops would stay, or they could refuse and he would return to the Netherlands, leaving them potentially open to the penalties for treason should James be restored. On 13 February 1689, William and Mary were offered the English crown as joint monarchs.

BELOW Medal commemorating the abdication of James II in 1688, showing him throwing the Great Seal of England into the River Thames, 1788 (MEC1319) OPPOSITE Royal coat of arms of William III, late seventeenth century (HRA0014)

The dynastic revolution in England had been achieved but this was far from the end of the military struggle. For one thing, England was an imperial power. Its monarchical authority extended not only across the rest of the British Isles, but included distant Caribbean and North American colonies. These too had to be secured for the new regime. Even more importantly, for both William and his nemesis, Louis XIV, the real conflict was not over control of the British Empire. This was ultimately peripheral to the central concern of both leaders, which was military mastery of continental Europe. The foreign-policy focus of Louis and William would have important ramifications both for James's attempt to regain the throne and for English naval activity. It would lead to a war at sea in which both sides scored notable victories but neither possessed the will or the resources to make the decisive breakthrough.

It was James who at first enjoyed greatest success in the naval struggle. The loyal regime of the Earl of Tyrconnel and the majority Catholic population seemingly made Ireland an ideal launching pad for an attempt to regain James's wealthiest former possession, England. On 12 March 1689, the ousted king landed at Kinsale. The English parliament was aware of the danger represented by leaving Ireland unprotected but it faced the additional problem that the English navy, as developed under Charles and James, had been fitted with ships suited to the conflict with the Dutch, the nation's main maritime rival in the 1660s and 1670s. These vessels were heavily armed but were not really seaworthy enough for fighting in the rougher waters of the Atlantic. As Admiral Edward Russell would later remark, the new conflict and a war with the Dutch were 'very different, for then bad weather was nothing, the fleet having it in their power to anchor, but now we keep the sea a thousand accidents attend it'.[5] William's administration took these problems seriously; in April 1689 a joint Anglo-Dutch navy had been created but the initial engagements nonetheless went the way of the French. On 1 May 1689, the commander-in-chief of the fleet, Admiral Arthur Herbert, joined battle with a larger force of French ships under the command of the Marquis de Château-Renault in Bantry Bay, south-west Ireland. The French fleet inflicted heavy damage on Herbert's ships, forcing them back out to sea but, tellingly, they did not press the advantage and instead returned to the bay and then back to the French naval base at Brest. As Herbert later wrote to the Earl of Nottingham, the secretary of state in charge of the navy, 'I must confesse that as long as I have gone to sea, I never saw soe much modesty in any men's behaviour as the French shewed upon this occasion...considering the advantage

of the place, the wind, their fireships'.[6] Ireland, meanwhile, was left virtually undefended from future French assaults.

Worse was to come the following year. In June 1690, a united French fleet under the command of the Comte de Tourville entered the Channel (see p. 33). Numbering seventy-five ships of the line, George Byng, 1st Viscount Torrington, could see that he was heavily outnumbered (his own force amounted to fifty-six ships) when he sighted the French fleet off the Isle of Wight on 25 June. A repeat of November 1688 seemed possible and Torrington was ordered to fight the French irrespective of the risk. On 30 June, the combined Dutch and English fleet formed a line of battle off

OPPOSITE Admiral Edward
Russell, by Godfrey Kneller,
oil on canvas, c.1710
(BHC2992)
RIGHT AND BELOW Full-hull
model of the *St Michael*, 90
to 98 guns, c.1672 (SLR0002)

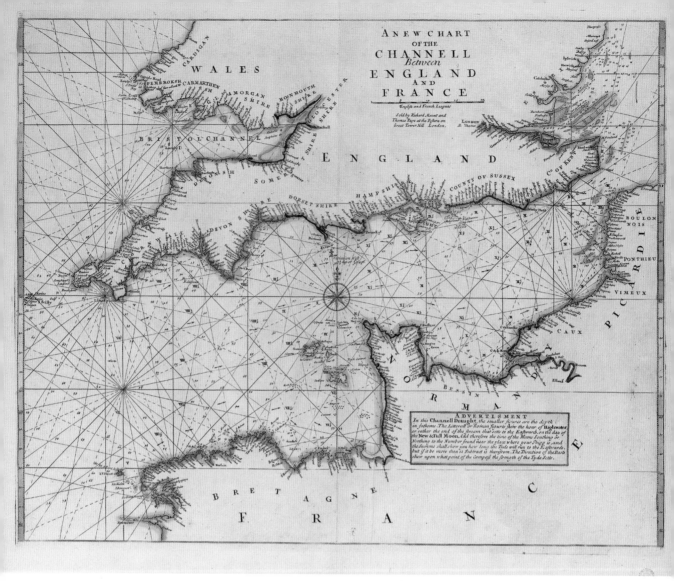

In this Channell Draught, the smaller figures are the depth in fathoms. The Litteral or Roman figures shew the hour of Highwater, or rather the end of the stream that setts to the Eastward, on the day of the New & Full Moon, and therefore the time of the Moon Southing or Northing is the Number found near the place where your Ship is, and the Lettens shall shew you how long the Tide will run to the Eastward, but if it be more then is Subtract is therefrom. The Direction of the Darts shew upon what point of the Compass the strength of the Tyde Setts.

Beachy Head. The Dutch led the attack but their squadron, led by Cornelis Evertsen, made a tactical error in engaging the French van at close quarters, allowing the unmarked leading division to encircle the Dutch, inflicting heavy losses upon them. The battle turned into a disaster for the allied fleet and Torrington was forced to burn seven more Dutch and one English ship as they retreated up the Channel. The defeat raised anxiety about a French invasion, heightened by real raids along the English coast such as the burning of the Devon port of Teignmouth on 26 July. In anticipation of a mass assault, the government raised 92,000 militiamen to defend the country.[7] Torrington, widely viewed to have deserted the Dutch in the battle, lost his post and was replaced as commander-in-chief by the triumvirate of Sir Henry Killigrew, Sir Richard Haddock and Sir John Ashby. The French had effective control of the Channel after Beachy Head but no invasion came. As had been the case after Bantry Bay, they did not exploit Britain's naval vulnerability. For James's Irish supporters, this lack of commitment was critical. Tyrconnel complained:

*The want of a squadron of French men of war in St George's Channel has been our ruin, for had we had that since the beginning of May, the Prince of Orange had been confounded without striking a stroke, for he could have sent hither neither forces nor provisions, and [the Duke of] Schomberg's army would have starved.*[8]

Without French naval support, the Jacobites were unable to overcome the besieged inhabitants of Derry, or prevent William from landing with 16,000 more troops to relieve the embattled Schomberg in June 1690.

Despite the failure to capitalise on the victory at Beachy Head, and the subsequent defeat of James and his supporters at the Battle of the Boyne, in July 1690, renewed plans were being made for a French invasion attempt in the summer of 1691. On the English side, Beachy Head had provoked a reorganisation of the navy, with the Commons voting money for twenty-seven new ships of the line, to be supported by the creation of new dry docks and shipyards at Plymouth and

OPPOSITE *A New Chart of the Channell Between England and France*, published by Mount & Page, hand-coloured engraving, 1702 (G223:1/2) LEFT *Monsieur Le Comte de Tourville Vice-Amiral.et Marechal de France* (detail), published by Antoine Trouvain, engraving, 1696 (PAD2672)

Portsmouth (though the design of some of these new ships, for instance the *Boyne*, may have left something to be desired).[9] By April 1692, news had reached England of a new plan to land 20,000 French troops at Torbay. Unfavourable winds kept the invasion force from setting out from La Hogue, giving the English fleet time to assemble under the command of Edward Russell. The Anglo-Dutch force had a considerable numerical advantage over the French, with some eighty-two ships against forty-four vessels on the opposing side. Despite his opponents' greater numbers, de Tourville decided to engage the allied fleet on 19 May, though he may have been misled as to the size of the enemy force due to the heavy fog that morning. Although the battle began well for the French, by evening the greater Anglo-Dutch numbers had forced a retreat. Twenty-two ships

escaped to St Malo but others, including the French flagship the *Soleil Royal*, were so badly damaged that they had be beached at Cherbourg only to be burnt subsequently with fireships. A further twelve French ships which sought refuge at La Hogue were also destroyed in later attacks on 23 and 24 May (see pp. 36–39).

The allied victory at Barfleur/La Hogue was not, however, followed by a successful descent upon the northern French coast as many English politicians hoped. The 14,000 troops assembled for this operation had to be dispersed and the only significant consequence of the aborted scheme was that Nottingham lost his job. The French response to defeat was to attack English shipping rather than attempt to compete with the larger Anglo-Dutch navy. The shift to a *guerre de course* had a significant impact on English trade:

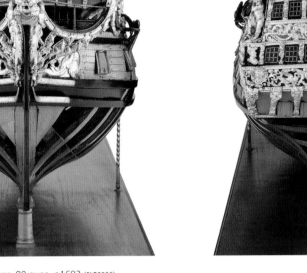

Full-hull model of the *Boyne*, 80 guns, *c.*1692 (SLR0006)

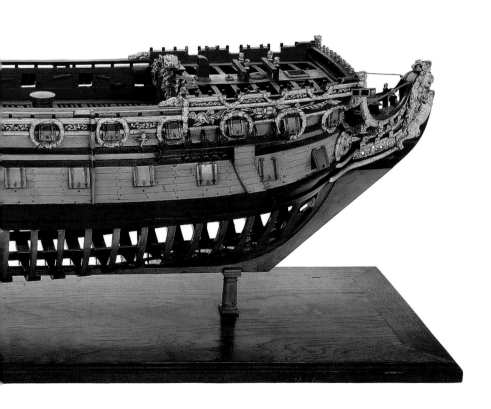

ABOVE The Battle of Barfleur, 1692, by Ludolf Backhuysen, oil on canvas, 1693 (BHC0331) OPPOSITE ABOVE Letter by John Lloyd, surgeon of the *Stirling Castle*, describing the Battle of La Hogue, 26 May 1692 (AGC/L/5) OPPOSITE BELOW Medal commemorating the Battle of La Hogue, 1692 (MEC0136) OVERLEAF The Battle of La Hogue, 1692, by Adriaen van Diest, oil on canvas, late seventeenth century (BHC0337)

by 1693–94 exports to the Iberian Peninsula, the Canary Islands and the Mediterranean had fallen by 25 per cent from their 1686 levels. As the country Tory MP Robert Harley remarked: 'We have had a glorious victory at sea; [yet] though we have had the honour of it, your enemy had the profit of it by taking our merchant ships.'[10]

Looking at the opening years of the Nine Years War (as the conflict with France between 1688 and 1697 came to be known), the overall impression is one of military stalemate. There were moments when it appeared that either William or Louis could gain the ascendency, but neither did. One reason for this was simply that naval resources were limited – strategic operations had to be balanced against the need for convoy protection of merchant shipping. And it was trade that provided much of the wealth that supported the navy:

customs revenues brought in two-thirds as much income as the land tax, and in 1693 revenue from the West Indies and Virginia fleets amounted to £200,000.[11] However, it was arguably because both William and Louis saw warfare in the British Isles as a sideshow compared to the 'main event' of the land war on the Continent that the opportunities presented by both Beachy Head and Barfleur were spurned. Firm evidence for this can be found in the rapidity with which William turned the English navy's focus away from 'home waters' to the Mediterranean. Indeed, John Ehrman has argued that this was always the king's goal but the need to secure his power base in England forced him to contest control of the Channel.[12] Again, this shift in policy was directed at supporting the land war, not achieving naval supremacy. The English fleet would be used to assist its allies by

bombarding fortifications along the critical coastal road that connected Spain, France and Savoy, and by providing supplies to the land forces. In doing so, it was hoped that the navy would open up a second front in the south that would divert French military resources away from the war of attrition being waged in Flanders.

While this shift in strategy did lead to some radical changes in naval operations, most notably Russell's fleet over-wintering in Cadiz in 1694–95 rather than returning to England, it did not dramatically alter the outcome of war. When peace was secured with the Treaty of Ryswick in September 1697, the gains for William were relatively minor – Louis agreed to recognise him as king of Britain 'by the grace of God', and his princely lands in Orange were restored to their pre-1678 boundaries. These were the major returns on a conflict which had cost some forty million pounds and led to the loss of 1,500 vessels, including fifty warships.[13] Yet if the war appeared to have achieved little in territorial terms, it did have a profound effect on the English state. Tax revenue had doubled from its pre-1689 levels but this increase alone was not enough to support an army that was more than twice the size it had been under James II. New financial machinery was created to help fund the war, most notably

The Battle of Vigo Bay, by Ludolf Backhuysen, oil on canvas, c.1702 (BHC2216)

the Bank of England in 1694, an institution with very close links to the navy: its first governor, Sir John Houblon, sat on the Admiralty Board, while Admiral Russell was one of the bank's major early subscribers.[14] Most of all, parliament, which under the Stuarts had enjoyed a precarious existence, came to play an integral part in government. It was notable that while military disasters, such as the destruction of the Smyrna fleet in 1693, could lead to the fall of a ministry, they did not end England's participation in the war. Indeed, while Whigs and Tories could disagree vehemently about the direction of foreign policy, neither side really seemed committed to securing peace.[15] This is not all that surprising – war did place a heavy financial burden on the nation and not all MPs

saw the wisdom of William's foreign policy. Yet it was war, and not the constitutional settlement of 1688–89, that ensured regular parliamentary sessions and elections, gave parliament increasing powers over royal finances and appointments, and finally allowed it to dictate the royal succession itself through the Act of Settlement of 1701. For all the emotional resonance of calls by men such as Halifax and Harley for England to adopt the position of an 'independent umpire' in European affairs, when Louis XIV repudiated the Treaty of Ryswick by

LEFT Bar shot believed to have been used at the Battle of Vigo Bay (KTP1127) ABOVE LEFT Admiral Sir Cloudesley Shovell, by Michael Dahl, oil on canvas, 1702 (BHC3026)
ABOVE RIGHT Vice-Admiral John Benbow, by Godfrey Kneller, oil on canvas, 1701 (BHC2546)

recognising James Edward Stuart as James III on his father's death, the Commons yet again voted the money for war. The English navy was once more at the forefront, with Admiral Rooke eliminating the Franco-Spanish fleet at the Battle of Vigo Bay on 12 October 1702, and in the ensuing years other admirals, such as Benbow and Shovell, would make their mark. The symbiotic relationship between trade, national wealth and the navy ensured that war at sea with France would continue. And this second 'hundred years war' not only forged the British imperial state, but also fashioned Britishness itself.

# 2

# PATRIOTISM, TRADE AND EMPIRE

## Kathleen Wilson

In the pantheon of British naval heroes, the name of Vice-Admiral Edward Vernon may not spring readily to mind. And yet for several years in the 1740s, Vernon was the focal point of a remarkable episode in British politics, arts and arms that drew in all sectors of society across the British Atlantic world. Son of a secretary of state to William III, 'Ned', as his father affectionately called him, volunteered for the Royal Navy when just sixteen and quickly rose through the ranks, becoming captain in 1706 and serving in the Mediterranean and West Indian theatres during the War of the Spanish Succession (1701–14). He was elected MP for Penryn in 1722, when on half pay from the navy, and became a forceful opponent of the Whig government headed by Sir Robert Walpole, speaking out against the salt tax, the proposed excise bill of 1733, and British weakness in the face of France's encroachments on British colonial possessions.

In 1729, some months after Admiral Hosier's disastrous attempt to take Porto Bello – an important Caribbean port of the Spanish empire in present-day Panama where Spanish galleons were loaded with silver, gold and other luxuries – Vernon asserted that Hosier's orders 'were given by those who understood nothing of the sea', and that he could take Porto Bello with six ships and 300 men. Horace Walpole called his speech 'noisy', 'blustering' and 'foolish', but Vernon went on to vindicate his prediction by capturing Porto Bello with six ships in 1739. Moreover, he reduced the fort of San Lorenzo and the town of Chagres in March 1740, and engineered a promising though ultimately unsuccessful attack on Cartagena in 1741. For the next three years, Vernon was the focus of national acclaim, expressed in street demonstrations and in the production of poems, ballads, plays, pamphlets, medals and ceramics, all of which commemorated his exploits and exalted his name as the greatest of British patriots. How did the bluff and garrulous Vernon become a symbol of patriotic virtue? This essay will probe the contexts of Vernon's popularity, and its ability to mobilise and express a widespread enthusiasm – among a socially diverse public – for colonies, trade, patriotism and the requisite amounts of 'British liberty' necessary to pursue them, unfettered by governmental inaction or rival nations.

England – or, after the Act of Union of 1707, Britain – had long regarded itself as a trading nation, sustained and safeguarded by the sea. And concepts of patriotism, rooted in classical ideals about citizenship and modified by early modern civic humanism, had a similarly long history, which demanded that various forms of masculine austerity, force and self-sacrifice be put to the service of the polity.[1] By the eighteenth century, the internal empire had been amalgamated through both the 'Glorious Revolution' of

# How to get Riches.

## Humbly Inscrib'd to the British Nation.

Thro' various Climes, & to each distant Pole,
In happy Tides let active Commerce rowl;
As our high Vessels pass their watry Way,
Let all the Naval World due Homage pay;
Let Britain's Ships export an Annual Fleece,
Richer than Argos brought to ancient Greece;
Returning Loaden with the shining Stores,
Which lye profuse on either India's Shores:

We then shall get great Riches, and if Sway,
To calm the Earth, and vindicate the Sea;
And by your Aid, our Potent Fleets shall go
As far as Winds can bear, or Waters flow;
New Lands to make, new Indies to explore,
In Worlds unknown to plant Britannia's Power,
Nations yet wild by Precept to Reclaim;
And teach 'em Arms, & Arts, in Britain's Name.

*Josephus Champion Script*

Nº XVII.     1736.     G. Bickham sculp.

*How to get Riches. Humbly Inscrib'd to the British Nation*, engraving by George Bickham of the poem by Josephus Champion, 1736 (PAI8047)

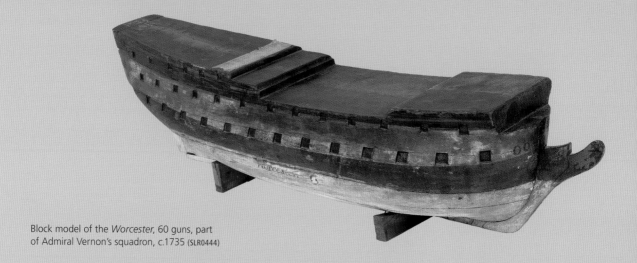

Block model of the *Worcester*, 60 guns, part of Admiral Vernon's squadron, c.1735 (SLR0444)

1688–89 and the Union with Scotland. Thereafter, both trade and patriotism took on new resonances that directly affected notions of the national character and the nature of British political leadership. An expansionist vision of Britain's destiny and a libertarian critique of the Whig state began to converge in public discourse.

Despite a long period of peace following the War of the Spanish Succession, Britons living throughout the Atlantic world in the 1720s and 1730s felt the pressures of national and imperial rivalries, manifested in threatened invasions, privateering or other encroachments on British markets and settlements. For example, in 1723 France had retaken the island of St Lucia from the British, and then battled with British Caribbean merchants over sugar production and the highly profitable, illegal trade with Spanish America and the British northern colonies. The great wealth produced by this contraband trade meant that Jamaican merchants in particular were disinclined to give up its pursuit, even when ordered to do so by the Treaty of Seville in 1729. When Spain retaliated by deploying *guardacostas* in Caribbean waters to search and seize British ships, the situation was pushed to a crisis point. In 1738, British West Indian and American merchants and shipowners

from a number of out-ports – including Kingston, Bridgetown, New York, Bristol, Glasgow, Lancaster, Liverpool, Edinburgh and London – bombarded parliament and the Board of Trade with memorials, addresses and petitions against the 'Spanish depredations', demanding redress.

These addresses were publicised in newspapers and pamphlets; prints circulated recalling the unfortunate fate of Captain Robert Jenkins, a Jamaican landowner and merchant whose ear had been sliced off by a Spanish guard in 1731. Edward Cave's *A New Map or Chart of the Western or Atlantic Ocean* allowed subscribers to follow the progress of these skirmishes in Caribbean waters (see p. 53). At the same time, broadsheets such as Josephus Champion's *How to get Riches. Humbly Inscrib'd to the British Nation* popularised the parliamentary opposition's view that only a 'blue-water policy' – a foreign policy that concentrated on maintaining Britain's naval power and colonial supremacy – was consistent with British liberty, property and prosperity (see p. 43). *The Craftsman* reported on the 'Sentiments of the Nation' in the following manner: 'The general cry is War, Revenge on the SPANIARDS, Restitution for our PAST LOSSES, satisfaction to our NATIONAL HONOUR, and above all, ample

Security to our FUTURE TRADE AND NAVIGA-TION.'[2] In October 1739, when efforts to negotiate a new treaty with Spain had come to nothing, the Walpole government was forced to declare war on Spain. The public reaction was electric: wildly joyful celebrations more appropriate to a national victory than a declaration of war broke out across the localities, and subscriptions were begun among the urban middle classes to pay for the defence of British merchant ships.

Vernon was called from his estate in Suffolk to be promoted to vice-admiral and put in charge of the six ships that were ordered to the West Indies to seize Spanish galleons. The government was hoping, perhaps, that Vernon and his small squadron would fail, and so render ridiculous the opposition's demands for greater aggressiveness against Spain. But, against the odds, Vernon was able to capture the town and fort of Porto Bello, destroy all the war stores held there and hold them to ransom against the Spanish. Vernon then launched a successful attack on Chagres and its fort, San Lorenzo, reducing both before begin-ning reconnaissance on the port of Cartagena in early March 1740. After a seven-hour bombard-ment, he forced a surrender of the castle and then returned to Porto Bello to await further rein-forcements from the navy and army. Of the latter, Vernon was not optimistic: '[O]ur Gentlemen of Parade, who having been long trained to nothing but Reviews, can't so readily shake off the rust of idleness', he wrote to the Governor of Jamaica on 20 March 1741, referring to the troops sent from Britain under General Thomas Wentworth (and who were, in fact, sickening and dying of fever in the Jamaican lowlands).[3] And indeed,

from May 1740 until January 1741, Vernon was unable to attempt any further attack on Spanish possessions.

Nonetheless, Vernon's ultimate failure to take Cartagena and St Iago in Cuba did nothing to dim the acclaim brought by the reduction of Porto Bello and Chagres, the first victories in the war. The news of Vernon's successes reached England in March 1740, and celebrations of these triumphs as well as of his birthday (12 November) punctuated the calendar for the next two years in fifty-four towns across Britain and several more in the West Indies, Ireland and America. In Stratford, Essex, an effigy of the Spanish admiral Don Blass, who according to many accounts

Medals commemorating Admiral Vernon, and his attacks on Porto Bello and Cartagena, after 1739 (MEC0890, MEC0986, MEC1025)

Small-sword thought to have belonged to the Spanish governor of Porto Bello, 1737–38 (WPN1248)

ABOVE Disc commemorating Admiral Vernon, c.1740 (JEW0028)
BELOW RIGHT *The Honble. Edward Vernon Esqr. Vice Admiral of the Blue. And Commander in Chief of all His Majestie's Ships in the West-Indies...*, by John Faber after Thomas Bardwell, mezzotint, 1740 (PAD4591)

depicted, against a background view of Porto Bello and men-of-war, a Spaniard on his knees offering Vernon a sword as a flag lies over Vernon's head with the gallant words *'veni, vidi, vici'*. This image was also reproduced on medals: indeed, more medals were struck in honour of Admiral Vernon than for any other figure in the eighteenth century (see p. 45). At least 102 of these were reproduced between 1740 and 1743, decorated with his head, and legends such as 'He took Porto Bello with Six Ships only' or 'The Pride of Spain humbled by Admiral Vernon'. Some were made in the form of badges that could be worn on hats, coats and jackets.

The press teemed with information on Vernon and his exploits, beginning with the Porto Bello victory. Prints, poems and ballads appeared at booksellers and print shops, and in London and provincial newspapers, glorifying Vernon and his plan of capture for Porto Bello and Chagres;

surrendered his sword to Vernon on bended knee, was burned in an enormous multi-storey bonfire as crowds round it sang 'Britons strike home'. In Wymondham, Norfolk, the rejoicing at news of Vernon's initial victory at Cartagena evinced the extent of pride in the hero:

> *Trees planted in the streets like a Grove: a grand procession was made through the whole town, where in the new rich flag belonging to the Town Society was carried before... after which a Person in a grand Manner representing ADMIRAL VERNON rode on a fine horse, and another in a despicable manner on an Ass Representing Don Blass... the whole was the general sense and free Act of the People, being in no way promoted by any leading Gentlemen.*[4]

In London, residents of Fleet Street put on a pageant in his honour, the main scene of which

*Admiral Hosier's Ghost*, Charles Mosley's hand-coloured engraving of Richard Glover's ballad, July 1740 (PAF3959)

in the more enterprising papers, maps and prints were provided gratis. On all counts, Vernon was exalted as Britain's sole salvation and the incarnation of patriotic virtue, a 'True Briton' and 'Son of Liberty' who dared to stand up to the Catholic powers of Europe, rivalling Ralegh and Drake as the greatest naval commander the country had ever known. A representative poem of the multitude written for his birthday in 1740 described him as 'the generous hero, and Country's praise': 'Let the [day] be devoted with Eternal Fame To Glory, Liberty and VERNON'S Name...[The day] which gave t'Immortalize a Brunswick's Reign, Britain's Avenger, and the Scourge of Spain.' Another song, entitled 'The True English-Boys Song to Vernon's Glory: Occasion'd by the Birthday of that Brave Admiral', was written specifically 'to be sung around the bonfires of London and Westminster' on that auspicious anniversary. The press thus disseminated information on Vernon's activities and demonstrations in his honour throughout the country, providing a calendar for the expression of allegiance and patriotic sentiment.

As in Wymondham, most festivities were planned and financed by the subscriptions of local merchants and tradesmen – the 'free act of the People'. In Liverpool, London and Newcastle, whole parishes made voluntary subscriptions to provide fireworks for their celebrations on Vernon's birthday. In Southwark, Hackney, Ipswich, Lymington, Durham, Sunderland and Norwich, the middling sorts gave money to buy candles, fireworks, bonfires, liquor, dinners or even to hire cannon for their celebrations. The taverns and coffee-houses of London and provincial towns were also sites where Vernon's supporters commonly met to express their allegiance to 'the Heroic asserter of British liberties' and his patriotic cause. Publicans were careful to expand their custom as much as possible by publishing advertisements as to the particular

Ceramic plates showing the taking of Porto Bello, c.1740
(AAA4352, AAA4353)

celebrations in their establishments, sometimes making available new ballads to sing to Vernon's honour. A few even provided free beer to drink to the patriot hero's health, apparently believing, as did a tavern keeper in Salisbury, that the great quantities of liquor consumed 'never would be employ'd better than in drinking the Health of Him who cannot but be the darling of every free born British soul'. Appropriately, Vernon's head became a favourite public house sign in the capital and provinces for decades.

This heady combination of profits and patriotism was exhibited in other aspects of his support. Advertisements such as the one that appeared in the *Norwich Gazette* in January 1741 were not at all uncommon: 'To be Sold, a parcel of old Havanna SNUFF, that comes directly from Admiral VERNON.' Moreover, the calendar provided by Vernon's birthday and the anniversaries of his victories created a predictable market for Vernon artefacts, and enterprising manufacturers were quick to exploit it. 'It is Admiral Vernon's birthday, and the city shops are full of favours,

ABOVE City of London freedom box presented to Admiral Vernon, 1740–41 (PLT0187)
BELOW Ceramic tea-pot and bowl, commemorating the capture of Porto Bello and Chagres, c.1740 (AAA4354, AAA4355)

the streets of marrowbones and cleavers, and the night will be full of mobbing, bonfires and lights!', the writer and diarist Horace Walpole wrote in 1741. Some of these 'favours' were made by potters, who introduced a whole array of relatively inexpensive Astbury, salt-glaze and delft-ware pottery to commemorate Vernon's glory. These objects allowed consumers to express their allegiance and solidarity to the British polity. Since the late seventeenth century, monarchs and military figures had been immortalised on plates, bowls and platters, but Vernon ceramics constituted the most prolific output of commemorative pieces since the century began, with virtually all the major potteries producing Vernon memorabilia, including Bristol, Brighton, Lambeth, Liverpool, Leeds and Stafford. Vernon's head, opposition mottoes and his flagship, the *Burford*, appeared on such useful items as plates, mugs, tea-pots, bowls, jugs, inkpots and

punchbowls – catering, it seems, for a middling-to-prosperous market of shopkeepers, tradesmen and merchants. The mottoes emphasised his role as Britain's sole and stalwart patriot hero: 'The British Glory Revived by Admiral Vernon, He took PORTO BELLO with Six Ships Only', was a popular legend. A more limited number of Vernon plates constituted a new departure in the design of ceramic wares, such as those made by Joseph Flower of Bristol, which displayed in minute and elegant detail the taking of Chagres and the destruction of the fort of San Lorenzo. Such attention to accuracy and realism were a far cry from the crude and often rude portraits that characterised commemorative pottery prior to this time.

Portraiture, seascapes, sculpture, gold boxes and dramatic tableaux also proved to be sympathetic mediums through which loyalty to Vernon and pride in Protestant Britain's seemingly inevitable dominion over her ancient Catholic rival were expressed and solicited. Gainsborough's portrait of 'Old Grog', as Vernon became known (for his fondness for wearing a grosgrain cloak and for the drink of diluted rum that he introduced), was painted in 1753 against a background of the Caribbean Sea. Another portrait, executed by Charles Philips and begun in the mid-1730s, had to be altered after Vernon was promoted to vice-admiral of the blue. The French sculptor and expatriate Louis-François Roubiliac, whose previous commissions included a statue of Handel for Vauxhall Gardens, did a bust of Vernon in about 1744 that portrayed him as austere and forward looking. Jewellers and goldsmiths got in on the

ADMIRAL VERNON

LEFT Admiral Edward Vernon, by Charles Philips, oil on canvas, c.1735–43 (BHC3068)
RIGHT Bust of Admiral Vernon, attributed to Louis-François Roubiliac, c.1744 (SCU0057)

act by engraving the dozens of freedom boxes presented to Vernon by towns across Britain; that given by the City of London was particularly elaborate (see p. 49), engraved with its coat of arms and motto *'Domine Dirige Nos'* ('Lord, Direct Us').

More kinesthetic representations occurred in metropolitan and provincial theatres: a popular production called *The Play of the British Hero: or, Admiral VERNON's Conquest over the Spaniards,* was staged in towns across the Atlantic world. In Norwich, the play included 'The whole View and Prospect of the Town, Fort and Castles of Porto-Bello, with a beautiful Representation of the Battle, also the Flight of the Spaniards out of the Town for Refuge', a scene that had already been usefully imagined in a painting by Samuel Scott in 1740 (see p. 52). The enduring hold that the Porto Bello victory had on the popular imagination is also demonstrated by the plethora of British Porto Bellos that sprang into existence after 1740. Hamlets and suburbs in Staffordshire, Sussex, Oxfordshire, Durham and Edinburgh, and a farm in London, appeared with that name in the decade after 1740; and in the American colonies, one Lawrence Washington named his Virginia estate in honourable allusion to his former commander, under whom he had served during the War of Jenkins' Ear, calling it Mount Vernon.

Through a variety of activities Vernon was appropriated as a national hero and patriot, one who restored national honour and protected British liberty and properties, at home and abroad. But although support for Admiral Vernon was not necessarily partisan, and court Whigs attempted to use the Porto Bello victory as proof of their vision of ministerial policy, it was as an *opposition* political hero that Vernon was celebrated, consolidating at least a decade of popular agitation over the role of trade and empire in the national destiny. During the agitation over the proposed excise bill of 1733, for example, opposition writers had reiterated the critical role of merchants in expanding and thus

Medal commemorating Admiral Vernon and the capture of Porto Bello. It shows the devil leading the prime minister, Sir Robert Walpole, into the mouth of an infernal beast; after 1739 (MEC0896)

ensuring the health of the national economy, and pro-Vernon memorabilia continued to associate the defeat of the excise bill with the government's disdain for the merchant community.

Walpole was also harshly criticised after 1739 for his administration's refusal to commit maximum military and naval resources to the war. 'It is not a little low piratical War, Gentlemen, but a vigorous Prosecution of the War...that will...maintain and defend our ancient Trade, Commerce and Navigation', complained the constituents of Nottingham in the instructions to their MPs in late 1739. Hence the successes at Porto Bello and Chagres, effected by a long-standing critic of Walpolean domestic and foreign policy, yielded maximum political capital as an opposition triumph, imparting direction and unity to instruction and petitioning movements in the constituencies, and to the 1741 parliamentary election.[5] 'We wish that every Member in the ensuing parliament might be a VERNON, or animated

by like Spirit', one Newcastle writer reflected after learning that Vernon had been nominated as parliamentary candidate in five boroughs and returned in three. 'We should see our Country Flourishing at home, and giving Laws abroad.'[6]

The support for Vernon, then, evinced a widespread view about the nature of the Whig state and the role of the people in the political process, as well as demonstrating the importance of trade and empire to national prosperity, liberty and greatness. The audience that this composite of principles and ideas appealed to was diverse, taking in the great and the poor, but was particularly appealing to urban commercial and middling classes. Merchants, shopkeepers and tradesmen, as well as their wives and daughters, funded many

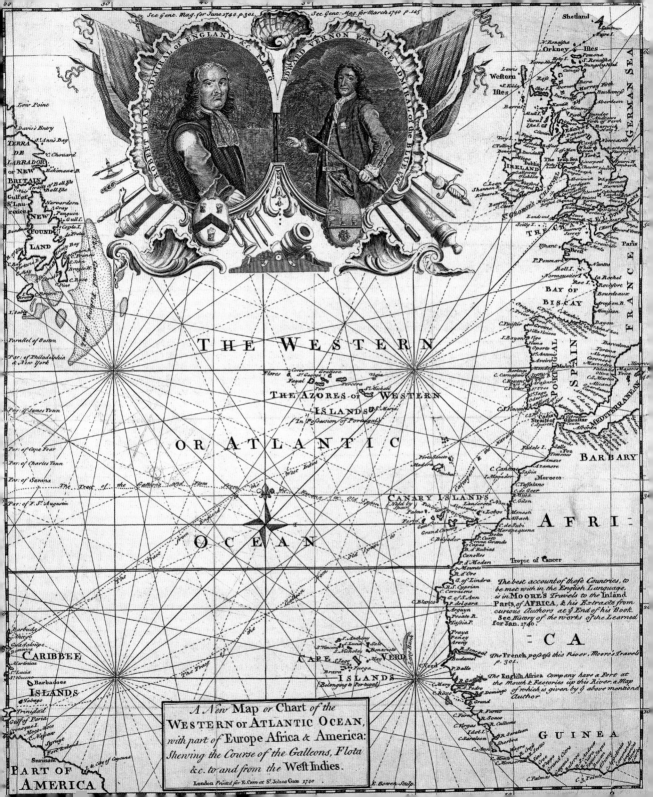

More than any previous naval hero, Vernon's fame spread across the nation. He was celebrated in towns and countryside, by men and women, rich and poor, and across the home kingdoms. One object above all brings this home, an ivory and paper fan manufactured with a colourful and exotic depiction of Vernon's capture of Porto Bello in the Caribbean. This was an overtly patriotic item, inscribed with verse that communicated ideas of national character, commercial potential and passionate celebration:

> Come my Lads with Souls befitting,
> Let us never be dismay'd;
> Let's revenge the Wrongs of Britain,
> and support her injur'd Trade.
> The true Spirit of the Nation,
> In our honest Hearts we bring;
> True tho' in an humble Station,
> To our Country and our King.
>
> Spain no longer shall asume Boys,
> The free Ocean as her own;
> For the time at last is come Boys,
> We've their Top-sails lower'd down.
> Tho' in Politics contesting,
> Round and round they veer about;
> All their Ships and Manifesting,
> We will with our Broadsides rout.

> Hark the British Cannon thunders,
> See my Lads six Ships appear;
> Every Briton acting Wonders,
> Strikes the Southern World with fear.
> Porto Bello fam'd in Story,
> Now at last submits to fate;
> Vernon's Courage gains us Glory,
> And his Mercy proves us great.
>
> May all English Lads like you Boys,
> Prove on Shore true Hearts of Gold;
> To their King and Country true boys,
> And be neither bought nor Sold.
> Let the Landsmen without Party,
> Act like Brethren of the Flood;
> To one Cause alone be hearty,
> And be that for Britains good.
>
> Then thro' all the mighty Ocean,
> Th' English Cross shall Honour find;
> Far as Wave can feel a motion,
> Far as Flag can move with Wind.
> Then insulting Monarchs shewing,
> More regard, shall humbler be;
> This old truth of Britons knowing,
> As they're Brave, they will be free.

That such verse could be found in the hands of a gentlewoman suggests that Vernon had an unprecedented social resonance. The nation had found its first fundamentally British naval hero. This is borne out by other testimonies that hint at the manifold ways in which Vernon was consumed. In 1742, Elizabeth Robinson Montagu wrote to her friend the Duchess of Portland and described a recent visit to a fair in Northfleet, near Gravesend in Kent:

*Under one booth, for the pleasure of bold British youths, was Admiral Vernon, in ginger-bread; indeed he appeared in many shapes there; and the curate of the parish carried him home in a brass tobacco stopper. I was a little concerned to see him lying in passive gingerbread upon a stall with Spanish nuts; but the politicians of our age are wonderful in reconciling the interests of nations.*

of the celebratory festivities attendant upon Vernon's successes. They published, manufactured, bought and sold the pamphlets, ballads and artefacts in his honour, offered their taverns for his birthday celebrations, and fluttered fans depicting the taking of Porto Bello as they discussed *guardacostas* and the importance of the blue-water policy that Tories had advocated since Anne's reign. They identified, in other words, with the 'trading interest', defined in propaganda as overseas merchants and wholesale and retail dealers at every level: as one pamphlet put it, 'the Merchants and wholsale Traders, as well as Shop-keepers, Innholders, Victuallers, Distillers, and other Retailers of imported Commodities'.[7]

British trade had trebled since 1650 and the most dynamic sector was in the colonial trade. Port books, diaries and account books bear witness to the prosperous but otherwise quite ordinary men and women in the provinces who invested in this trade, apparently convinced of its profitability in providing markets or commodities. In Bristol, Dartmouth, Plymouth, King's Lynn, Lancaster and Newcastle, for example, the individuals involved in colonial trade in the first three-quarters of the century, either as direct investors in cargoes or as lenders to merchants or shipowners, included haberdashers, grocers, hoopers, sugar-bakers, printers, gunsmiths, apothecaries, tobacconists, yeomen and widows. Shopkeepers in even remote locales, such as Abraham Dent of Kirkby Stephen, sold imported goods, purchased from distributors in Manchester, Lancaster, Whitehaven, Liverpool and Bristol. Individuals such as these, and several thousands like them throughout Britain and its dominions,

were fervently interested in that 'empire of goods' which, as historians have argued, linked the producers, distributors and consumers of Britain on both sides of the Atlantic, and provided the impetus for imperial growth and prosperity in the eighteenth century. They were thus receptive to the arguments that, as members or supporters of the trading interest, they would benefit from an aggressive commercial policy, and that, indeed, 'domestick Welfare is inseparable from Success, Prosperity and Glory Abroad'.[8]

Vernon's popularity and significance must be seen in these contexts. He was, first of all, a naval hero, and as such represented the kind of war and military policy that the majority of the nation felt Britain should be fighting. The British hatred of a standing army was grounded in the belief that land forces were the invariable agents of absolutism (a fear that Britain's wars with Louis XIV of France and his successors had done little to ameliorate), and thus antithetical to the mixed and balanced constitution of king, lords and commons for which Britain was celebrated around the world. The navy and the militia were alone acclaimed as the most appropriate agents to protect the interests of a trading nation. Vernon, vice-admiral of the blue, represented by his actions the epitome of British spirit, integrity and intrepidity in a mercenary and venal age. Daring to confront Britain's imperial rivals, hostile to the profiteering that riddled the Royal Navy and disdainful of the emoluments of title (he declined an offer of a knighthood in 1742), he was also a just commander, mindful of the needs of the sailors aboard his ships, willing to implement reforms to improve morale and health and to press their rights in parliament. In this respect, too, his humane treatment of the inhabitants of Porto Bello, as well as his speedy restoration of trade relations between Jamaican merchant ships and the Spanish West Indian settlements, received full press coverage and added to his already considerable popular acclaim. Eschewing private gain in favour of the public interest and national honour, Vernon thus restored faith in Britain's moral fibre in a time perceived by many to be marred by enervation and corruption.

As such, he was also an *imperial* hero, both in the geographic extent of the admiration for him and in his efforts to preserve and extend empire. Vindicating the substantial promise of an aggressive blue-water policy in the Americas for British commerce, Vernon was the ultimate 'Free Born Briton, truly Brave! Born to revenge our wrongs, and Glory Save; To Teach the World Britannia Rules the Main', as one poet described him in 1740. He thus not only symbolised British maritime ascendancy in the world; he also coaxed consolidation of a British imperial identity, one in which the Irish, Scots, Welsh and Americans, as well as the English, could participate.

The Vernon episode displayed the readiness of ordinary citizens in the capital, provinces and colonies not only to interest themselves in affairs of state and foreign policy, but also to see themselves as part of a broader British polity, extending across the sea and protected by a strong navy. Vernon's acclaim also reveals to us how empire, trade and patriotism had become intertwined in domestic politics and public political sensibilities, and endowed the idioms of patriotism and trade with important new meanings. It was scarcely coincidental that it was in 1740, on the heels of Vernon's victory at Porto Bello, that 'God Save the King' was first sung in Britain, and that the same year brought the first publication of Arne's rendering of 'Rule Britannia'. In a period when Great Britain was a contested concept and British monarchs were foreigners, Vernon illustrated how naval heroes could supplant and eclipse monarchy in the imaginaries of ordinary British people. He provided a template through which future wars, battles and commanders could be endowed with specific political meanings, standards of patriotic conduct could be recalibrated, and the nation, state and people rendered as distinct, and not necessarily compatible, entities.

It is, perhaps, appropriate that Vernon ended his career at odds with the government. Accused by the Admiralty of having published state correspondence in two pamphlets, Vernon refused to acknowledge or deny the charge, for which he was struck from the list of flag officers in April 1746. 'I thank God I have hitherto discharg'd my Duty to the Crown in every Station I have been called to Serve in, with a diligent Care, and Attention to His Majesty's Service', he wrote in reply to the allegations, before going on to remark that his refusal to answer was part of 'ye common Privledge which was due to every British Subject'.[9] He died in 1757, a year after a string of British defeats in the Ohio Valley, Calcutta, and Minorca and two years before the *annus mirabilis* of British worldwide victories, capped by the mortal triumph of General James Wolfe at Quebec, promised a new world order of British supremacy. Yet Vernon's legacy as a patriotic hero would be drawn on by future naval figures, not least by Horatio Nelson.

# 3

# DOCKYARDS AND INDUSTRY

## Brian Lavery

Between 1689 and 1815, Britain's royal dockyards became the greatest industrial organisation in the world, employing 15,598 men on six main sites at their peak in 1814. The country was at war for more than half the period and the navy grew from 173 ships in 1688 to 936 in 1815. It was the job of the royal dockyards to support these ships. Large sums were spent in expanding them, buying new land, civil engineering works, buildings, docks, offices, houses and fortifications.[1] Unlike shipbuilding, this was a long-term endeavour – many of the buildings survive to this day – while ships rarely lasted for more than about thirty years without very expensive preservation. An effective dockyard relied on a sound financial system, such as the one set up after the 'Glorious Revolution' of 1688. This support was often contested: periodically, public pressure would force a series of commissions and reforms that aimed at limiting expenditure.

All the home dockyards were in southern England. Deptford and Woolwich on the Thames were mostly building yards rather than operational naval bases. Deptford was four miles by water from London and could not handle the largest ships because the river was so narrow, but it was useful for special tasks, such as fitting out Captain Cook's *Endeavour* in 1768. It was rather old-fashioned in that most of its buildings, apart from the Grand Storehouse in the centre

of the yard, were in wood, with a great risk of fire. Woolwich dockyard was five miles further downstream and spread along a length of river frontage. It could build larger ships, including the 100-gun first rate *Royal George* in 1756, but it worked mainly with smaller vessels such as frigates. Between 1801 and 1805, only thirteen seventy-four-gun ships of the line were dry-docked there, compared with fifty at Portsmouth and fifty-two at Plymouth.[2]

Chatham had been England's primary defence base during the wars with the Dutch in the seventeenth century, but it was less important in wars with *ancien régime* France. Nevertheless, the yard was developed in the first half of the eighteenth century with new storehouses, workshops, dry docks, offices and officers' houses. The process continued with a new ropery and storehouses in the 1780s. According to Lord Sandwich, the yard was to be 'kept singly to its proper use as a Building yard'. As such it had a 'great extent of yard' facing the river, and 'room to moor half the fleet of England'.[3] Its operational role revived during the French Revolutionary and Napoleonic Wars when an invasion fleet was prepared in the Netherlands. Sheerness at the junction of the Medway and Thames had a strategic position near the Nore anchorage where fleets for the North Sea assembled, but its site was both exposed and restricted, and unable to handle large ships.

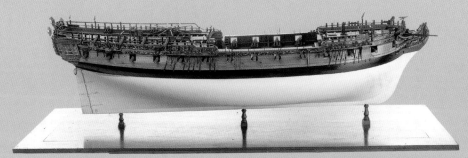

TOP A third-rate warship on the stocks at Deptford, thought to be the *Buckingham*, by John Cleveley the Elder, oil on canvas, 1752 (BHC3762) ABOVE RIGHT Full-hull model of an *Amazon*-class frigate, 32 guns, c.1780 (SLR0315) RIGHT Combined full-hull and frame model of the *Royal George*, 100 guns, c.1772–77 (SLR0336) OVERLEAF The *Royal George* at Deptford showing the launch of the *Cambridge*, by John Cleveley the Elder, oil on canvas, 1757 (BHC3602)

Plymouth dockyard, by Nicholas Pocock, oil on canvas, 1798 (BHC1914)

Portsmouth dockyard had the best facilities in many ways, a self-contained base with a good harbour and anchorages, and facing the main enemy coast across the English Channel. Its chief problem was that it was too far east to service a fleet blockading the main French base at Brest. It was expanded in the course of the century, with much of it rebuilt in brick rather than wood after an American rebel sympathiser, 'Jack the Painter', caused a major fire in 1776. It employed more than 4,000 men by 1814, more than a quarter of those employed in the royal dockyards.[4] Plymouth was the newest of the dockyards, founded in 1690 to meet the needs of the wars with France. Sited on the Hamoaze in the River Tamar, it started off as a single wet dock leading to a dry dock, with a terrace of officers' houses overlooking it. It was expanded partly by levelling land to the south, until by 1793 it had three single dry docks and one double, with four building slips. It was the second yard in terms of numbers employed, with 3,869 in 1814.

In addition, there were several overseas yards. Minorca, taken in 1708, had a great natural harbour and could support a blockade of the French in Toulon. Despite vast fortifications it changed hands six times in the course of the century. Gibraltar was also taken from the Spanish; it was easier to defend but it had a very poor harbour. English Harbour

Model of the royal dockyard at Plymouth (detail), 1772–74 (SLR2149)

in Antigua provided refuge from hurricanes, and Port Royal in Jamaica was the main base in the western Caribbean. Several good harbours were lost with the American Revolution but forces were maintained at Halifax and Bermuda. Other bases taken during the conflict included the Cape of Good Hope and Malta.

A dockyard was mainly about the building and upkeep of ships and it was the core of a fully fledged naval base, for many other facilities were needed. Ships of war hardly ever came alongside except for major repairs, so they needed sheltered water in which to rest, particularly a river or a natural harbour where they could be laid up

or await repair. It would probably only have one entrance and exit, and a fleet might be trapped in it if the wind was not favourable, so each base also needed an inner anchorage, less sheltered but more convenient as an exit. It also needed an outer anchorage where the fleet was sheltered from the prevailing winds but ready to put to sea the moment it was needed. In addition, a naval base usually had numerous depot ships and hulks moored in the harbour, holding newly pressed seamen, stores and prisoners of war. There was typically an armament store nearby operated by the Ordnance Board, which supplied guns and ammunition to both the army and the navy.

ABOVE AND OPPOSITE ABOVE Artisans thought to be producing munitions at Woolwich Arsenal, watercolour, 1740–60 (PAI0745, PAI7701) OPPOSITE BELOW Munitions workers in Laboratory Square, Woolwich Arsenal, watercolour, 1740–60 (PAI0746)

Gunpowder storage was not popular with local inhabitants: in 1750 the people of Greenwich petitioned to have a magazine removed.

Since they were some distance from London and other naval bases, Portsmouth and Plymouth both had a full range of facilities. For victualling, Portsmouth had offices, a brewery, a bakehouse and a slaughterhouse dispersed around the town, with the main store in the Weevil Yard across the harbour in Gosport. The Ordnance Board premises followed a common pattern by moving from the ancient Square Tower into Priddy's Hard on the western side of the harbour, and expanding the gun wharf on the east. Originally the marines were quartered in inns and houses, until an old cooperage was taken over as a barracks in the

1760s. A hospital was opened at Haslar in 1753, on a peninsula so that convalescent seamen would find it more difficult to desert. Plymouth was equally well equipped, with two breweries and a slaughterhouse on the Cornwall side of the Tamar, and the main victualling store at Lambhay in the town itself. The marine barracks at Stonehouse was purpose-built and opened in 1783, while the hospital nearby was built during the Seven Years War.

Taken as a whole, the Thames and Medway complex had the main naval victualling yard at Deptford, from where cattle could be bought from Smithfield Market, slaughtered and salted in casks. There was a subsidiary yard at Chatham, mainly used for ships in harbour which were on

'petty warrant' victuals. The main ordnance depot was at Woolwich, with a smaller one at Chatham. There were Royal Marine barracks at Chatham and later Woolwich.

The dockyards were controlled by the Navy Board, which was subordinate to the Admiralty. Dockyard management was a confusion of overlapping responsibilities, originally created in an unsuccessful attempt to prevent corruption. Ships and sailors in commission were under the command of the port admiral who reported to the Admiralty and was technically outside the dockyard system. The commissioner was the most senior figure; he actually had little direct power but a good deal of status and a very grand house.

His main responsibility was to inform the Navy Board what was going on, and to liaise between the dockyard and the port admiral. The dockyard itself was run by the senior officers. The master shipwright was responsible for shipbuilding and repair, and managed the largest part of the workforce, for instance the shipwrights, sawyers and caulkers. The master attendant was in charge of the ships afloat and in dry dock, and of the riggers of the yard. He also acted as harbour-master and was responsible for pilotage and buoyage. The clerk of the survey was responsible for contracts; the clerk of the cheque was the finance officer; the storekeeper was much grander than his title suggests and was one of the five principal officers.

The dockyard took in all kinds of supplies – different timbers for shipbuilding, iron for making anchors, hemp for rope, canvas for sails, tar, nails and many others.

Ship repair was the most important function of the dockyards, particularly work which involved the ship's bottom, and therefore needed a dry dock. The docks were the 'unique selling point' of the yards and gave them their name. They had to be dug out, lined with brick or wood and fitted with more or less waterproof gates, so they needed much more investment than a building slip, which was essentially a flat piece of ground close to a river or natural harbour. Privately owned dry docks were comparatively rare and could not handle the biggest ships. In any case, the navy did not trust private enterprise with repair work, which needed more detailed supervision than new building.

One advantage of British waters was the rise

ABOVE Watch that belonged to Matthew Smith, a rope-maker from Woolwich, c.1805 (JEW0256) BELOW Print showing the process of rope-making, by Robert Benard, engraving, c.1787 (PAI8126)

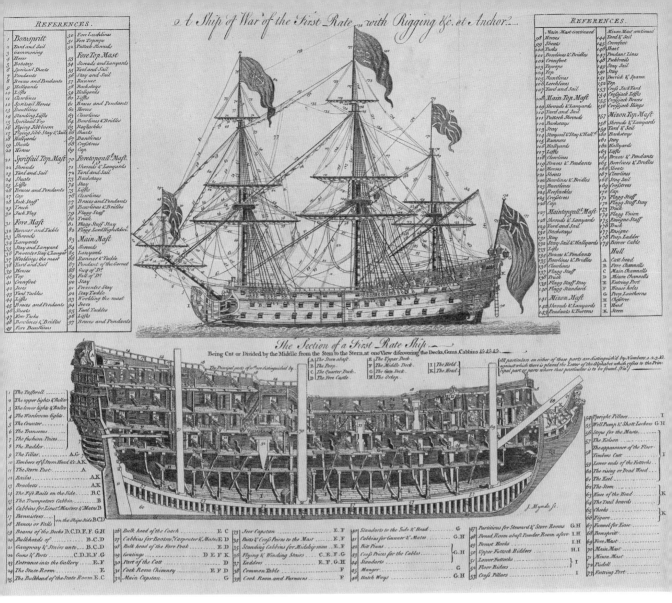

*A Ship of War of the First Rate with Rigging &c. at Anchor,* by J. Mynde, engraving, mid-eighteenth century (PAI2630)

and fall of tides, which could fill and empty the docks. In the relatively tideless Mediterranean, ships usually had to be careened by heeling them over to one side and then the other. The British home dockyards operated to a fortnightly cycle, using the high spring tides to lift ships over the sills of the docks. A ship might be put in for a quick cleaning for less than twenty-four hours during successive tides. It might remain in the dock for a fortnight between spring tides for a small

repair, or for a much longer period for a medium or great repair. The seventy-four-gun *Bellona* was built at Chatham between 1758 and 1760, and was docked for short periods in July 1760, February and November 1761. In June 1763, at the end of the Seven Years War, she was fitted as a guardship at Portsmouth. She was docked for fourteen days in 1764 and six weeks in 1767.

The royal dockyards also built new ships: approximately half those used by the navy during the century. Originally the master shipwrights designed the navy's ships themselves, within tight limits imposed by the establishments of dimensions. That function was taken away in the 1740s, and they and their assistants subsequently supervised building according to plans prepared by the surveyor of the navy in London. The largest ships – three-decker first rates of 100 guns or more, and second rates of ninety to ninety-eight guns – were invariably built in the dockyards, often in dry docks where they could be floated out slowly rather than launched, with less danger of accident in a narrow and often crowded river. Apart from that, new ships were generally built in the dockyard in peacetime to keep the labour force together, especially during the long peace of 1714–39. During these years, old ships were often 'rebuilt' – an ambiguous term which came increasingly to mean that few or none of the ship's existing timbers were retained. This was a process that the navy did not trust to private enterprise, so rebuilding was always done in the dockyards. It did not survive the start of war in 1739, when there was no time even to go through the motions of taking an old ship to pieces (in a valuable dry dock) before starting the new one. The practice of building ships by contract was revived, as it was in all subsequent wars.

*An exact Representation of Launching the Prince of Wales Man of War, before their Majesties, at Portsmouth*, by John Barlow after Joshua Cristall, engraving, 1 October 1794 (PAD6038)

The size and complexity of naval ships made them objects of wonder and symbols of national power and prestige. As a result, the launch of a great warship was often a spectacular public occasion. For example, the launch of the *Nelson* at Woolwich in 1814 was a grand event, attended by the first lord of the Admiralty and the great Prussian Field-Marshal Blücher.

*By two-o'clock the tide had flowed nearly high enough, and at 32 minutes past two the usual signal was given, the remaining shores were taken away, and the Nelson began to move. She went off the slips and glided into the river, amidst the shouts of at least 20,000 spectators. Having been named with the usual ceremony of throwing a bottle of wine against her bows, she drifted into the middle of the river, and dropped anchor...the bands played martial music, and the launch ended.*[5]

The dockyards also looked after ships 'in ordinary', which had been laid up in peacetime in the expectation that they might be needed in a future war. At the end of the Seven Years War in 1763, for example, the yards had to cope with the problems of the fleet after years of hard service. Although the reduction in ships was relatively moderate, the number of men voted by parliament was rapidly reduced between 1762 and 1764. This meant that most of the ships, particularly the larger ones, would rarely put to sea. Instead they were laid up in the dockyard ports under the supervision of the master attendant. Their guns were taken out, and their rigging and fittings were put in the extensive dockyard storehouses, labelled and still allocated to the individual ships. At Chatham in December 1768 it was reported that, 'Ships in ordinary at this port are laid up extending from Rochester Reach to the lower part of Gillingham'.[6] In May 1771, there were twenty-one ships laid up in the Medway. They included the new 100-gun *Victory*, for after her launch she was moored in the river under the care of her standing officers: the boatswain, carpenter and gunner.[7]

The guardships were one level of readiness above the ships 'in ordinary', manned with about three-fifths of the normal crew, rigged and fitted with guns so that they could put to sea at short notice if there was a sudden crisis. Perhaps the most famous was the seventy-four-gun *Triumph*, in which the young Horatio Nelson served as a midshipman. Not content with the static nature of the service, he had himself appointed to command a boat: 'Thus by degrees I became a good pilot... from Chatham to the Tower of London, down to the Swin, and the North Foreland.'[8]

Considering his vital role in national defence and imperial expansion, remarkably little was written about the ordinary shipwright and his skills. There were plenty of books on naval architecture but far less on the cutting of wood and the assembly of the hull. In theory, all the shipwrights were members of the same profession, but in practice distinctions set in as soon a boy was indentured. As early as 1664, Edmund Bushnell wrote,

*Although some* [shipwrights] *have many servants, and by Indenture (I suppose) bound to Teach them all alike the same Art and Mystery that he himself useth; Yet it may be he may Teach some one, and the rest be kept ignorant, so that those Ship-Wrights, although bred by such knowing Men, yet they are able to teach their Servants nothing, more than to Hew, or Dub, to Fay a Piece when it is Moulded to his place assigned, or the like.*[9]

A boy was apprenticed to an individual rather than the organisation; if his master was a master shipwright or his assistant, he would learn the secrets of design. If he was an ordinary workman, the boy would become a highly skilled manual worker. However, our best description of the shipwright's life comes from a young woman, Mary Lacy, who disguised herself as a man and began an apprenticeship in Portsmouth dockyard in 1763. As soon as her indenture was signed, 'my master went and bought me a saw, an ax and chizzel, which made me very proud to think I had some new tools to work with'. Such tools required professional skill and expertise. There were no mechanical aids or twist drills in those days and soon, despite having spent some years at sea, she found the work was very hard. 'The first work I was called upon was, to bore holes in the bottom of a ship called the Thunderer, which, as I was at first unacquainted with the method of doing it, proved hard work for me. This occasioned me to think I should not be able to serve out my time without being discovered.'[10] The apprentice's wages were paid to his master, who was responsible for feeding him (or her). When Mary Lacy's master became bankrupt, she had to endure hardship: 'My master now became so poor, that he was not able to buy me a pair of shoes.'[11]

Shipwrights were fiercely protective of their craft. In February 1741, Commissioner Richard Hughes heard 'three loud acclamations or huzzas'. He soon found that 'the shipwrights had received...intelligence that one William Ainell... had not regularly served his time to the trade, and for the reason aforesaid horsed him out of the yard; that is...the shipwrights surrounded him, put a piece of quarter [timber] beneath his legs, took him up on their shoulders, carried him just without the gate, then sat him down, gave three shouts as above, and returned to their duty'.[12]

Shipwrights had the privilege of taking home 'chips', or pieces of wood that were too small to be useful in shipbuilding. The definition expanded over the years, until in 1755 the commissioner at Chatham decreed that a piece which could be carried under a man's arm was lawful, one which had to be carried on the shoulder was not. Security was increased on the gate but the 'men with chips on their shoulders' forced their way through. This led to several days of rioting, during which marines were called in to restore order. The alleged ringleaders were pressed illegally into the navy, then taken round to Portsmouth where they were released to find their own way home.

Shipwrights formed about a quarter of the total dockyard workforce, though they regarded themselves as the elite. Labourers were the next biggest group, followed by sawyers who cut the

BELOW Fid, used for working canvas and splicing, nineteenth to twentieth century (TOS0412) OPPOSITE ABOVE Grease horn containing needles, and a sail-maker's needle case, nineteenth to twentieth century (TOS0911, TOS0907) OPPOSITE BOTTOM Cream-ware mug inscribed 'Success to the Sailmakers', c. 1800 (AAA6332)

there, though this was felt much less in the vicinity of an expanding metropolis like London than in an outpost such as Plymouth. A dockyard usually boosted the local shipbuilding industry, for the navy preferred that contract-built ships should be kept close to the dockyards where naval officials could keep an eye on them. The Thames already had many private shipbuilders, including the Blackwall yard, the largest in the country, which also built East Indiamen and other large merchant ships. Medway shipbuilders were far less prolific in naval work, but Greaves of Frindsbury near Rochester built the famous seventy-four-gun *Bellerophon*. The best-known private yard in the Portsmouth area

timbers to shape, or 'sided' them, in sawpits. There were hundreds of caulkers who filled the spaces between the planks of ships with oakum and tar, sail-makers, and joiners and house-carpenters who fitted out the interiors of ships and buildings. More than thirty other trades were represented, including bricklayers, glaziers, hair-bed manufacturers, painters, and trenail mooters who made the wooden pegs which held the ships together. Woolwich, Chatham, Portsmouth and Plymouth also had roperies employing hundreds of men.

A dockyard was a benefit to local employment that went far beyond the workers employed

was Buckler's Hard on the Beaulieu River, where Henry Adams built Nelson's *Agamemnon*. However, this was an object lesson in the dangers of becoming too dependent on naval work, which dried up almost entirely in peacetime, and the shipyard closed after the war ended in 1815.

Many other industries supplied the needs of the dockyards. Timber was rarely sourced close to the dockyards by the eighteenth century, and the Navy Board spread the search for it further afield as time went on, with much coming from the Baltic. But there was still work for the barge-masters who might bring the timber up to the dockyard wharves. One industry that flourished in the dockyard areas was the carving of figureheads and other decorations. In the 1760s, Richard Chicheley was under contract for carving work at Chatham and Sheerness, and the head he produced for the *Victory* was 'executed in a masterly manner'.[13] Even the weakest in society might find some kind of employment, and the poor of the Chatham area were collectively paid £100 per annum for picking oakum.

The royal dockyards were often regarded as deeply conservative institutions but they produced their share of innovation. Wooden ships were plagued by weeds and barnacles, which grew on their bottoms and reduced speed, and by shipworm, which might enter a hull in tropical waters and eat its way along the timbers. Many solutions were suggested but the ideal one was to sheath the hull in copper, which was first done with the frigate *Alarm* in 1761. It dealt with weed and worm but the electrolytic action between copper and iron bolts and rudder gear caused alarming decay. Nonetheless, in 1780 it was decided to go ahead with coppering the whole fleet, using tarred paper to keep the two metals apart. This greatly increased the ships' performance. It was enough

Naval figurehead representing a lion, c.1720 (FHD0088)

to keep the fleet in order for the remaining three years of war but it could not last forever. In 1786, it was decided to drive out every iron bolt below the waterline as ships came in for repair, and replace them with an alloy of copper and zinc. The programme was practically complete by 1793, just in time for the next war with France.

Innovation was given a boost by the appointment of Sir Samuel Bentham as inspector-general of naval works in 1796. He introduced steam power for machinery and trialled many inventions. Marc Isambard Brunel, the father of the great Victorian engineer, designed highly innovative machinery to make rigging blocks at Portsmouth in an early form of mass production: forty-three machines were installed by 1806, so that six men could do the work of sixty. When Robert Seppings became master shipwright at Chatham in 1804, he too saw ways of improving dockyard and shipbuilding practice. Now that ships did not stick rigidly to line-ahead formation in battle, the light construction of their bows and sterns became increasingly vulnerable. After Trafalgar, Seppings began to investigate reinforcing the main structure of the bow right up to the forecastle. His work on sterns

was less popular, as it reduced the comfort of the officers' cabins. His main contribution, however, was to recognise that there was no diagonal element in ship construction, ignoring the principle well known to the meanest mechanic that a triangle is much stronger than a rectangle. Beginning with the *Tremendous* in 1810, he applied a method of diagonal bracing to the interior of the hull, greatly reducing hogging or sagging at the ends. It became standard for all ships.

It is only within recent decades that the royal dockyards have begun to receive sustained historical attention. Naval history was previously about battles rather than logistics, and was largely written by naval officers or those who read their reports and interviewed them. The dockyards were regarded as dens of corruption and incompetence, and were unjustly blamed, for example, for the slowness of British ships and the loss of the *Royal George* in 1782. Modern research has produced a far more balanced picture. The royal dockyards were not without faults but they serviced the greatest fleet in the world, as well as contributing to local employment and industry, and supporting several key inventions.

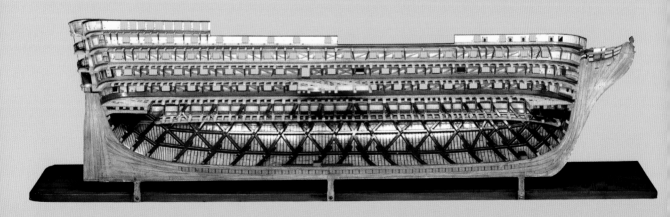

Half-hull model of the *Caledonia*, 120 guns, showing diagonal bracing, c.1828 (SLR0120)

The *Bellona* of 1760 was one of the first British seventy-four-gun ships, using a highly successful layout that originated with the French navy and was developed by Sir Thomas Slade to meet the Royal Navy's needs. The *Bellona* was the first of the type with a 168-foot gun deck, which became standard for more than twenty years. In 1761, she fought a famous single-ship action and captured the French *Courageux* – another vessel that would have a great deal of influence on British design. The *Bellona* served in the Royal Navy until 1814, an unusually long life. Ships with the same basic layout formed the greater part of all contemporary battle fleets, not least Nelson's fleets at the Battle of the Nile in 1798 and the Battle of Trafalgar in 1805.

These three models of the ship are all different in style and function. The block model from about 1760 was a type that could be made quickly and cheaply, and may have been used to approve the design (see top right). The framing model from about 1770 has a conventional system on its port side and a slightly more innovative method to starboard (see bottom right). It was presumably used to demonstrate an idea which was never executed, and it is an invaluable source for mid-eighteenth-century shipbuilding practices. It shows the framing of the hull completed with most of the wales, or thicker planks, in place. The constituent parts of the wales are interlocked for strength, a system known as 'hook and butt', which was intended to give greater longitudinal

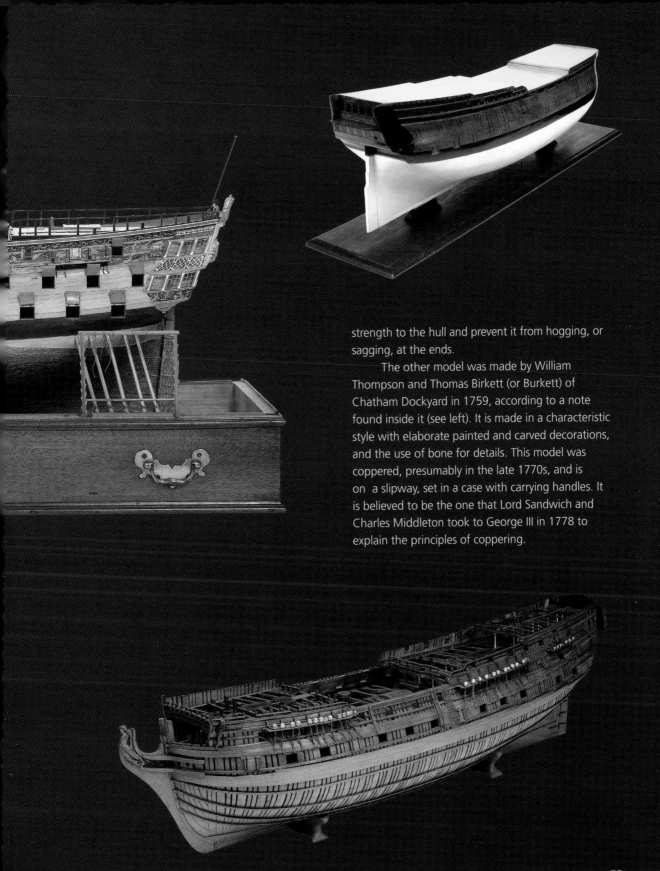

strength to the hull and prevent it from hogging, or sagging, at the ends.

The other model was made by William Thompson and Thomas Birkett (or Burkett) of Chatham Dockyard in 1759, according to a note found inside it (see left). It is made in a characteristic style with elaborate painted and carved decorations, and the use of bone for details. This model was coppered, presumably in the late 1770s, and is on a slipway, set in a case with carrying handles. It is believed to be the one that Lord Sandwich and Charles Middleton took to George III in 1778 to explain the principles of coppering.

# 4

# LIFE AFLOAT

## Quintin Colville

The Royal Navy profoundly shaped British culture and society during the eighteenth century, and yet for most British people during this period the identities and daily activities of its sailors remained mysterious and wreathed in stereotype. Even those who did come face to face with the 'Jack Tar' in the streets of a port town or city might not have seen past his carefully cultivated image. One seaman, Robert Hay, has left us with an engaging portrait of the sailor as he appeared ashore in Plymouth:

> The jolly tar himself was seen with his white dimity trousers fringed at the bottom, his fine scarlet waistcoat bound with black ribbon, his dark blue broadcloth jacket studded with pale buttons, his black silk neckcloth thrown carelessly about his sunburnt neck. An elegant hat of straw, indicative of his recent return from a foreign station, cocked on one side; a head of hair reaching to his waistband; a smart switch made from the backbone of a shark under one arm; his doxy [girl] under the other, a huge chew of tobacco in his cheek...thus fitted-out, in 'good sailing trim', as he himself styles it, he strides along with all the importance of an Indian nabob.[1]

The fact that this finery had been fished from the depths of a sea chest in the excitement of leave-going, and was never intended to be worn at sea, was lost on the casual observer. The compelling image that it presented – at once hearty, generous, charismatic and exotic – may not have been untruthful, but it was a carefully and creatively edited version of naval life. The aim of this chapter, however, is to look beyond the ignorance of the landlubber and the selectivity of the seafarer to the experience of naval service itself. The wooden world that emerges is certainly one that was packed with idiosyncrasy. At the same time, though, the navy's social norms closely reflected the conventions of the nation from which its manpower was predominantly drawn. From the start, therefore, we can say that life afloat was never entirely life apart: the Royal Navy was an evolving compound of difference and sameness, familiarity and strangeness.

Before going any further, it is useful to consider how and why the navy's rank-and-file personnel found themselves in His Majesty's service in the first place. After all, the experience of life afloat was likely to be informed by the circumstances that made this existence a reality. Within the public imagination it is the activities of the press gang which have become most closely associated with manning the navy and, as a result, violent compulsion rather than personal choice has often appeared the deciding factor. This starting point has, in turn, frequently inflected

An Indian silk neckerchief that belonged to Samuel Enderby, a sailor who fought at the Battle of Trafalgar c.1805 (TXT0284)

our broader picture of naval service in this era. Men ripped from their families and forced to sea against their will must surely have become sullen and recalcitrant crews, who could only have been rendered compliant through unremitting and brutal discipline. The oppositional and oppressive character that this applies to the institution is, though, partial and misleading. In reality, and across the century, the majority of those on board British warships chose to be there and, we may assume, saw the occupation as compatible in one way or another with their own interests.[2]

For some – not least the impressionably young – the navy appeared a direct route to a life of novelty, romance and adventure. Recalling his childhood in the 1750s, William Spavens wrote:

> *I thought sailors must be happy men to have such opportunities of visiting foreign countries, and beholding the wonderful works of the Creator in the remote regions of the earth...I thought of nothing but pleasant gales and prosperous voyages, and indulging a curiosity which seemed implanted in my nature.*[3]

Another seaman, Samuel Leech, remembered the tales his sailor cousins 'used to tell of wild adventures and hairbreadth escapes, spinning out the winter evening's tale to the infinite delight of their willing listeners';[4] and John Nicol, apprenticed to a cooper, found that 'while my hands were hooping barrels my mind was at sea, and my imagination in foreign climes'.[5] Others responded to the rousing, patriotic rhetoric deployed on volunteering posters, such as the example shown here, or to their customary subtext that joining up was the mark of manliness. But the majority – from green novices to seasoned merchant mariners – are likely to have been attracted by more quantifiable returns. The navy paid a good and more importantly a dependable wage, often with a bounty for

the new recruit. It provided shelter, three meals a day, medical attention if required, and the promise of a pension in later life. Moreover, a pre-eminent inducement in the minds of many sailors was the fact that the entire crew of a warship stood to benefit from the sale of an enemy vessel captured as a prize (along with any cargo it might be carrying). In addition, those used to working on board merchant ships were well aware that the far larger crew of a warship meant that daily duties were less onerous and spread more thinly.

At the same time, while the supply of unforced labour to the navy's lower deck might sustain peacetime needs, the expanded requirements of war were a very different story and a dangerously exposed Achilles heel. Helping to fill the shortfall that invariably occurred was the particular contribution of the Impress Service. Organised into predominantly coastal districts, each with a regulating captain and a gang of sailors or hired hands, the press targeted those experienced in working at sea: the scrawny tailor featured in the satirical print below would not have been high on the list. One Cornish seaman has left us with a highly coloured, early nineteenth-century account of its activities:

> *I have...deeply engraven on the memory of my boyhood the apprehensions and alarms that were experienced amongst the inhabitants of our town regarding the press-gang during the war. The cry that 'the press-gang was coming' was sufficient to cause all the young and eligible men of the town to flock up to the hills and away to the country as fast as possible, and to hide themselves in all manner of places till the danger was supposed to be over. It was not always, however, that the road to the country was open to them, for the authorities sometimes arranged that a troop of light horse should be at hand to cut off their retreat when the press-gang landed. Then might the soldiers be seen, with drawn cutlasses, riding down the poor fishermen, often through fields of standing corn where they had sought to hide themselves, while the press-gang were engaged in diligently searching every house in order to secure their victims.*[6]

The bitter harvest of the press gang therefore made up a significant but not dominating component of the navy's human material. The irony that a service popularly celebrated for preserving national liberties routinely did so at the expense of personal freedoms was not lost on contemporaries. Presuming, though, that all pressed men remained indefinitely resentful would be a mistake. Carried on board one of Admiral Vernon's ships destined

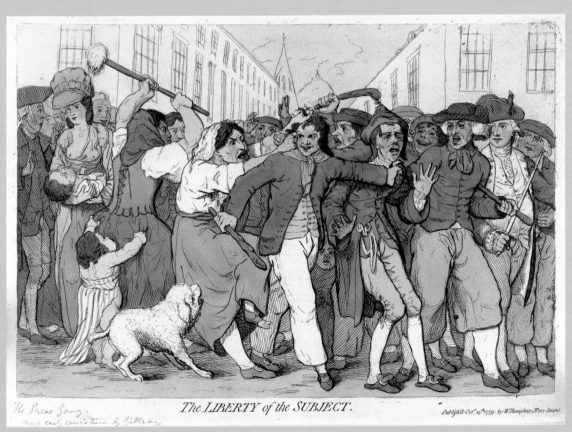

The Press Gang.
sure early caricature by Gillray

*The LIBERTY of the SUBJECT.*

Publish'd Oct.r 15.th 1779. by W.Humphrey N.º 227 Strand.

Presentation sword given by Lloyd's Patriotic Fund to Captain Charles J.M. Mansfield, commanding officer of the *Minotaur* at the Battle of Trafalgar, 1805 (WPN1491)

for the Caribbean in 1739, Henry Roberts seems to have warmed to the task at hand:

> *My Deare Life,*
> *When I left you, heven nose it was with an akin hart for I thout it very hard to be hauld from you by a gang of rufins but...I soon overcome that when I found that we were about to go in earnest to rite my natif contry and against a parcel of impadent Spaniards by whom I have often been ill treted and god nows my heart I have longed this four years past to cut off some of their ears and was in hope I should haf sent you one for a sample.*[7]

It is worth noting, by contrast, that no such *force majeure* was required to swell the navy's officer corps – the nation's gentry provided a usually reliable stream of candidates for this status

(significantly supplemented by those promoted from the lower deck). The explanation does not lie in the nature of an officer's job, which was dangerous and unfashionably technical; nor in his living conditions, which were austere, socially constrained and far removed from the clubs and drawing rooms of elite society. Instead, what recommended the position of officer were its affordability and its prospects, combined with a sufficient air of gentlemanliness. Rather than requiring a substantial financial outlay to open the door of preferment, a boy on the road to officer rank was trained without charge and paid into the bargain. Family connections could also smooth his path to promotion considerably, although patronage was rarely bestowed indefinitely on those without merit. Furthermore, if blessed with good fortune, considerable rewards lay within an officer's reach. A warship's commanding officer was entitled to

City of London freedom box presented to Vice-Admiral Sir John Jervis, 1794–95 (PLT0075)

Tankard commemorating Captain William Pierrepont's part in taking the Spanish frigates *Thetis* and *Santa Brigida* – with £600,000 of treasure – off Cape Finisterre in 1799, 1799–1800 (PLT0169)

a quarter of the value of any prize captured, and this meant wealth for many and wholly trans-formational riches for a lucky few. The role of naval officer was, in consequence, tailor-made for respectable families on the make. For those who stood to inherit great titles and fortunes, though, its concomitant perils and hardships were a price they did not feel compelled to pay.

The seamless interweaving of self-interest and public service that this reveals was entirely consistent with eighteenth-century notions of office-holding, from diplomacy and politics to the royal court and the church. Indeed, an un-ashamed appetite for personal gain helped to drive eighteenth-century naval achievement in a way that the Victorian and Edwardian officer corps, with its cult of selfless and professionalised duty, would come to find deeply problematic. No such scruples troubled Admiral Boscawen, who

wrote of his new house, 'I flatter myself to make the French pay for this building this summer. I have got at least one-fifth of it already, and another trip to the southward will bring three or four sugar ships more in our way'.[8] Officers' fortunes were also boosted by a close and symbiotic relation-ship with the powerful mercantile companies and City corporations whose vessels and trading net-works they protected. Presented to naval officers from just such sources, the glittering objects above reveal that, during this period, the rewards for valour could be rather more tangible than just the thanks of a grateful nation.

Nonetheless, whatever an individual's back-ground or ambitions, the bewilderment of stepping on board a warship for the first time was surely an experience common to all. If, for instance, we take as an example the workhorse of the late eight-eenth-century Royal Navy, the seventy-four-gun ship of the line, the first impression must have been of a formidably complex and superficially chaotic environment. Within the, approximately, 160 feet of its length and fifty feet of its beam, a crew of 600 to 700 lived and worked, surrounded by the myriad provisions required to sustain them, and the vast paraphernalia without which the vessel would be unable to sail or fight. Moreover, far from being an undifferentiated pool of humanity, the crew was stratified and clustered not only by rank but by age, skill, trade and status. The patchwork of self-contained but interlocking communities that resulted was perhaps as opaque to the newcomer as the regime of an antheap.

If a flagship, then an admiral or commodore stood at the pinnacle of formal authority, with the captain and his lieutenants comprising the vessel's remaining commissioned officers. All received their appointments directly from the Admiralty, and conceived their duties as, in general terms, commanding and fighting the vessel. Beneath them stood a range of more specialised personnel termed warrant officers. These comprised the master, who navigated the ship; the purser, who managed the foodstuffs consumed by the ship's crew; and the surgeon, gunner, carpenter and boatswain – the latter responsible for, among other things, all sails and rigging. A subordinate tier of officers included men such as the armourer, the cook, the gunsmith, the sail-maker, the schoolmaster and the master-at-arms, as well as the midshipmen and master's mates, who might in due course expect promotion to higher, and often to commissioned, rank.

The remaining majority of the ship's company was subdivided in accordance with an additional and complex set of demarcations. Some men formed dedicated teams under the control of, for instance, the sail-maker or carpenter, or were detailed to assist others such as the cook, armourer and cooper. Large numbers were required to handle the vessel itself, each of whom was allocated a station in areas of the ship such as the forecastle

towards the bow, amidships in the waist, aloft in the tops, or on the quarterdeck as part of the afterguard. Known as landsmen, some of these were novices without seagoing experience, who would be kept at a safe distance from any duties requiring individual skill. After a year afloat such men might be rated as ordinary seamen, and after two as able seamen; rungs on the ladder that brought increased pay, greater respect and more demanding roles. From the latter category the captain would also select men to become petty officers, a rank that included, for instance, coxswains (responsible for the ship's boats), and boatswain's mates (who assisted in maintaining daily routine and discipline). Another significant group on board were the servants attached to the captain, the wardroom, the midshipmen and the warrant

Portrait of a seaman, attributed to James Gillray, watercolour, late eighteenth century (PAD8576)

officers. Finally, the ship would carry a detachment of marines – whose continuous existence as a corps dates from 1755 – which was complete with its own commissioned and non-commissioned officers. In addition, though, the entire edifice of officer and non-officer roles and responsibilities was bisected by a fundamental distinction. For those who actually worked the ship, from the lieutenants to the newest and greenest member of the afterguard, daily life was broken into periods on or off watch. By contrast, specialist non-seamen such as the surgeon, the purser, the schoolmaster, the carpenter and, where relevant, their crews and assistants, could maintain the normal routine of a working day and a night's sleep.

Setting out the navy's ranks and ratings can only take us so far into the texture of life afloat. In order to explore further, we should consider some of the social and cultural dimensions of naval service and the ability of the ship itself to shape the experiences and relationships of those on board. In this connection, the greater proportion of the crew of a seventy-four-gun warship ate, slept and passed their leisure time on the lowest of the vessel's gun decks. The vital requirement for structural strength and integrity meant that head height was limited, and the massive, receding forms of cannons on their heavy wooden carriages and rows of hammocks slung from the deckhead dominated the long cramped space.

To the volunteer Robert Hay, the human cargo of this universe was beyond anything he had known. and he noted that while most sailors were English, Scottish, Irish or Welsh, men from many lands and racial backgrounds literally rubbed shoulders:

> It would be difficult to give any adequate idea of the scenes these...decks presented: complexions of every varied hue, and features of every cast, from the...African, to the...Asiatic; the rosy complexion of the English swain, and the sallow features of the sunburnt Portuguese; people of

*Olaudah Equiano or Gustavus Vassa, the African,* by Daniel Orme after W. Denton, published by Vassa in his autobiography, stipple engraving, 1789 (ZBA2657)

> every profession and of the most contrasted manners, from the brawny ploughman to the delicate fop; the decayed author and bankrupt merchant who had eluded their creditors; the apprentices who had run from servitude; the improvident and impoverished father who had abandoned his family, and the smuggler who had escaped by flight the vengeance of the laws. Costumes ranged from the kilted Highlander... to the knuckle ruffles of the haughty Spaniard, to the gaudy and tinselled trappings of the dismissed footman, to the rags and tatters of the city beggar...To the ear came a hubbub little short of Babel: Irish, Welsh, Dutch, Portuguese, Spanish, French, Swedish, Italian, together with every provincial dialect prevailing between Land's End and John O'Groats.[9]

# WATERCOLOURS OF NAVAL LIFE
## BY GABRIEL BRAY, 1774–75 (PAJ1998, PAJ1989, PAJ2024, PAJ2018)

Born in 1750, Gabriel Bray was a naval officer with an extraordinary, and perhaps unequalled, artistic gift for capturing the ordinary and everyday moments of Royal Naval life during the eighteenth century. The four examples of his work shown here belong within a collection of more than seventy drawings purchased for the National Maritime Museum by the Macpherson Fund of the Society for Nautical Research in April 1991. The majority of these date from the period 1774–75, during which Bray served under Captain the Honourable William Cornwallis as second

lieutenant of the forty-four-gun frigate *Pallas*. The voyage took him to Tenerife and a number of West African destinations – to support British commercial interests there, including the slave trade – before making for Barbados and finally Jamaica.

When duties permitted, Bray used these months to observe and record the people and circumstances that surrounded him. The results are remarkably unconfined by artistic convention, picturesque sensibility or, indeed, by his own social position. Instead, an evident and sympathetic curiosity in human life propelled him to make ordinary sailors, Royal Marines and servants as much the subjects of his sketches as his brother officers. In a series of fresh and lifelike 'snapshots' we see, for instance: a steward weighing some beef for a wardroom dinner;

a sailor bringing up his hammock from below decks to air; a man dangling a fishing line from the end of a cannon; a midshipman dozing on the ship's taffrail; and a group of marines eating a meal while seated on their sea chests. Both directly and indirectly, Bray also turned the lens on himself. One watercolour shows him shaving with the assistance of a travelling mirror, his creased and rumpled shirt testifying to the casual dress of an officer at sea. Another depicts the master's mate of the *Pallas* examining Bray's sketchbook. Nor was the world ashore any less a source of fascination. In the weeks before he set sail on the *Pallas*, Bray painted a range of scenes that place his naval work in a broader context, for example: a bootblack, a street vendor and a country reaper with his sickle and keg of ale. Once in Portsmouth, where the *Pallas* was fitting out, he also created a wonderful representation of

a greengrocer's shop, with autumn fruit stacked in baskets and bundles of clay pipes on a shelf.

Perhaps lacking the necessary patron, Bray never advanced beyond the rank of lieutenant. He was given command of a number of cutters: the *Sprightly* in 1779, the *Nimble* in 1782, and the *Hind* in the early 1790s. However, these were his last postings, and he spent the rest of his life on half pay. Gabriel Bray died in 1823, aged seventy-three, at Charmouth in Dorset.

Indeed, a record from the *Caledonia* in 1811 indicates that Danish, Swedish, African, Portuguese, Chinese, West Indian, Brazilian, German, Polish and Italian sailors were among the crew.[10]

Before long, this seething mass resolved itself into something more ordered and comprehensible. Between each pair of cannon a table was laid at mealtimes, and the six or eight men that sat around it constituted a 'mess', the basic social building block of the lower-deck world. Beyond any doubt, part of the glue of these small communities was food. In the words of Samuel Pepys:

> *Englishmen, and more especially seamen, love their bellies above anything else, and therefore it must always be remembered in the management of the victualling of the Navy that to make any abatement in the quantity or agreeableness of the victuals is to discourage and provoke them in the tenderest point, and will sooner render them disgusted with the King's service than any other hardship that can be put upon them.*[11]

The standard of victualling achieved by the second half of the eighteenth century suggests that Pepys's sentiments had been thoroughly digested. The ingredients that were casked and stored in a ship's hold were generally of a high quality. A sailor's weekly diet comprised bread or biscuit, pork, beef, pease, butter, cheese and oatmeal, to which might be added suet, raisins, vinegar, stockfish and fresh vegetables or fruit when available. In the substance and nutritional value of their meals, the navy's lower ranks fared better than most of their peers ashore. A daily quantity of alcohol was also provided, in the form of beer, rum, wine or brandy.

ABOVE Ship's biscuit inscribed 'This biscuit was given – Miss Blacket at Berwick on Tuesday 13 April 1784, Bewick' (AAB0003) RIGHT Sailor's love token, late eighteenth century (MEC1641)

It was also in the context of the mess that sailors enjoyed their recreation. Men sang, danced and played musical instruments such as fiddles, fifes and drums; they gambled, wrestled and spun yarns in which embroidered inventiveness was often prized more than accuracy. As a result of this inescapably close-knit interaction, the community of the mess generated loyalties that typically outweighed more conceptual allegiances to the nation, the Royal Navy, or even to the ship. At the same time, and notwithstanding the glare of this incessant communality, sailors were also able to cultivate moments of interiority and reflection: painstakingly crafting ornaments from bone or metal, or applying the skill that most developed with needle and thread to making and mending the distinctive items of a sailor's clothing. For the significant numbers who were literate, reading and writing were also popular and potentially private pastimes, valued above all as a means of communicating with loved ones ashore. The majority of lower-deck sailors were young men between the ages of eighteen and twenty-two with few attachments beyond the mess itself. However, for those who were older and married, the competing claims of home and family could make the sending and receiving of letters particularly precious.

Once at anchor in port, though, a sailor's life was transformed. Watchkeeping was not always observed, duties tended to be less arduous and, while leave might not be granted, leisure time was usually extended. Under these

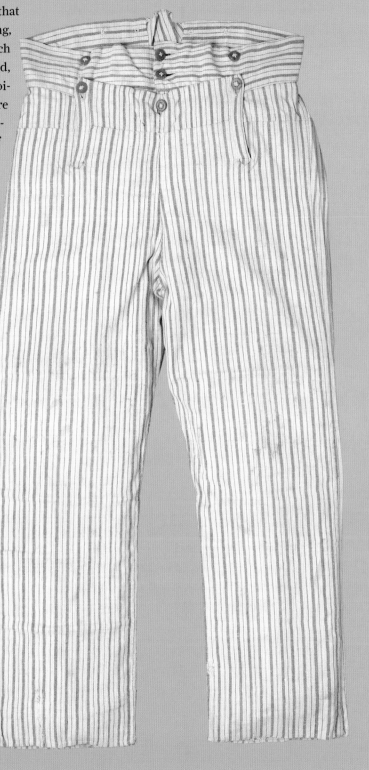

Pair of trousers as worn by lower-deck sailors, c.1810 (UNI0092)

conditions, flotillas of small boats were permitted to approach a warship, some transporting wives or relatives, others with a range of usually over-priced goods for purchase, and many carrying prostitutes. Daniel Goodall's description of the latter casts sailors improbably as the passive and powerless victims of female predation:

> No sooner had the 'Temeraire' cast anchor off Plymouth than she was surrounded by shore boats, for the fact that a ship's company was coming in to receive pay spread somehow with a rapidity and certainty that would have seemed marvellous to those who did not know how numerous were the harpies that preyed upon poor old Jack, and how keen was their scent when plunder was in prospect. The first arrivals were, of course, the fair sex, who set up the most clamorous demands for admission on board, each claiming to have a husband amongst the crew. Some of them, it is true, really were the wives of men belonging to the ship, but, if all had been admitted who set up the claim of connubial right, it would have been a clear case of polygamy, for there could not have been less than a proportion of three or four to every man of marriageable age and position on board. As it was, three days sufficed to see fully more than two hundred of the Delilahs of Plymouth settled amongst the crew.[12]

As this print begins to convey, albeit rather decorously, the male camaraderie of the lower deck was thus dissolved. In fact, when the *Royal George* sank at its moorings off Portsmouth in 1782, as many as 300 women lost their lives. This should not be taken to imply that women were excluded

*A Scene on the Main Deck, of A Line of Battle Ship in Harbour,* by Thomas Sutherland, published by J.B. East, hand-coloured aquatint, 1 June 1820 (PAH7339)

T.Sutherland Sculp.

A SCENE ON THE MAIN DECK,
*of*
*A LINE of BATTLE SHIP in Harbour.*

London Published June 1st 1820 by J.B. East & Co Fenwick Court Strong Square.

from ships at sea. The wives of petty, warrant and commissioned officers frequently lived on board and, on occasion, served alongside men in action by carrying powder to the guns or assisting the surgeon. For example, Ann Hopping, Elizabeth Moore, Ann Taylor, Sarah Bates and Mary French are all recorded among Nelson's squadron at the Battle of the Nile in 1798.

While it was certainly the largest, the lower deck was only one of many living environments on board a ship of the line. Indeed, the navy's system of role and rank found important expression through the diversity of on-board accommodation. For the relatively lowly petty officer this might

ABOVE Sketch between Decks May [17]75, probably showing midshipmen studying and writing letters, by Gabriel Bray, watercolour (PAJ2026) RIGHT Octant that belonged to Lieutenant James Campbell, c.1770 (NAV1344)

My dear Papa & dear Mamma

        I take this Opportunity of writing
to you to inform you that I shall go on board
the Sabrina the first opportunity that offers
itself Mamma, I assure you that I did not forget
the Promise that I made forgeat some Christmas
Pye and Drunk all your healths and wished you
all a long, happy and merry life this letter besides
Contains my best love and a kiss to all well
fare you all with a thousand times and good bye

          I remain

          Yours very dutiful Son
Portsmouth
December 25th     George James Perceval
   1806    A merry Christmas

Decr 25th 1806 from
George at Portsmouth

No 26

Right Honble Lord Arden
Bruton Street
Berkeley Square
London

THE INTERIOR OF A MIDSHIPMAN'S BIRTH

ABOVE *The Interior of a Midshipman's Birth*, published by George Humphrey, hand-coloured aquatint, 12 August 1821 (PAF3730)
OPPOSITE Letter from midshipman George Perceval, perhaps showing the effects of a Christmas party, 25 December 1806 (PER/1)

simply mean a little more room in which to sling his hammock. Midshipmen, on the other hand, occupied a discrete space known as the gunroom. The route into the navy taken by these young-sters was often fast-tracked by family contacts, but could still involve several initial and menial years as a captain's servant. Membership of the gunroom was therefore a significant elevation, and its atmosphere was often characterised as an uneasy cohabitation of adolescent exuberance with pretensions to the dignities of adulthood. Warrant officers were allocated cabins to them-selves in various parts of the ship; the surgeon, for instance, below the waterline on the orlop deck, and the carpenter beneath the forecastle. By custom, though, the ship's commissioned officers congregated at the stern. The more junior occu-pied rows of cabins within an area towards the rear of the main deck known as the wardroom; while the captain – and, if present, the admiral

– could possess spacious quarters comprising day, dining and sleeping cabins as well as elegant stern galleries overlooking the vessel's wake. Given the premium placed on space within a warship, the scope this afforded senior officers to house and display personal possessions (including furniture, silverware, uniform, paintings and books) under-scored their authority (see pp. 92–93).

Contrasting this relative opulence with the lot of an ordinary seaman, whose worldly goods might be kept rolled in his hammock, could suggest that naval life was defined by an exploitative and adversarial relationship between officers and men, 'haves' and 'have nots'. The more convincing inter-pretation, though, is that shipboard society was experienced as a finely graded hierarchy, rather than a binary battleground. Those occupying different rungs on this ladder were not surprised to receive different conditions of service and dif-ferent rewards: structured inequality was part

LIFE AFLOAT **91**

of the bedrock of contemporary British society. The crucial point is that the interests of everyone on board – beginning with their simple physical security – were best served by an efficient, well-trained and harmonious ship. Captains keen to make a name for themselves understood this full well, and endeavoured to gather a following of skilled officers and sailors who might accompany them from one command to the next. These men, in turn, saw a talented or well-connected leader as the surest guarantee of their own fortunes. By the same token, the man sentenced to a dozen lashes was not necessarily the victim of officer prejudice.

Whether through theft, drunkenness or negligence, the disciplinary code that he breached was one in which all ranks had at least some investment. To be sure, the eighteenth-century navy was no stranger to tyranny, oppression and brutality, from the institutionalised cruelties of the press gang to the individual sadism of some naval officers. Addressed in a later chapter, the mutinies that erupted in 1797 also show that the shipboard community could and sometimes did break down altogether. In general, however, life afloat was marked more by stability and consensus than by conflict.

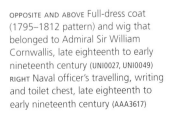

OPPOSITE AND ABOVE Full-dress coat (1795–1812 pattern) and wig that belonged to Admiral Sir William Cornwallis, late eighteenth to early nineteenth century (UNI0027, UNI0049) RIGHT Naval officer's travelling, writing and toilet chest, late eighteenth to early nineteenth century (AAA3617)

# 5

# EXPANSION AND VICTORY

## Dan Snow

It was early summer in the Gulf of St Lawrence but, as so often in those waters, banks of fog made it feel like anything but. A British fleet had been prowling off the coast of Newfoundland for weeks, hoping to snap up French ships bearing reinforcements to New France – King Louis's vast North American empire. Seizing valuable cargoes would please their masters in London, but also bring the crews riches. On 8 June, the British spotted three French warships. They closed to hailing distance. The commander of the French ship, *Alcide*, shouted to enquire whether the two nations were at peace or at war. Richard Howe, captain of the *Dunkirk*, roared back, 'At peace, at peace', even though their respective North American colonists had been exchanging vicious blows for just over a year. To the consternation of the French, this assurance was followed by thundering broadsides as three British warships opened fire and sent around a ton of iron crashing into their hulls. The *Alcide* fought bravely but was eventually captured along with another vessel as the third escaped to spread the tale of Albion's latest perfidy.

The bloody squabbles of unruly colonials were one thing, the considered broadsides of His Majesty's ships were quite another. It was 1755, and Britain and France were now at war, although the politicians delayed the official declaration for nearly a year. It was a dishonourable start to the Seven Years War, in which a small island nation with a modest population, no superabundance of precious minerals, and a temperate if oft-lamented climate, did something no other kingdom – republic or empire – had ever done before. Britain became a global hegemon, capable of sustaining fleets and armies engaged simultaneously across five continents. This success shapes the world to this day. The globalised economy, the omnipotent English language and the constitutional arrangements of the majority of the world's population all stem from Britain's victories – victories delivered by the Royal Navy. The navy defeated enemy fleets, strangled their trade, landed amphibious forces, captured colonies and kept allies supplied.

By the 1750s, France's navy was but a remnant of the mighty force with which Louis XIV had once dominated the seas. The French navy was about half the size of the Royal Navy through the War of the Austrian Succession (1740–48), and by 1755 the French had fifty-seven ships of the line to the Royal Navy's 120, although the number of ships that were actually seaworthy was considerably less. The return of war saw the British either order or commence building another twenty-two by the end of the year, while the French were hobbled by lack of funds. France's navy received only half what was spent on the army, whereas in Britain a strong navy was the one policy capable of uniting a fractious political class.

Dress coat of a lieutenant (1748–67 pattern), 1748 (UNI0003)

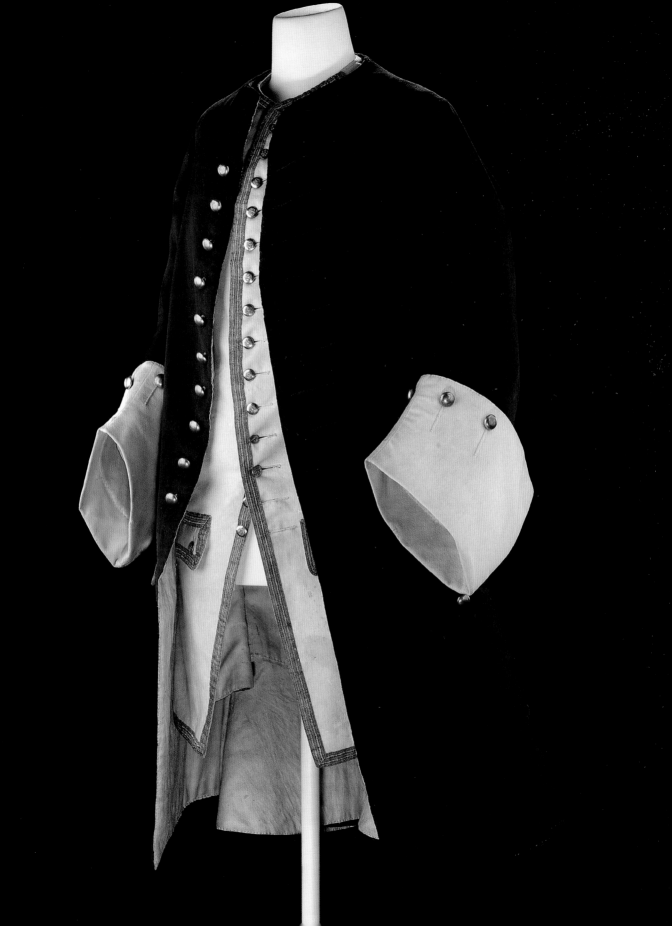

*The English Lion Dismember'd Or the Voice of the Public for an enquiry into the loss of Minorca with Adl. B—g's plea before his Examiners,* hand-coloured etching with engraving, 1756 (PAF3986)

The Royal Navy's superiority rested on more than just its numbers: it was run by men who knew their business. George Anson had been a first-rate fighting admiral who had evolved into a brilliant administrative head. As first lord of the Admiralty, he had ensured that ships in reserve were subjected to regular inspections, discipline was tightened, ship design vastly improved and the officer class rigorously purged of the old and incompetent. Government offices were usually used to buy political allies, but the navy was different. In 1757, the politician Henry Fox summed up the navy's exceptionalism: 'Capacity is so little necessary for most employments that you seem to forget that there is one where it absolutely so

– viz. the Admiralty...the First Lord of the Admiralty must be a man of real ability.'[1]

Knowing that over a long war Britain would inevitably crush the French navy and throttle its trade, France looked to do just enough to protect its colonies, and concentrated instead on winning victories in Europe that would force Britain to give up its conquests. A complicated strategic situation in Europe saw Britain, Hanover (which was the hereditary possession of the current dynasty of British kings) and Prussia lining up against Austria, France, Russia and others, although Britain was officially at war only with France. British fortunes were effectively tied to Frederick II of Prussia: if he prospered, the Royal

Navy could roam the world's oceans unfettered, but if Frederick was defeated Britain would have to concede the spoils of the naval war.

The British were focused on the threat of invasion, and hoarded their naval strength in home waters. French planners seized this chance to capture the island of Minorca, 220 miles southwest of Toulon, where a British garrison had long nurtured a nest of privateers – state-sanctioned private raiders – and encouraged them to harass French shipping. Admiral John Byng was sent out to the Mediterranean with a small, undermanned fleet, which was all that could be spared by nervous policy-makers with their focus on waters closer to home. Byng engaged the French fleet off Minorca on 20 May 1756. After an inconclusive skirmish in which no ships were lost, Byng failed to renew the action and sailed back to Gibraltar for much-needed repairs. This handed the French a notable strategic victory, one of their few of the century. Control of the sea proved decisive – starved of aid, the British garrison surrendered.

Coming alongside setbacks on the Continent, the government collapsed. The British public was unused to defeats at sea and howled for a scapegoat. Byng was court martialled and shot (see pp. 120–21). Through the rest of the Seven Years War the British hurled themselves at the enemy, often with utter disregard for the balance of forces. Arthur Gardiner, in command of the sixty-four-gun *Monmouth*, had been a protégé of Byng's, serving under him off Minorca. He closed with the eighty-gun *Foudroyant* off Cartagena in southern Spain in February 1758, despite knowing that the *Monmouth*'s broadside of around 500 pounds was puny compared to his enemy's of over 1,200. His temerity won him fame, but cost him his life.

The French minister of marine, Jean-Baptiste de Machault, tried skilfully to manage the situation. Louisbourg, France's wind-blasted fort on a bleak outcrop of Cape Breton Island at the mouth of the Gulf of St Lawrence, was saved by a squadron of ships which accompanied an amphibious assault force. When this fleet returned to Brest, however, it brought typhus. Known as 'ship fever', and carried by lice, it thrived in cramped, filthy conditions. The French were not as rigorous with ship cleanliness as their British counterparts, and this was partially responsible for an epidemic so severe that it damaged the French navy as seriously as losing several ships in battle. Nearly half of the 12,000 men on board died, and it spread ashore when they returned, killing perhaps 5,000 civilians. By contrast, the British system for protecting the health of their sailors was way ahead of their enemy's. A giant hospital was opened at Haslar near Portsmouth in 1753 which was the largest brick building in Europe. In 1760, the base at Plymouth received a similar facility. Both were pioneering attempts to reduce sickness by an application of scientific principles. Patients were well fed and kept in hygienic conditions.

The French navy's finances were in grave crisis by 1758. It received around forty million *livres* to spend. The Royal Navy's budget was £4.8 million, equivalent to 115 million *livres*. The British had now put nearly 100 ships of the line into service, crewed by more than 60,000 seamen. Success on the world's oceans required gold, and the French government had more pressing priorities than its navy. Bad French decision-making piled even more pressure on their navy. Machault, an effective minister, was removed from his job, largely thanks to the enmity of Louis XV's former mistress and current confidante, Madame de

Pompadour. The navy had always suffered at the highest levels of the French state from being faintly unfashionable. The army was unassailably the senior service. Princes and dukes dreamed of winning glory at the head of an army across the Rhine, not in the teeth of an Atlantic gale. French ministers of marine tended not to be senior statesmen and were often excluded from the highest levels of royal policy formation, and this deficiency was exacerbated by the regular changes of personnel. Ministers were dismissed with a regularity that exposed the arbitrary nature of absolute rule – a contemporary French commentator bemoaned the fact that ministers changed 'like scenery at the opera'. There were five ministers of marine during the war. The contrast to Britain was notable: first lord of the Admiralty was a position of the highest importance, and once in office he would be responsible for his conduct not only to his royal master but also to his colleagues in the cabinet and parliament itself.

By 1758, shortages of dockyard supplies meant that a French fleet designed to protect the North American empire was sent out piecemeal, as each ship overcame huge problems just getting to sea. Many vessels were captured by the British, and only six ships of the line ended up in Louisbourg to defend it against the expected British assault. The French were terribly outnumbered by the twenty-three Royal Navy warships. Powerless to challenge the superior British force as had happened off Minorca, the French commander sent his sailors ashore to make themselves useful in defence of Louisbourg's walls. When the town fell the ships, as well as their valuable crews, were all lost with it and 20,000 French sailors were now prisoners of war. By midsummer the French were so short of men that they could only crew twenty-five of their sixty ships of the line, giving the British an actual advantage of four to one. In the Caribbean, ten British ships of the line operated virtually unopposed. France's sugar-producing islands – Guadeloupe, Martinique and St Domingue – had been worth more than seventy-five million *livres* to the French economy before the war, and were now blockaded. In India, British naval vessels helped Robert Clive capture the French trading post of Chandernagore, up-river from Calcutta, in a riverine operation that demonstrated the skill in pilotage and navigation that would become a hallmark of the Royal Navy, and allow it to bring decisive influence to bear further inland than had been thought possible. In western Africa, the British captured Gorée and Saint-Louis in what is today Senegal, and a fort at the mouth of the River Gambia – all important slaving stations.

As this begins to demonstrate, a vigorous, powerful and deeply bellicose lobby of merchants, planters, MPs and naval officers – linked by family, investments and patronage – had cemented itself into the British political establishment. The wars of the eighteenth century were as much about the ruthless asset-stripping of competitor nations as they were about the European balance of power. This often frustrated Britain's Continental allies, like Prussia, who were fighting for the altogether simpler goal of national survival. However, as the British government reminded their ambassador in Berlin: 'we must be merchants while we are soldiers...our trade depends upon a proper exertion of our maritime strength...trade and maritime force depend on each other, and the riches which are the true resources of this country depend upon its commerce.'[2]

By the start of 1759, only a handful of British sailors had been killed in combat with the French. However, because of desertion and death from disease, the Royal Navy still needed to find more men. For the first time in history the navy had 300 ships in service, and by February an all-time record of 71,000 men were serving in them, which was still around 9,000 short of the required total.[3] Even at this swollen size the navy would be stretched. The government – dominated by the eloquent, if faintly messianic, William Pitt the Elder – had grandiose plans. Pitt envisaged giant blows against the French colonial empire that would lead directly to its total destruction.

In France, Étienne-François, Duc de Choiseul, had emerged as a war leader and, after gaining the confidence of the king, tried to bring direction where there had been little. His solution for the maritime war was bold: marshalling all of France's dwindling naval resources to invade Britain. Pitt's global plans meant that there was a danger that Britain would be overextended and leave the homeland vulnerable to Choiseul's desperate gamble. In Brest, Admiral Conflans somehow managed to put twenty-one ships of the line into service. The French navy was still seriously short of experienced crewmen, so coastguard troops and peasants – untrained landlubbers all – were forced aboard.

This moment of crisis forced the British to do something remarkable. Navies had long attempted to blockade and keep an enemy fleet penned up in harbour to prevent it from operating. But a systematic blockade had always proved impossible, as sickness and malnutrition forced fleets to return home after a matter of weeks. The Seven Years War had already seen significant progress in the Royal Navy's ability to keep ships on station. In 1756, Admiral Boscawen noted that, 'this ship has now been at sea twelve weeks, which is longer than I ever knew any first-rate ever at sea'. In his experience, 'our cruisers would not keep the sea above a fortnight, till one or two of them were broken for it, now three months is but a common cruise'.[4]

Anson knew that 'the best defence...for our colonies as well as our coasts, is to have such a squadron always to the westward as may in all probability either keep the French in port, or give them battle with advantage if they come out'.[5] Anson himself had taken direct command of the western squadron off Brest in 1758, but had been forced to return to Britain after six weeks, as his crews grew weak, ravaged by scurvy and fever. He did, however, conduct one experiment with re-victualling at sea, which was considered enough of a success to attempt a far more ambitious

programme of resupply the following year. The British fleet would blockade Brest and would remain there until the autumn gales made any cross-Channel enterprise too risky. Nothing like it had ever been attempted before. From the end of May, transport ships were sent out from Plymouth with fresh turnips, onions, cabbages, live animals and beer, and the navy conducted history's first systematic replenishments at sea. The western squadron, under command of Edward Hawke, allowed ships to be detached back to Britain to rest the crews and scrape the hulls, dramatically increasing performance.

This system of blockade and replenishment was nothing short of revolutionary, and its effect was decisive. While the main French fleet was ensnared, France's global position utterly collapsed. The attritional effect of years of warfare had gravely weakened France's navy and empire: 1759 was to see its eclipse. In Canada, a mighty amphibious assault was sent up the St Lawrence. More than 100 ships, spearheaded by twenty-two ships of the line, carrying tens of thousands of soldiers and sailors, sailed up an uncharted river through hundreds of miles of hostile territory that was thought impassable by the French and colonial defenders of Quebec, the primary settlement of French North America. The Royal Navy took meticulous soundings and ensured not a single naval vessel was lost in a river that had proved the graveyard of at least one previous British fleet.

French fire-rafts attacking the English fleet off Quebec, 28 June 1759, by Samuel Scott, oil on canvas, 1767 (BHC0393)

Once they had arrived before Quebec, the army – commanded by the inexperienced and highly strung James Wolfe – made heavy work of the siege. The Canadian capital was pounded and incinerated by artillery as the landing forces were repulsed, and operations bogged down into a brutal war of insurgency against Native American and Canadian irregulars. Wolfe eventually decided to use his absolute control of the river to launch a surprise amphibious assault just to the west of Quebec, up a perilous ravine leading from the river to the heights above. In an impressively co-ordinated operation, a naval force under the command of Admiral Sir Charles Saunders sailed far up-river and transferred the assault infantry into flat-bottomed boats, which then dropped back down-river on the ebb tide until they reached the landing zone. All this was conducted at night, in absolute silence, exactly on schedule. The French were shocked into action before they could muster their full strength; their infantry was annihilated and within days Quebec surrendered. Although it took another year of campaigning, the fate of the French Canadian empire was sealed. Wolfe's successor wrote, 'I should not do justice to the admirals and the naval service if I neglected this occasion of acknowledging...how great a share the navy has had in this successful campaign'.[6]

In the Caribbean, the sugar island of Guadeloupe fell to the British, largely because the navy totally controlled the waters around it. Back in the Channel, Hawke's blockade was still closely enforced – no fleet in history had ever stayed at sea for so long, in such rude health. Hawke sent

*A Plan of the River St. Laurence...with the Operations of the Siege of Quebec; under the Command of Vice Adml. Saunders & Majr. Genl. Wolfe, 5th. Sept. 1759,* by J. Cary, etching, c.1759 (PAD5267)

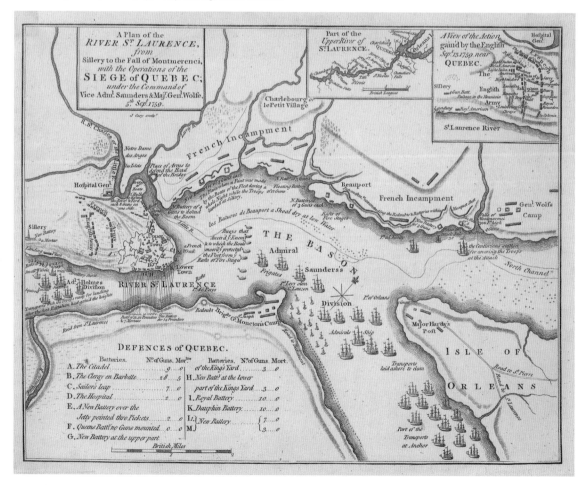

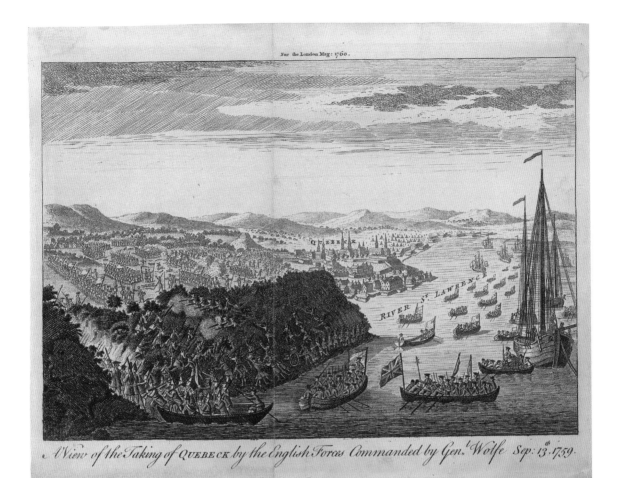

*A View of the Taking of* QUEBECK *by the English Forces Commanded by Gen.ᴵ Wolfe Sep: 13ᵗʰ 1759.*

TOP *A View of the Taking of Quebeck by the English Forces Commanded by Genl. Wolfe Sep 13th 1759*, published by the *London Magazine*, etching, 1760 (PAD5270) ABOVE Medal commemorating the capture of Quebec, 1759 (MEC1305) RIGHT Admiral Sir Charles Saunders, by Richard Brompton, oil on canvas, 1772–73 (BHC3011)

# MODEL OF A TROOPBOAT, MID- TO LATE EIGHTEENTH CENTURY (SLR0499)

Amphibious assaults in shallow waters into the teeth of enemy defences were challenging operations, requiring suitable vessels, hydrographical knowledge and logistical support. They also required close cooperation between the army and navy. Seaborne forces had unique mobility, allowing surprise attacks in far-flung imperial regions. In principle, the naval force transported and convoyed the military contingent and, on arrival, secured mastery of local waters. It was then the army's responsibility to conduct the main land attack. The gradual strengthening of landward defensive positions required ever-larger (and hence more cumbersome) forces to overcome them, so it took time for Britian to perfect the art of amphibious warfare.

The effective bombardment of coastal positions, and organised landing of troops, had been attempted many times before the Seven Years War. In 1741, Admiral Vernon was naval commander of an amphibious assault on Cartagena, in what is now Colombia, which resulted in a devastating British defeat. Such landings were often well prepared and implemented but forces could struggle to sustain themselves once ashore. After 1756, the challenge of fighting a worldwide war saw British governments increasingly favour amphibious operations, though not necessarily with any greater success. In 1757, for instance, a British attack on the French port of Rochefort ended in fiasco.

The sheer quantity of amphibious assaults launched after 1757 enabled administrators and commanders to improve their effectiveness. Britain introduced doctrines for landing troops on a hostile shore, and encouraged close fire support from naval ships involved. Specialist landing craft were built; shallow-draft, flat-bottomed boats with a gun in the bows to cover their landings. They were capable of carrying up to seventy infantrymen, or marines, who could disembark with their powder dry, ready to engage the enemy immediately. This model shows the fruits of the designers' efforts, and is typical of the type of vessel used in amphibious operations during the Seven Years War.

Crucially, between 1759 and 1763, British amphibious operations were rarely threatened by the arrival of significant enemy fleets. This allowed lines of support to stay open, and also freed up naval crews to help operations on land. At Louisbourg in 1758, and at Quebec in 1759, Britain mounted seaborne attacks that captured the two great French fortresses along the St Lawrence River. However, while the British honed their application of these complex operations, they could still become mired in difficulty. The capture of Havana in 1762 was not only an impressive achievement of British logistical might but – both financially and in its high casualties owing to tropical disease – also a costly reminder that successful amphibious landings were always prey to local conditions.

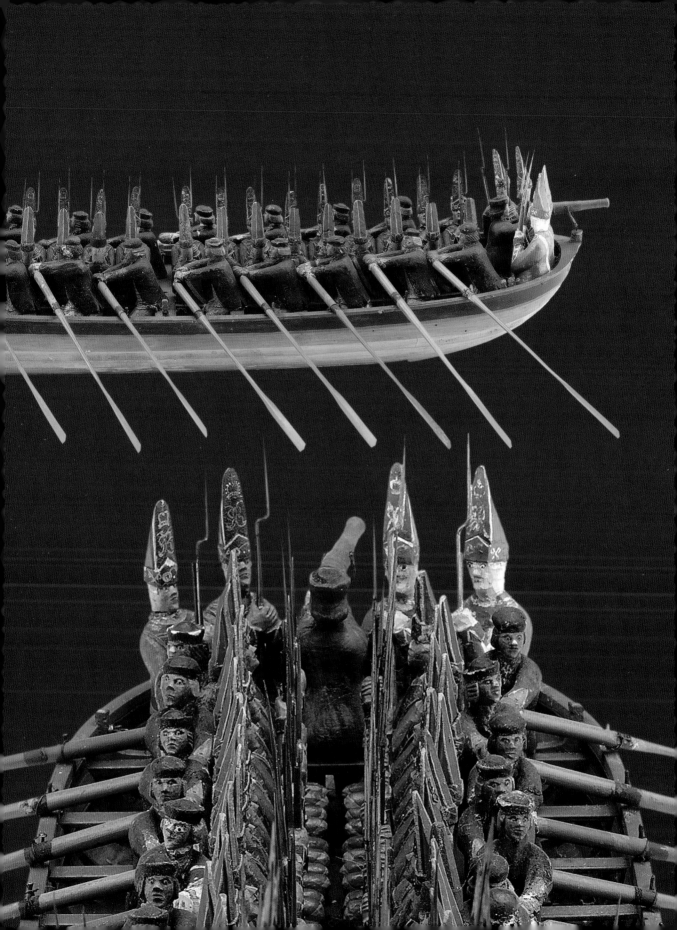

a squadron of frigates virtually into the mouth of Brest, flaunting British superiority. In conditions just as dangerous as the St Lawrence, with the fastest tidal race in Europe to contend with, among other challenges, the Royal Navy demonstrated a mastery of inshore pilotage that was underpinned, yet again, by highly qualified officers who had created meticulous charts and surveys. Hawke was able to report that Brest was 'blocked up in the strictest sense'. The commodore in command of the frigates reported that, 'I think, sir, you have insulted them in a manner that they were never before used to, or that any history can give an account of'.[7]

The odds were now even more stacked against the French, and a potent mix of pride and desperation drove them to press ahead with the invasion of Britain. On 14 November, late in the season, and taking advantage of a gale that had temporarily blown the British fleet off station, the French commander, the Comte

de Conflans, left Brest with twenty-one ships of the line, heading for southern Brittany where the invasion transport vessels were assembled. He would then escort this fleet to Britain and knock France's implacable enemy out of the war. Hawke's force immediately set off in pursuit with twenty-three ships of the line, which included a 100-gun ship and two ninety-gun vessels, their crews drilled to the highest state of perfection after an entire summer afloat.

At dawn on 20 November, the French fleet arrived off Quiberon Bay in Brittany, but by 8:30am sails were spotted to the west and Conflans realised that Hawke had caught up with him. The French admiral had no stomach for battle in the teeth of a west-north-westerly gale, on a dangerous lee shore, and with a larger and better drilled enemy fleet. He made for Quiberon Bay itself, guarded by ship-killing shoals, intending to anchor and force Hawke to withdraw rather than follow the French into the hazardous waters with the sun setting. Horrified, the French watched as Hawke threw the British fleet into a headlong pursuit. Hawke ordered more sail to be crowded onto his ships' groaning rigging, and the entire fleet ran into the unknown waters. It was one of history's most aggressive naval decisions. The British caught the slowest French ships and mauled them as they rounded Les Cardinaux rocks at the mouth of the bay. With the light failing, the British poured broadsides into French stragglers: the *Formidable* surrendered, the *Thésée* was caught by the wind as she tried to open her lower gun ports and capsized, *Héros* surrendered but then also ran aground, the *Superbe* simply sank as Hawke's flagship blasted two broadsides into her at point-blank range. As night fell, ships dropped anchor and fighting continued sporadically as ships drifted near enough

ABOVE Admiral Sir Edward Hawke, by Francis Cotes, oil on canvas, 1768–70 (BHC2754) OPPOSITE ABOVE Belt plate commemorating the Battle of Quiberon Bay, 1759 (MEC1099)
OPPOSITE BELOW The day after the Battle of Quiberon Bay, 1759, by Richard Wright, oil on canvas, 1760 (BHC0402)
BELOW Medal commemmorating the Battle of Quiberon Bay, 1759 (MEC1306) BOTTOM Medal commemorating the British successes of 1758–59, 1759 (MEC1138)

to identify friend from enemy. Some French ships risked all and sailed out blind rather than face a certain British storm of iron the next morning. The *Resolution* went aground as she tried to flee, other French ships broke their backs on mudbanks. Those that did escape jettisoned their guns to allow them to take refuge up the River Vilaine where the British ships could not follow. The French flagship, *Soleil Royal*, tried to flee, with the *Essex* in hot pursuit – both went aground and were wrecked on the same shoal. The Comte de Conflans abandoned his flagship and gave the order to burn it.

It was a stunning British victory. Six French ships of the line had been destroyed, others had been scattered and battered, as 2,500 Frenchmen lost their lives. The two British losses were ships of the line that had run aground in their haste to close with the enemy. Hawke had placed the national interest over the fortunes of individual vessels in spectacular fashion. The spectre of Minorca had been banished, and the French navy had been dealt a psychological blow that would resonate for years to come.

The invasion, always unlikely, was now impossible. Britain was safe to enjoy its 'year of victories' as success in Quebec and the Caribbean was joined by victory at the Battle of Minden in Germany, which prevented the French from seizing Hanover to make up for its disastrous losses elsewhere. But nowhere was the effect of the defeat more profound than at the pinnacle of French power. The French

government was furious at the navy's inability to deliver a victory, and effectively demobilised it. Spending was slashed to around twenty-three million *livres*, more than half of which had to be used to settle debts from previous years. The story goes that there was not even enough money to pay for food for the dockyard cats.

In 1761, fear of British hegemony brought the Spanish into the war. Had Spain and France combined fleets from the start they would have posed a very considerable threat; instead their untrained crews and untested ships made easy pickings for the veteran British fleet. Both kingdoms were powerless to prevent the British seizing Martinique, Grenada and St Lucia. In 1762, the heart of Spain's Caribbean empire, Havana in Cuba, was attacked by another large amphibious force under the command of Admiral Sir George Pocock. The British fleet sailed through the apparently

PREVIOUS PAGES The capture of
Havana, 1762: storming of the
Morro Castle on 30 July, by
Dominic Serres, oil on canvas,
1770–75 (BHC0412)
OPPOSITE The Capture of
Havana, 1762: landing cannon
and stores on 30 June, by
Dominic Serres, oil on canvas,
1770–75 (BHC0411)
FAR RIGHT Wine-glass
commemorating the capture
of Havana, c.1762 (GGG0297)
RIGHT *Sr. George Pocock
Admiral, of the Blue-Squadron
of His Majesty's Fleet...*, by
James MacArdell after Thomas
Hudson, mezzotint, 25 March
1762 (PAF3685)
BELOW The capture of Havana,
1762: storming of the Morro
Castle, 30 July: a closer
view of the final assault, by
Dominic Serres, oil on canvas,
1770–75 (BHC0413)

impassable Old Bahama Passage, 100 miles long and only fifteen miles wide. The fleet stayed clear of both the rocky coast of northern Cuba and the reefs on the southern tip of the Great Bahama Bank, appearing off Havana to the utter consternation of the defenders. A quick assault would have taken the city but the general in command was too slow and it only fell after an attritional siege (see pp. 108–11) in which thousands of British troops died of disease. The jewel of Spain's eastern empire, Manila in the Philippines, fell to a British force from India escorted by eight Royal Navy ships of the line. In India, after the capture of Gheria and Calcutta earlier in the war, the key French base at Pondicherry was taken in January 1761 after an effective naval blockade.

Peace came in 1763; even the British had grown weary of war. The national debt was soaring and the long conflict was hurting British trade. France and Spain had some of their confiscated colonies restored, but nothing could disguise Britain's dominance over the world's oceans. The European struggle for India and North America had been decisively won by Britain. France, in the words of a contemporary soldier, 'was never more reduced in its naval power...their ships are now diminished in their numbers...from British capture, from being subdued or destroyed...the French are at this instant but seldom seen upon the ocean...because they have been beat and burnt out it by the English'.[8] These victories stemmed not from superior courage – both French and Spanish crews often fought with a bravery that was admired by their British antagonists – instead, it was a triumph of organisation. The British were a century ahead in the unglamorous fields of logistics, administration, infrastructure, surveying and health: the Royal Navy was shaping the modern approach to warfare.

None of this would have been possible without a government able to deliver vast sums of money from direct taxation and through borrowing. The bond markets were much happier to lend money to Britain, with its government that was answerable to parliament, than to absolute monarchies where there was no institutional way to secure redress or scrutinise budgets. But the sum spent by the British government during the Seven Years War had exhausted even its treasury. At

The Battle of the Saintes in 1782, which saw Admiral Rodney defeat a French fleet during the American War of Independence, by Thomas Whitcombe, oil on canvas, 1782 (BHC0445)

the onset of peace, desperate politicians slashed the naval establishment from 76,000 men to just 17,500 within a year.[9] London also attempted to oblige the North American colonies to shoulder a share of the costs of their defence. Some colonials realised that with French and Spanish power destroyed, the protection of their imperial overlord was no longer required, and they worked successfully to provoke a confrontation between Britain and its colonies. Just a generation after the triumphant end to the Seven Years War, Britain's empire was at war with itself over who should bear the cost and who should enjoy the spoils. Britain's embittered rivals noted with glee and rushed into another war. So great was the desire of France, Spain and others to undermine Britain's newly won hegemony that they charged headlong into conflicts that would lead to suffering, revolution and occupation on a previously unimaginable scale.

# 6

# NAVAL PERSONNEL
# IN POPULAR CULTURE

## Margarette Lincoln

The navy had a tremendous impact on popular culture in the eighteenth century. This is hardly surprising given the vast sums government allocated each year to naval expenditure, the range of vested interests that merchants and naval suppliers had in the navy and its dockyards, and the numbers of families who had loved ones at sea, whether serving voluntarily or against their will. Public support for the navy drew on a variety of arguments and emotions: an understanding that its role in protecting trade was vital to the economy, intermittent fear of invasion, simple pride and patriotism. Throughout this period the navy was firmly associated with what seemed to be obvious benefits: Protestantism, political liberty and financial profit. Even so, when events at sea became implicated in parliamentary power struggles, the avid party politics of the time could influence public reaction to the exploits of individual officers.

Fighting for the DUNGHILL — or — Jack Tar settling BUONAPARTE.

by Thos Tegg III Cheapside London.    Price One Shilling Coloured

JACK JOLLY steering down Wapping in Ballast trim.

OPPOSITE *Fighting for the Dunghill – or – Jack Tar settling Buonaparte,* by James Gillray, published by John Miller, hand-coloured etching with aquatint, 20 November 1798 (PAD4792) ABOVE *Jack Jolly steering down Wapping in Ballast trim,* published by Thomas Tegg, hand-coloured etching, 1813 (PAF3787) OVERLEAF Sailors fighting in a tavern, hand-coloured aquatint, c.1819 (PAD4769)

Britain was at war for much of the century, which also helps to explain why representations of the navy and its personnel were so important. Politicians and the public at large had to be persuaded to support it through each successive war effort. Importantly for a nation under such strain, each victory was wildly celebrated, and each defeat needed a scapegoat. After 1688, society increasingly valued civility and 'politeness'. Gentlemanly behaviour was redefined as the ability, based on natural goodwill, to seem at ease in varied social situations, and converse affably and with propriety on a range of topics. The representation of naval officers, whose profession was brutal warfare, consequently reflected a growing

unease about changing concepts of masculinity and the effect of war on human nature. The representation of Jack Tars, seamen from the lower deck, was also conflicted and at times contradictory, as these two illustrations show.

Popular interest stimulated a commemorative industry that was able to respond to topical events and which, in turn, influenced taste and fashion. The representation of the navy in this period is firmly entwined with the growth of consumerism. As technologies were refined that allowed prints, ceramics and jewellery to be produced for different markets, so images of celebrity officers and of Jack Tar burgeoned and themselves became talking points. At the beginning of the century,

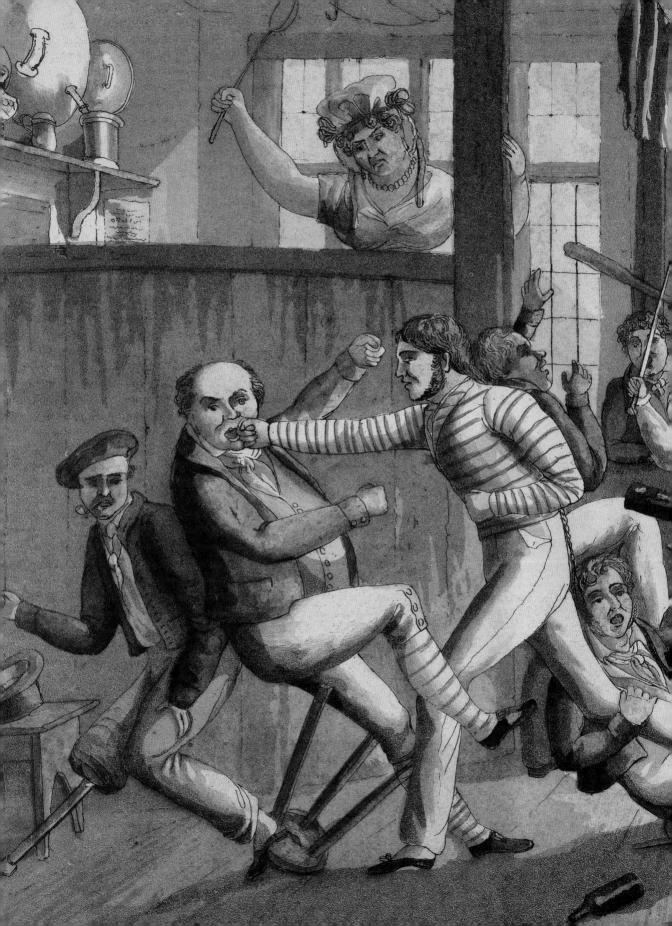

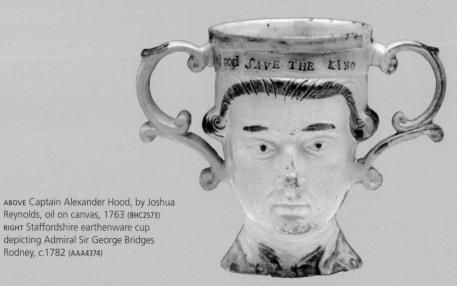

ABOVE Captain Alexander Hood, by Joshua
Reynolds, oil on canvas, 1763 (BHC2573)
RIGHT Staffordshire earthenware cup
depicting Admiral Sir George Bridges
Rodney, c.1782 (AAA4374)

naval heroes were celebrated in popular ballads and, more rarely, in prints. By around 1800, those who wished to exhibit the latest trends in patriotic display could choose from a range of commemorative items: from mugs, plates, figurines, fans, purses, clocks and lockets to ribbons, curtains and wallpaper. A wide spectrum of society visited dramatic spectacles relating to recent naval engagements including panoramas, mock sea battles between model ships in real water (*naumachias*), gallery shows and theatre pieces. Upper-class women vied with each other to entertain naval officers at social gatherings. Women in general, unable to take an active role in public life, found that they could improve their social standing by publishing poems in praise of the navy or wearing fashions that clearly marked their support for officers who were public figures. Naval monuments erected in St Paul's Cathedral soon became visitor attractions. Enthusiasm for the navy did not begin to wane until 1815, when Wellington's great victory at the Battle of Waterloo temporarily put the army in pole position.

Early in the eighteenth century, once it became axiomatic that Britain owed its position in the world to trade and sea power, the stage was set for successful naval officers to attain celebrity status. After Edward Vernon's popular victory at Porto Bello in 1739 came George Anson's celebrated circumnavigation of the globe (1740–44), which included his capture of a Spanish treasure ship. This feat inspired renewed confidence in the skill of British seamen, and bolstered national self-esteem. Both events were marked by festivities up and down the country, and by the production of record numbers of commemorative objects for public consumption.

It was soon obvious that popular opinion about individual naval officers could be manipulated for political ends. In 1756, at the beginning of the Seven Years War, the French invaded Minorca, a British possession. Admiral John Byng failed in

ABOVE *Jack Oakham throwing out A Signal for an Engagement*, published by Robert Sayer and John Bennett, hand-coloured mezzotint, 24 May 1781 (PAF4039)
TOP Earthenware tile with a scene of a sailor's return, mid-eighteenth century (AAA4501)

his attempt to relieve the island. True, government orders had compelled him to leave for the Mediterranean in ships that were unseaworthy and undermanned. Yet, after an inconclusive battle, he allowed the French fleet to slip away, then retreated to Gibraltar for repairs. He intended to obtain reinforcements there before setting out in pursuit of the enemy but was peremptorily relieved of his command. At home, the catastrophe spurred a weak ministry under the Duke of Newcastle to cover up its administrative failures: both the delay in dispatching a force against the enemy and the poor state of the fleet. Byng was brought back to England and imprisoned. Newcastle's ministry published Byng's dispatches in the *London Gazette*, a government newspaper, omitting any passages that showed him in a favourable light and all criticism of government preparations. The government's aim was to foist all the blame on Byng to save itself from collapse.

The public, which had anticipated naval victory, was already deeply disappointed. Even before Byng reached home, derisive ballads were being sung about him in the streets, hinting at cowardice. Unflattering prints of him were circulated, captioned with memorable, doggerel verse:

*We have lately been told*
*Of two admirals bold,*
*Who engag'd in a terrible Fight:*
*They met after Noon,*
*Which I think was too soon,*
*As they both ran away before Night.*

Byng was charged with 'failing to do his utmost' in battle. Neglect of duty was a capital offence: mobs roamed the streets of London chanting, 'Swing, swing Admiral Byng'. Newcastle's unpopular ministry fell, but public opinion was so hostile towards Byng that even his political friends could not secure him a royal pardon. Byng's frustrated defenders were angered by the level of debate. One complained that ministers had encouraged public demonstrations against Byng in order to shield themselves from blame: 'Money has been given and distributed to the Mob, to dress a Figure in the Sea uniform, to make Fires, and burn him; and thus to keep the Popular eye on B—g only.'[1] He was executed by firing squad on the deck of his former flagship, the *Monarch*. He faced death bravely, only persuaded to wear a blindfold out of consideration for his executioners, firing

The execution of Admiral Byng, 14 March 1757, British school, oil on canvas, c.1760 (BHC0380)

at close quarters. Voltaire commented sardonically that Byng was shot 'to encourage the others'. His quip proved more accurate than perhaps he intended. The execution had a dramatic effect on the spirit of contemporary British naval officers, who afterwards fought with unwavering aggression. Byng's fate was proof that not even political friends in high places could save an admiral who refused to fight.

The navy did much to influence its own image. Officers extolled the service and its role in society. In the wake of the Byng fiasco, naval professionals sought to establish an honourable tradition for Britain's supremacy at sea. In 1766, 'a society of naval gentlemen' wrote *Britannia Triumphant: or, An Account of the Sea-Fights and Victories of the English Nation from the earliest Times, down to the Conclusion of the late War, under the following noted Commanders, viz...Drake, Raleigh...Hawke...Anson*. They argued that Britain had exerted dominion over the seas from the earliest times, and included plates of famous admirals to personalise their achievements. Rather pointedly, their account of Admiral Hawke's victory over the French in 1759 ends: 'Perhaps there never was a naval engagement of such extent, in which no captain was accused,

nor even in any degree suspected of misbehaviour or cowardice.'

In such an arena, ambitious officers soon noted public opportunities for self-promotion. They aimed to ensure that visual representations of battles were accurate, and that their own position in the fighting was well represented, if not enhanced. Portraiture was central to fame. So, when Admiral Augustus Keppel was acquitted at his controversial court martial in 1779, Joshua Reynolds seized the moment and sent his portrait of Keppel to an engraver so that it could be copied and circulated as a print. Keppel had been given command of the Channel Fleet on merit, rather surprisingly since he belonged to a group, the Rockingham Whigs, who opposed the government's position on the American Revolution and refused to fight the colonists until France came into the war. He then failed to secure a decisive victory against the French off Ushant in 1778. Afterwards, Lord Sandwich, first lord of the Admiralty and a supporter of the government, suspected Keppel of failing to clinch a victory in order to discredit the administration and its naval strategy. Keppel, for his part, feared he had been set up to take the blame in a situation where victory was always doubtful. In the battle Keppel's junior, Sir Hugh Palliser, had failed to bring up his damaged ships in time to engage the French. Palliser was both a key aide of Sandwich at the Admiralty and a staunch supporter of the Tory government. Now he feared that his own name would be tarnished and demanded that Keppel be court martialled to make public the facts of the battle.

Keppel's trial in Portsmouth was little short of public entertainment. The press reported the case in detail; readers eagerly followed each twist in the drama. His trial was viewed as a political affair, indicating incompetence and corruption at the heart of government. Leading opposition Whigs and their wives ostentatiously travelled to Portsmouth to support their naval champion.

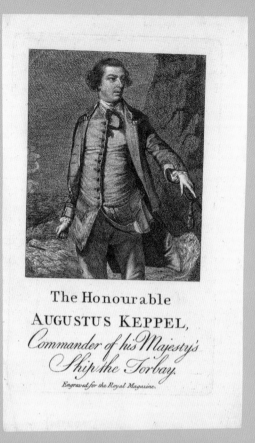

ABOVE *The Honourable Augustus Keppel...*, after Joshua Reynolds, etching, c.1760 (PAD2936) OPPOSITE Captain the Honourable Augustus Keppel, one of various portraits of this officer by Joshua Reynolds, oil on canvas, 1752–53 (BHC2823)

This flamboyant display cheered Keppel's sympathisers and encouraged public criticism of the ministry. When Keppel was acquitted, there was a procession around the town during which supporters proudly wore the light blue ribbons of the Rockingham Whigs. Such a ritualistic display and the use of symbols meant that even ordinary people, ineligible to vote, felt they were participating in the political process.

While hundreds bought Reynolds's print of Keppel, eager to display their allegiance to his cause, others wore commemorative medals and counters, just as they had done to celebrate Vernon's victory. Josiah Wedgwood secured a good

profit from speedily produced portrait medallions of Keppel. Those with money to spare could also buy earthenware plates, wall plaques and table linen, all commemorating the admiral's success. Keppel found keen supporters among those with merchant and trading interests. On his acquittal, a resolution was passed at the Guildhall to award him the freedom of the City of London. The lord mayor and aldermen commissioned a presentation box of oak covered with gold mosaic work, and publicised the award ceremony by distributing a pamphlet describing the box and detailing Keppel's services to his country, particularly to trade. In 1780, less controversially, the Guildhall awarded Admiral Rodney the freedom of the City of London in a gold box, for his victory over Spain when he relieved the siege of Gibraltar. This, too, was widely publicised to reflect well on giver and receiver.

Women's support for naval heroes became established. There were well-publicised instances of aristocratic women adopting naval motifs as ornament. Admiral Lord Howe, in command of

the Channel Fleet when war was declared against France in 1793, had reason to welcome such support. Until the Battle of the 'Glorious First of June' in 1794 his command had been largely ineffectual, and attacks against him in newspapers and prints had been so severe that he had been contemplating resignation. Although both sides claimed the battle as a victory, popular opinion at home helped the navy to declare it a triumph. When King George III visited Howe's flagship on his return, ladies in the royal party wore gold anchors on chains round their necks (see p. 16). Upper-class women set the trend and commemorative jewellery rapidly became a fashion item after important victories.

Women's magazines and almanacs promulgated the latest seasonal fashions for headdresses, ornaments, fans and gowns. These were regularly adapted to celebrate victories and leading naval officers, stimulating the domestic market for commemoratives. Nelson's victories produced a flood of such items. Women wore gold anchors to mark his victory at the Battle of the Nile in 1798, engraved with the name and date of the engagement. Painted ivory lockets were also produced to celebrate the victory, and women helped to promote Nelson's increasing popularity by wearing such trinkets. The images on some lockets depicted the loyalty of Nelson's seamen to their commander (important since mutinies in the fleet had taken place in the previous year). Others suggested that naval victories brought lasting fame to British officers. Haberdashers and fan-makers were as swift to make money from the celebrations surrounding the Battle of the Nile, reflecting the growing commodification of the navy.

The public flocked to ship launches, which became popular spectacles, attracting crowds of as many as 100,000 people if royalty were present (see pp. 68–69).[2] These events carried a political message about the power of the nation, a key theme expressed in visual representations of the moment of the launch. The colour and excitement of the day is conveyed in contemporary prints and newspaper reports, which helped to communicate the patriotic enthusiasm of these dockyard events to an even wider audience.

The victory culture of the period was encouraged by government, but also flourished because of simple economics. Early in 1798, print-sellers were mocked for being 'among the most considerable contributors to that British bulwark, the navy – They have fitted out all their old *Hawkes* and *Rodneys*, as *Howes* and *Duncans*, and have turned all their *marine still-lifes* into the most *tremendous engagements*. There are no bounds to human industry'.[3] Items produced to celebrate some topical event might have a fairly short shelf-life, which may explain why naval heroes (who might reasonably be expected to stay famous for some time) were depicted more often than their individual victories, although sometimes manufacturers seem to have had scant regard for accuracy in portraiture as they hurriedly produced goods to celebrate a topical event. From the 1770s, many of the larger potteries in the north of England had agents supervising their warehouses in the metropolis. These individuals sent the latest prints by coach back to the factory so that, in theory, china could be produced more accurately to match the latest event. As soon as news of the Nile reached Birmingham, its potters set about producing commemorative tea-trays, cream-jugs, beer cans, tobacco- and snuff-boxes.

Over the years, the ordinary seaman, so often a problematic, disruptive figure, was made safe and acceptable as Jack Tar, a comic caricature that glossed over sailors' loose morals and capacity for violence. This was the image promoted in prints, in Charles Dibdin's sea songs, and on the stage where such songs often formed part of the entertainment. Seamen liked the popular theatre – after all, many plays were inspired by contemporary naval incidents. One commentator wrote, 'In sea-port towns, where Play-houses are frequently to be found, it may be observed, how sailors are perched in abundance in the upper gallery. Music and dancing they are fond of'.[4] Sailors formed a lively, participatory audience whenever plays with a nautical theme were staged.

OPPOSITE Ceramic plate with a portrait of Admiral Keppel, c.1770 (AAA4409) ABOVE LEFT Anchor pendant, converted into a brooch, celebrating Admiral Lord Howe and the Battle of the 'Glorious First of June', 1794 (JEW0278) ABOVE CENTRE AND RIGHT Pendants (ribbon a later addition) commemorating Nelson's victory at the Battle of the Nile, c.1798 (JEW0145, JEW0140)

# THE GREENWICH PENSIONER

PUBLISHED BY N. CARPENTER WITH TEXT FROM A SONG BY CHARLES DIBDIN, HAND-COLOURED MEZZOTINT WITH ETCHING, LATE EIGHTEENTH CENTURY (PAH3329)

This jolly print, designed for a popular, sympathetic audience, illustrates Charles Dibdin's song 'The Greenwich Pensioner'. The words of the song are printed below the image. Greenwich Hospital was established by royal charter in 1694 to house old and infirm naval seamen. The first pensioners arrived in 1705. Created as an act of royal bounty, the Hospital was largely funded by seamen themselves, both merchant and naval, who paid sixpence from their monthly wages towards its upkeep. Successive monarchs liked to demonstrate strong support for this national institution but tended to be frugal in practice. Often their donations came from chance confiscations. For example, in 1705 Queen Anne allocated to it the remaining effects of the pirate Captain Kidd, executed in 1701. The Hospital duly received a gift of £6,472 and 15 shillings in the queen's name. Kidd's loot could not decently be transferred into royal coffers, so instead Queen Anne assigned it to the Hospital in a flamboyant gesture of generosity. The charity was put on a more stable footing in 1735 when the crown endowed it with estates and lead mining rights in Northumberland and Cumberland. Increasingly, it also provided support for seamen's widows and helped to educate their children.

The Hospital soon became a national icon, emblematic of the importance of the navy to Britain and reproduced in many prints. Its location on the site of the old royal palace at Greenwich, and its impressive Baroque architecture designed by Christopher Wren and his assistant Nicholas Hawksmoor, elevated both naval seamen and the benevolence of the state that cared for those who could no longer serve. The artist James Thornhill, instructed to include naval episodes, decorated the ceiling of its refectory from 1708 to 1727. His long labour produced a striking visual tribute to the Protestant succession but permanently displaced pensioners to dining in the undercrofts below. Naval families donated paintings of officers and battles to this gallery. These great works, much visited in the nineteenth century, are held in trust at the National Maritime Museum, and form the core of its art collection.

This print not only capitalises on the iconic significance of Greenwich Hospital but also on the popularity of naval songs and ballads during the French wars. Ballads were sold cheaply on the streets by hawkers who performed them to attract a crowd of purchasers. Most naval ballads were rousingly patriotic. Arguably they did much to encourage recruitment and, more widely, a national, maritime identity. Dibdin composed over 100 sea songs and claimed that 10,750 copies of *The Greenwich Pensioner* alone were published. Inevitably, there were many disabled seamen on view. Prints of the day helped to reconcile people to these distressing casualties of war and guided their response. Most prints of Greenwich Pensioners show them in their blue uniform, happily reminiscing in spite of their injuries. Other, more pathetic prints of maimed seamen underlined the importance of charitable giving to those in need.

## The GREENWICH PENSIONER.
### By Mr. DIBDIN.

'Twas in the good ship Rover,
   I sail'd the World around,
And for three years and over,
   I ne'er touch'd British ground:
At last in England landed,
   I left the roaring main;
Found all relations stranded,
   And went to Sea again.

That time bound strait to Portugal,
   Right fore and aft we bore;
But, when we made Cape Ortugal,
   A gale blew off the shore,
She lay, so it did shock her,
   A log upon the main,
Till saved from Davy's locker,
   We put to Sea again.

Next in a Frigate sailing
   Upon a squally night,
Thunder and lightening hailing
   The horrors of the fight,
My precious limb was lopped off,
   I, when they'd eased my pain,
Thanked God I was not popped off,
   And went to Sea again.

Yet still I am enabled
   To bring up in life's rear,
Altho' I'm quite disabled,
   And lie in Greenwich tier,
The King, God bless his royalty,
   Who saved me from the main,
I'll praise with love and loyalty,
   But ne'er to Sea again.

Published by N. Carpenter, 60 Spencer St. London.

ABOVE *Jack, hove down – With a Grog Blossom Fever*, published by Thomas Tegg, hand-coloured etching, 1811 (PAF3752)
BELOW Earthenware figure group of a sailor and his lass, c.1800 (AAA6058) OPPOSITE A sailor's return in peace, by Thomas Stothard, oil on canvas, c.1798 (BHC1125)

Sailors' willing participation in the theatre may have helped to endorse a view of Britain's 'jolly tars' that actually made it easier for the public to ignore the real hardships of their life at sea. Conditions in a warship were not well known to those who had never served, but could broadly be assumed to be unpleasant. It made people less uncomfortable to foster an image of the navy composed of devil-may-care, cheerful heroes. Seamen themselves seem to have internalised this image and tried to live by it. Officers also valued 'your jolly, merry-making, don't care sort of seamen' because they were good for morale.[5] Occasionally, the image of Jack Tar was used with radical intent in subversive prints but it was never entirely free of sentimentality. Even when caricatures alluded to the damage sailors inflicted on their health by excessive drinking, they made both the seaman

ABOVE *Jack's Return after Lord Howe's Glorious Victory*, showing a sailor holding a purse of coins, mezzotint, c.1794 (PAF4026) RIGHT *The Neglected Tar*, published by Robert Sayer & Co., mezzotint, 1 October 1791 (PAF4019) OPPOSITE *A Mid on Half Pay*, a dramatised representation of the prospects for officers in peacetime, by C. Hunt, hand-coloured aquatint, 1 June 1825 (PAF3722)

and his doctor figures of fun. For example, *Jack, hove down — With a Grog Blossom Fever* shows Jack rejecting treatment from an incompetent doctor, declaring, 'You may batter my Hull as long as you like, but I'll be d—m'd if ever you board me with your Glyster pipe' (see p. 128). By the end of the eighteenth century, the dominant, popular image of the sailor was of a bluff, cheerful lad who lived for the present.

As numbers of seamen grew with the expansion of the navy, they were increasingly represented in sentimental terms. This trend may reflect a wish to deflect or neutralise the threat that boisterous seamen could pose to social order when ashore. Some sea songs mention a girl in every port but by Nelson's time prints, ballads and chinaware were more likely to feature jolly Jack Tars faithful to one girl who waited at home. Sailors were

portrayed as brave, true, and fatalistic about their chances of survival. The songs rehearse various scenarios: the sailor's joyful return, his shipwreck and death, or the loss of a limb leading to beggary and want. These options were repeated in many songs with only slight variations, and possibly helped to normalise disruptive events that affected many families. The government recognised that such songs were good for public morale. Dibdin was awarded a pension of £200 a year for keeping his London theatre open nightly, and was also '*instructed* to write, sing, publish, and give away what were termed War Songs'.[6] The situations depicted in the songs are reflected in the prints and ceramics of the period, notably in porcelain and earthenware figures of the sailor's parting and his return (see pp. 128–29).

It is difficult to estimate the volume of naval commemorative ware that might have been in circulation. In the later eighteenth century, when the technique of transfer-printing was used for

A MID _ on                HALF PAY.

TOWER                      HILL.

Engd & Pubd June 1, 1825 by C. Hunt, 18 Tavistock Stt Covent Garden.

commemorative pieces, we know that considerable numbers of each decorated item would have been produced in order to justify the expense of having a copper plate engraved for the printing of china. A copper plate would easily yield 10,000 prints, and it has been estimated that thousands more would be possible with careful handling and a few touch-up repairs here and there.[7] In the British print market, they had come down in price since the early eighteenth century, when only the privileged had been able to afford them. The aspiring classes bought portrait prints out of curiosity to see what famous people looked like, but also to associate themselves with these prominent individuals by using such images to decorate their homes. Displaying naval prints was regarded as a form of patriotism, so the nationalism and social ambition of the middling sort came to influence the British print market. Mezzotints, suited to portraits because of their wide tonal range, were most common between 1750 and 1780. Representations of contemporary admirals including Keppel and Rodney were popular, but earlier commanders such as Anson and Blake were also produced, contributing to a sense of pride in Britain as a maritime nation.

Ambitious oil paintings of naval victories were displayed in shows and galleries, attracting crowds who wanted to view contemporary works of art but who also wished to be seen in fashionable civic spaces. Prints of naval heroes and significant battles were displayed in print shop windows, which functioned as galleries for the poor since the prints were on view to all passers-by regardless of their ability to purchase or hire them. We know that the wives of famous naval officers owned commemorative prints and often decorated their homes with these and other items that celebrated their husbands' achievements.

A rekindled patriotism from the 1750s cut across political divisions and the middling sort

were at the forefront of many of its expressions.[8] Patriotic display was good for business, and not only reinforced existing social status but also signalled an individual's ambition to attain the social heights reserved for the elite. The merchant class, for example, displayed art in their own homes as a means of demonstrating and even enhancing their social importance. The possession of artworks served as a badge of gentility, provided these objects conformed to standards of good taste. Successful merchants were important patrons of English artists and often included in their collections marine paintings that reminded them of their commercial interests.[9] They also bought paintings of naval scenes since patriotic feeling was heavily focused on the navy.

In an age of regular church attendance, clergymen also shaped public views of the navy. The clergy was a major force in forming popular opinion, one of the most numerous professions in Britain, and the only one to address ordinary people through the spoken word on a weekly basis. Openly religious sailors were sometimes marginalised by shipmates, possibly due to prevailing shipboard concepts of masculinity, and because seamen were encouraged to adopt a devil-may-care attitude. Yet in the wake of the 1797 naval mutinies, the navy was represented as increasingly receptive to religious influence. In published sermons, James Stanier Clarke, chaplain and librarian to the Prince of Wales, pictured the British seaman calmly reading his Bible in the midst of a rolling ocean that served to remind him of the power of God. By 1814, evangelicals reported that ships' crews were often found reading religious literature. Seamen's willingness to buy such works even made the Religious Tract Society consider breaking with its custom of only giving away Bibles. The navy's global reach, and its role in the protection of commerce and the extension of

*Billy Waters*, a naval sailor who lost a leg after falling from aloft and later became a well-known street performer, by T.L. Busby, hand-coloured etching, c.1820 (ZBA2698)

support for the navy as an institution, another naval doctor, Thomas Trotter, vigorously complained about the treatment of ordinary seamen liable to impressment and poor treatment. Holding up the spectre of the 1797 naval mutinies, and making a case for creating a more contented body of men, he contended that the popular celebration of British seamen was both hollow and cynical:

> *The seaman is like the victim in sacrifice, that is gilded and decked out to be consumed; for his valour is blazoned with triumphal songs and feats, while himself is dragged from his home and his endearments, and ultimately consigned to neglect.*[10]

In the years after the Napoleonic Wars, the public image of naval service became even more sentimentalised. But arguably there had always been a dichotomy between public recognition of the navy as an institution, and public understanding about the realities of life at sea which could never wholly be overcome. In the post-war period, retired seamen were gently ridiculed in various media for their tendency to live in the past; the anniversaries of naval victories were no longer depicted as occasions of heartfelt thanks. A gap opened up between the nation's old seafaring culture and the evolving entrepreneurial culture of pre-Victorian Britain. In the eighteenth century, various forms of material culture had helped to support the morale of a nation at war, while the navy had helped to provide a market for a variety of goods that fostered a sense of national belonging. The place that the navy held in the public consciousness was set to endure in differing forms for another 100 years and more, but it would never again be so central to public discourse or so fine an indicator of social relations.

empire, now allowed the service to be represented as an agent of benevolence, helping to spread the benefits of a civilised society.

Towards the end of the century, the writings of naval doctors helped to publicise the development of a more paternalistic ethos of command in the navy, which they had helped to effect. The Scottish physician Gilbert Blane especially encouraged a paternalistic relationship between officers and men. He thought that a crew's health depended more on the power of officers than on doctors. Such views began to alter public attitudes to the navy. After the Napoleonic Wars, when there was less pressure to demonstrate patriotic

# MUTINY AND INSECURITY

## James Davey

For as long as Britain has had enemies abroad, its population has worried about invasion. The long eighteenth century was a period of great international turmoil in which years of war outweighed those of peace. For the British public, the threat of the enemy across the water was a daily reality. With only the small stretch of the English Channel separating Britain from the European continent, national defence fell almost exclusively on the shoulders of the Royal Navy. This fear of invasion was particularly prominent in the 1790s and 1800s, when Britain faced a renewed threat from abroad. The loss of the American colonies at the end of the American War of Independence in 1783 served as a reminder that Britain's position in the world was neither secure nor guaranteed. This blow to national pride had also revealed a French navy that had grown in strength and confidence. Mutual distrust between the two nations remained: in the years that followed, the governments of William Pitt the Younger spent vast sums on shipbuilding programmes that placed the Royal Navy on a par with the combined fleets of France and Spain.

When in 1789 the French Revolution broke out, it was initially welcomed in Britain. Some observers were happy to see the nascent French democracy aping British parliamentary institutions, while others were content to spectate as Britain's great rival was consumed by civil strife.

However, as the revolution became ever more radical and entrenched, there was increasing concern that popular radicalism might spread across the Channel. In 1792, the first democratic organisations for political reform sprang up in Britain, with memberships drawn from the artisan and working classes. Politically motivated corresponding societies emerged across the country, which bridged social and geographical distances, and raised for the first time the spectre of mass political activity. There was an ever-flowing stream of radical pamphlets, and an increase in petitioning and workers' protests. Fears of political subversion prompted unprecedented state repression, including a proclamation against 'Seditious Writings and Publications' issued in 1792, successive suspensions of *habeas corpus* after 1794, and the eventual outlawing of the London Corresponding Society. The 'Gagging Acts' (1795) restricted the size of public meetings to fifty people and made it possible to arrest on grounds of treason anyone overheard criticising the monarchy. This anxious mood was captured in a memorable passage in Jane Austen's *Northanger Abbey*, written in the late 1790s. Henry Tilney's description of a country 'where every man is surrounded by a neighbourhood of voluntary spies', was at first comforting, but also an uneasy recognition of national paranoia.[1]

In February 1793, the new French republic's avowed motive of spreading revolutionary ideas

Defeat of the Spanish Armada, 1588, by Philippe-Jacques de Loutherbourg, oil on canvas, 1796 (BHC0264)

across Europe led to a declaration of war on Britain. This was not the traditional enemy of old, but a new and more threatening adversary. As one pamphlet put it, Britain was facing 'an Enemy of a new kind...who fights not to subdue States, but to dissolve society – not to extend Empire, but to subvert Government – not to introduce a particular Religion, but to extirpate all Religion'.[2] Eighteenth-century Britons were familiar with the story of the Spanish Armada, which had become a symbolic event in Britain's national memory, a moment when foreign threats were decisively annihilated. In the tumultuous climate of the 1790s, the events of 1588 served as a reassuring

point of reference. British security once again rested on its navy, charged with containing the French fleet in port, and destroying any attempt to land an army. People across the country came to rely on the Royal Navy. While its officers were celebrated as national heroes, its seamen – 'the bulwark of Great Britain' – were represented as brave, loyal and constant servants to the national interest. The British people were content to pay for fleets, funded by high levels of taxation, which promised protection from external threats. This unwritten contract between navy and nation would be tested to its limits by the challenge of revolutionary warfare.

For the first two years of the war, Britain watched uneasily as French armies marched across the Continent, and secured advantageous treaties with Austria, Prussia, Spain and Russia. It was only a matter of time before the French turned their attention northwards. Few doubted the navy's ability to defend the shores of the British Isles. One observer, Maria Stanley, described the navy's competence with considerable nonchalance: 'Papa says Invasion is much talked of in London...I do not feel much alarmed, for I cannot think that our Navy is reduced so very low as to suffer the French to land in any number so as to do much damage.'[3] By 1796, however, the French had begun seriously to plan an invasion of Britain, though they would struggle to overcome the logistical and geographical challenges that confronted them. In December of that year, a fleet of French transports carrying 15,000 troops was intercepted after being stranded in Bantry Bay, Ireland; twelve ships were captured or wrecked in harsh winds and blizzards and the would-be invasion ended in disarray. Two months later, in February 1797, Britain's coastal defences were again put to the test when French frigates landed over 1,000 troops on the Welsh coast at Fishguard. The small and ill-disciplined invading army was quickly rounded up by Welsh militia, but the potential consequences of another more successful attempt were felt across Britain, prompting a run on the banks, a financial crisis, and widespread public alarm.

It was in this climate of uncertainty, with accounts of external threats disseminated across the country, that the naval fleets stationed around southern England mutinied: at Spithead, the Nore, and finally at Yarmouth. Seemingly at once, the nation's protector against invasion was rendered impotent. These were uprisings on a greater scale than had ever been seen before. Naval mutinies during the eighteenth century rarely took the form of the violent usurpations of legend. Generally resembling a strike, they were labour disputes

resolved consensually and quickly, normally without recourse to punishment. The mutinies of 1797, though, took on a more dangerous appearance. Coming in the politically charged atmosphere of the 1790s, and in such number, they appeared radical, revolutionary and subversive. Each successive uprising became more extreme and saw the aims of the mutineers expand. Whereas the first was marked by a speedy resolution with minimal violence, the later mutinies saw political radicalism, conflict and ruthless retribution.

The first mutiny at Spithead (Portsmouth) fell into a broad tradition of collective action in the navy. The seamen's petitions ignored, on 16 April 1797 the signal was given for a refusal to weigh anchor. The fleet was immobilised, while two delegates from each ship were elected and sent to negotiate, first with the fleet's commander, Admiral Bridport, then with the Admiralty, led by Lord Spencer. Their principal demands – an increase in wages, and improvements in the quality and quantity of food – were quickly granted by the Admiralty. There was little violence or disorder, and the delegates strongly rejected any suggestion that they had political motives. Throughout, the mutineers insisted on their readiness to sail if the French fleet put out from Brest. A delay in securing their demands briefly raised the suspicions of the crews and saw mutiny break out anew. Vice-Admiral John Colpoys ordered the officers and marines of the *London* to fire on the mutineers, mortally wounding several of them. Fortunate to avoid violent retaliation, Colpoys and his fellow officers were confined to their cabins, and later sent ashore. Following the announcement that a bill had been passed which answered the delegates' grievances, the mutineers returned to their posts, amid much rejoicing and celebration. The crew of the *Mars* wrote a lengthy document to their officers, signed individually, that apologised for their conduct and hoped that shipboard relations

An Address to Alexander Hood Esqr. and his Officers Commanding
On board H.M.Ship Mars Dated June 27, 1797

Honoured Sir,

It is the Unanimous Wish and Desire, of the Seamen and Marriners, of H.M. Ship
Mars, to testifye, this our Zeal and Gratitude, to you And your Officers in General. and
to inform you that our past Conduct, has been Uncivel and that the Contempt that
has been Shewn to you. And the Officers in General. in Open and Direct Violation to the
laws of our Country. And more Spirticularly to Gentlemen of your Humanity and Conduct
and who has Ever been Forward in promoting our Care and Welfare this Sir we are Sorry
to Say has been the Case. but believe that Contempt which has been Shewn to you and
the Officers in General. was totally Exhibeted by those Unthinking Men. who was totally
led away by false Notions. Errors for which those very Men at this time Are particularly
Sorry for. And Ernestly hope for a General Forgiveness. And who now being Consious of that Error
and being brought to a proper Sense of their Duty. And Good Will towards you And
the Officers in General. your Ships company has taken this Opportunity to testifye our
Intentions and Good will towards our Officers in Future. that we are Determined Never to
Violate our orders. or behave any ways Contrary to the Wishes of our Superiours in
any Case Whatever. And Furthermore we are Determined to do our Duty Done in the
Most Satisfactory Terms. both to the Satisfaction of our Captain. and Every Officer who
has the Honnor to Command Us. And are Determined to Support you And your Officers
to the utmost of our power And As a Proof of our Obedience to your Command. Never
more to be led away by any Notions. or Misrepresentations. or any Messages. by word of
Mouth. or by Letter. from any Ship or Ships. in H. Majestys Navy. that may tend to
Corrupt. or Inflame the Minds. of any of your Ships Company. And that you may be
Purfectly Satisfied. you will have the pleasure to See the Future Duty of your Ship
Done. with the greatest pleasure and satisfaction to you and your Officers in General
And Furthermore to Shew our Loyalty. and Affection. to our King and Country. and
to proclaim to the World in General. our Good Disposition that wee Are Willing
to Lay down our lives. for our Officers. And in Defence. of our King and Country

## A List of the Ships Companys Names — Michl. Newton

Wm Heather | Willm Daniel | David Stevenson | George Ellis x | Thos Perkins x | Samuel Farr
James Brownfield | Richard Clark | James Smith | Edm Greenbank x | Thos Roe x | Lowrence Hyser
Mark Thornton x | The mark of William Kingsell | Robert Lyell | John Wilkinson | Peter Templeman | Bengamen Ashley x
George Sole | The mark of Dudley Hood | Charles Watson | George Henry yeary | Edgerton x | John Walther x
James Eyon | | Thos Whitfield | Theodore Bick | John Marvell x | William Taylor x
William Price | Thomas Broadfoot | John Tuson x | Wm Falconer | James And... | John Walsh
Lewis Gearst | Charles Copland x | Edward cnell x | Thomas Harris | William Brown | William Foy
James price | John weather tin | Samuel Glover x | Pitter Goulden | Sevenh | Donovan | John Kelley

Robert Gent | Henry Ellis | Me Battersbee | George Otto | George Laing | John Ess | James Fowle | Wm Tucker x
George Laytney | James Fowles | Thos Tame x | Thomas Teller | John Tort | | James McMulen | Hen Roberts +
William Skeock | William Say | Gc Rutherford | Robert Wilmot | James Bond x | William Dixcon | William Wilson | Abraham Wood x
William Howeath | Thomas Cook | Mikl Regan | James Evans | John Kelly + | Jo Poise x | James Hanner | John Bootle
| | Wm Cowen | Andrew Brown | Edm Underwood | Tom Maysoot | George Chambers | autndee Price
| | Hartin Roja | Michl Johnson | Thomas Good | Rhea Wilson | Thomas Derviah | Robt Anderson x
| | Lewis Wms | Geo Webber | Thomas Don | Rich Warfield | John Rose | Jas Shephard x
| | Rhea Richardson x | Th Amson x | Philp Tollard | Henry Roberts | Robert Roberts x | Benl Mcneind
| | John Valley | Henry Sulivan + | Thos Dann | Ralph Webley x | Charles Treep x | John Dummitt
| | Rd Stephens + | David Vennew | Wm Wright | Thomas Wilbey + | James Armstrong | James Beach
| | Thos Joanes x | Rich Admans | Abraham Clear | John Yaken + | Saml Jennings | Wm Howeeh
| | Jas Hyars | Wm James Neesbey | James Gallagher | John Hues + | David Bolton | Geo Pees
| | Wm Johnson | George Goulding | Jno Doherty | Jas Hudd x | Abner Barnet | Nick Reiman
| | Hector McCloud + | Jno Knowles | Geo Stott | Walter Campl | John Ratkin | Richard moeert
| | Wm Myars | Si Fe Updell | Geo McGinny | Alex Johnston | John Brown | Francis Hay
| | Thomas Stepford | Lea Grest | Bengn Ryser | Phillip Foth | Samuel Herbert | Thos Treey
| | Sam Dyre | William Warsis x | Thomas Smith | Jno Gill x | Rich Gill | Wm Hall
| | Edw Shelly | Joseph Corcel | Henry Kinnent + | John G Witt | Conrai Ichray | Rich Whoelar x

would be restored to normality.[4] On 17 May, the fleet left port, and took up station off Brest.

However, the mutiny exposed Britain's vulnerability for all to see. Martha Saumarez, wife of a naval captain, wrote to her husband describing her relief at the satisfactory ending to the mutiny. Britain, she said:

> *has weather'd one of the greatest perils that ever threaten'd her By the late alarming Mutiny in the Fleet, with heartfelt pleasure I acquaint Thee that Discipline & Order are once more restor'd... This Mutiny while it stands recorded as the most serious that has ever threatened this Country must at the same time excite the astonishment of the World at the regularity with which these men conducted themselves who at other times, when left to their own Conduct...are the most Disorderly Beings upon the Earth! It is a great satisfaction to perceive that there was no disaffection amongst them – for on the contrary they express as fully attach'd as ever to their Country & and are gone to Sea with Hearty Wishes. They may have the opportunity of giving the French a sound Drubbing.[5]*

She well understood how close Britain had come to disaster, and how intertwined the nation's interests were with the conduct of her seamen.

As the mutiny of Spithead ended, a second broke out at the Nore, off Sheerness dockyard. The sailors demanded further indulgences to those granted at Spithead, among which were: shore leave for every sailor, selection of their own officers, courts martial run by sailors and marines, advanced wages for pressed men, and a more equitable distribution of prize money in which the majority would go to the lower deck.

The *Clyde* arriving at Sheerness after the Nore mutiny, 30 May 1797, by William Joy, oil on canvas, 1830 (BHC0497)

To twenty-first-century eyes this may not seem unreasonable, but to the eighteenth-century Admiralty these requests threatened to undermine the very fabric of shipboard discipline. Unlike the Channel Fleet at Spithead, the smaller fleet at the Nore had little political leverage. The Admiralty refused to accede to any of the demands. This served only to agitate the mutineers further. It was reported that 'the Mutiny at the Nore seems to have attained the most dangerous and alarming height. The Seamen appear to enter into open hostility against their Country'.[6]

The uprising was strengthened by the mutiny of Admiral Duncan's fleet at Yarmouth, which sailed to join the ships at the Nore. Responsible for the blockade of the Dutch fleet, the mutiny of this strategically crucial squadron exposed the entire south-east coast of Britain to invasion. The Admiralty refused to blink and cut off all communications and supplies from the shore. Whereas the seamen had initially been united in their designs, the crews became increasingly hesitant. Individuals, then ships, began to desert the mutiny. In one last attempt to force a decisive result, the order was given to sail to a French port. No ship obeyed it. Isolated from their supporters on land, starving and unable to sail anywhere else, the loyalist elements of each ship's crew began to seize control. Fighting broke out and by 13 June the mutinous ships had been captured.

The mutinies were over, but they left an uncertain legacy. The press and the London pamphleteering circle lost no time in highlighting the explicitly political motivations of the seamen, and blamed the influence of Irish, French and radical agitators. However, almost without exception, the mutineers were able seamen and seamen petty officers of long experience, rather than newly recruited and politically charged landsmen

Drum believed to have been used on board the *St Fiorenzo* during the Nore mutiny, late eighteenth century (AAB0233)

recently brought into the navy through the Quota Acts of 1795–96. There is some evidence of ideological motivation: for instance, at the court martial of seaman George Shave, he reportedly shouted at an officer 'that his country had been oppressed for these five years, that the war had been too long, and now was the time to get themselves righted'.[7] It is hard to judge how representative these beliefs were, though it is important to remember that seamen did not live in a political vacuum, nor were they unaware of the long-standing practice of collective lobbying on board naval ships.

Whether radical political events or not, the mutinies were certainly perceived as such by the British population. For all that its end was anticlimactic, with the majority of sailors returning to their ships, the national reaction to the Nore mutiny was one of fear. One distant observer, writing to her friend the month after the event, warned against the nation's dependence on its

caricatures of naval events were routinely published in tandem with, and even anticipating, official dispatches and news reports. This journalistic concern for current affairs ensured that caricature served as both a barometer of, and a guiding force for, British public opinion. The radical undertones of the 1797 mutinies, though often exaggerated, proved irresistible for satirical artists. This print appeared during the Nore mutiny, but played on deeper-seated concerns present since the first outbreak of insurrection at Spithead, merging the mutinies into one awful spectre of naval rebellion. *The Delegates in Counsel* shows the ringleaders of the Nore mutiny sitting at a cabin table while an Admiral – likely to be Admiral Buckner – stands to hear their demands. Buckner had been sent aboard the *Sandwich* to be received by Richard Parker, the alleged 'president' of the delegates. The artist reinterprets the scene, creating a picture of disharmony and unease, reversing the normal pattern of shipboard relations. While Buckner waits hat in hand, the delegates hold guns and swords, some displayed prominently on the table. The dangerous appearance of the assembled seamen is exaggerated by their unkempt look, their red jackets and their aggressive, purposeful stances. On the far right, a sailor pours from a jug of grog and expresses the group's determination to overturn the social make-up of the navy: 'Tell him we intend to be masters', he says. In the background a portrait of Britannia hangs upside-down, a graphic symbol of the social order being turned on its head.

Cruikshank's presentation of the British seaman is in notable contrast to the dutiful, constant sailors described in the ballads of the time, or the comical figures of fun preferred by other caricaturists. Here, the seamen take on a threatening appearance, showing how the nation's bulwark had suddenly become its greatest danger. Two song sheets are shown ripped and shredded on the wall. Those named, 'True Blue' and 'Hearts of Oak', were traditional songs that celebrated the courage and loyalty of the British sailor. In showing them torn, the artist was making a direct comment on the damage done to the sailor's image across British society. Four days after this print was published, the Nore mutiny came to a violent end, leading to relief and recrimination in public and in parliament. Aware of its political resonance, the artist added a partisan twist to the image. Underneath the table (see detail) the politician Charles James Fox mutters supportively with his fellow Whigs, admitting to their complicity in recent events. The Whig party, guided by Fox, had been early sympathisers of the French Revolution, and vocal opponents of the war. Although their support was tempered by the extreme violence of the Terror of 1793–94, Fox and his closest allies were unable to escape their reputation as Francophile revolutionaries. The mutinies of 1797, with their undercurrent of radicalism and subversion, were placed firmly at Fox's door. In this, the threat to the social configuration of the Royal Navy mirrored precisely the political dangers facing the nation.

RICHARD PARKER.

PRESIDENT of the DELEGATES in the late MUTINY in his MAJESTY'S FLEET at the NORE...
For which he suffer'd DEATH on board the SANDWICH the 30th of June 1797
York Published as the act directs July 8th 1797 by J.Harrison & Co.

*Richard Parker. President of the Delegates in the late Mutiny in his Majesty's Fleet at the Nore...*, by William Chamberlain, published by J. Harrison & Co., hand-coloured etching, 8 July 1797 (PAH5541)

*Richard Parker who was executed on board the Sandwich off Sheerness, on Friday June 30th. 1797...,* by F. Sansom after John Bailey, published by S.W. Fores, stipple engraving, 21 July 1797 (PAD3034)

navy. 'I was never so much alarmed by any circumstances of our political situation, as by the horrid mutiny of our sailors', she wrote:

> *It may teach us humility...when, what we considered as our greatest human defence, was turned against ourselves...It must be hoped, that such as are the least guilty, and escape capital punishment, may be entirely banished from the country, which they have endeavoured to destroy.*[8]

Pamphlets were produced that alleged a nationwide conspiracy to undermine the navy and the

nation it defended.[9] Officers who had helped to dissolve the mutiny were gratefully rewarded by mercantile and City companies, while the mutinies' dissolution was celebrated with a mixture of relief and wariness. Celebratory patch-boxes were sold alongside prints warning the sailors about their future conduct. It was recognised that the bond between the British people and its navy had been temporarily fractured.

Those in government were also shocked by the events. Eyewitness reports to the Admiralty confirmed their worst fears. Sir Charles Grey, the commander of the Sheerness garrison, had watched in horror as the mutineers paraded through the town with red flags flying: 'everything bore the most unpleasant, and alarming appearance...I trembled...for the consequences that might have ensued.'[10] In an exercise of deterrence and ruthless retribution, the Admiralty moved quickly to punish the leaders of the Nore mutiny. Altogether twenty-nine were hanged and many others disciplined for their actions. The trial of the mutineer Richard Parker excited much public interest. Pamphlets – many sympathetic to his plight – were published describing his trial and execution. Deemed to have been the ringleader of the mutineers at the Nore, he was hanged on 30 June on board the *Sandwich*.

For the navy, the events at the Nore transformed the relationship between officers and their

Presentation small-sword given to Captain W. Daniel by the Committee of Merchants & Co. of London following his conduct at the Nore mutiny, 1797 (WPN1553)

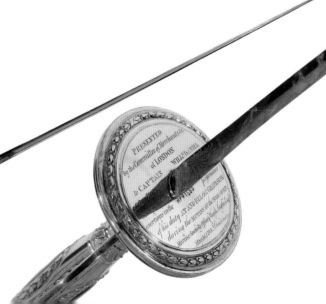

crews. The nation's sure shield had briefly threatened to become its Achilles heel. Instructions were issued by the Admiralty that reinforced 'the enormity of the crime of Mutiny', and warned that from henceforth those who failed to resist uprisings would also be deemed guilty of the crime. At the same time, special mention was made of the companies that had not mutinied: 'if the very great majority of Good Men in every ship were to conduct themselves in the same manner, the few ill-disposed who may be among them, would find it impossible to succeed in their wicked designs.'[11] Four months later, the vessels and crews involved fought and won the great victory of Camperdown against the Dutch navy. It would take years, however, before seamen and officers would fully trust each other again.

The mutinies proved to be a unique and unprecedented moment of shipboard disharmony.

ABOVE Ceramic plate celebrating a sailor, Jack Crawford from Sunderland, for his heroism at the Battle of Camperdown, late eighteenth to nineteenth century (ZBA4377) LEFT *An Address to the Seamen in the British Navy*, letterpress, 1797 (MKH/15)

AN

ADDRESS

TO THE

SEAMEN

IN THE

BRITISH NAVY.

LONDON:

PRINTED FOR W. RICHARDSON, AT THE
ROYAL EXCHANGE.

JULY, 1797.

In the years that remained of the French Revolutionary and Napoleonic Wars, there were no further widespread outbreaks in the navy. With invasion fears continuing to escalate, various Britons took it upon themselves to rehabilitate the image of the British seaman as a brave, loyal and trustworthy patriot, rather than the scurrilous radical suggested by recent events. One pamphlet, *An Address to the Seamen in the British Navy*, aimed to 'cast a veil' over recent events, and suggested how 'British seamen' might resurrect their image 'of being respected at home, and feared abroad'. The balladeer Charles Dibdin wrote over 100 songs celebrating the manly virtues of Jack Tar, while the caricaturist James Gillray would resuscitate the British seaman by drawing him punching a Frenchman from the face of the world (see p. 114). Jack Crawford – a seaman widely celebrated for nailing fallen colours to the shattered topmast of his ship at the Battle of Camperdown – was transformed into a national hero, not least on ceramics.

This was not the stereotypical naval sailor so often found in bawdy and patriotic prints, but a real person, in an individual act of valour. For the first time the ordinary British seaman had a name and a face.

For all these efforts, the navy's position as the nation's defender had been undermined by recent events. In the months after the mutiny, reports of French invasion plans continued to circulate through British society, given greater credence by further French Continental successes and a seemingly disloyal Royal Navy. Exaggerated tales of vast invasion craft spread across the nation, fanned by uncertainty and rumour. Prints were published with absurdist configurations of windmills, paddle wheels,

*An Accurate Representation of the Floating Machine Invented by the French for Invading England…, by Robert Dighton, hand-coloured etching, c.1798 (PAH7433)*

citadels and armaments, as artists attempted to convey the imagined, unquantifiable threat from across the Channel. Some of the reports verged on the ridiculous. *The Star* reported on 10 February 1798 that in St Malo:

> *a Raft, one quarter of a mile long, proportioned breadth, and seven balks deep, mounting a citadel in the centre, covered with hides, was nearly finished; and that a second upon a much larger scale, being near three quarters of a mile long, was constructing with unremitting activity…desperate as an expedition of this nature appears, it is not impossible that they may attempt it.*

Two days later, the *True Briton* poured scorn on the idea of such invasion craft: 'We have seen Letters of a recent date from Jersey, which state…

AN ACCURATE REPRESENTATION of the FLOATING MACHINE Invented by the FRENCH for INVADING ENGLAND. and Acts on the principals of both Wind & Water Mills. carries 60-000 Men & 600 Cannon.

that the French had no means whatever on the opposite Coast of transporting their Troops. There are no Boats even at St Maloes, nor have they the means of building any, much less a floating Machine of such magnitude as that represented.'[12] Caricatures mocked the idea of invasion, while conveying a patriotic image of a strong, unbending and invincible navy – images that reached a still wider audience when displayed on penny tokens. But while the idea of a full-scale invasion was often greeted with ridicule, even the most outlandish reports from across the Channel exploited a genuine and well-founded fear of attack. Gillray's print series, *Consequences of a Successful French Invasion*, was hugely popular. In it, various symbols of nationhood – parliament, the countryside, and the church – are shown submitting to French soldiers set upon destroying the British way of life. The credibility of the reports ushered in a series of military reforms that ensured an invasion force would

*Consequences of a Suc———cessful French Invasion.*

Nº 1. Plate 2ª. "We explain de Rights of Man to de Noblesse." Scene. The House of Lords.

Description. — A Guillotine, which is placed on the Throne; the royal Chairs being removed, pour accommoder les Etrangers, (in English) To accommodate the Strangers. Two Turkish Mutes, with strangling Bowstrings, each his Hand on his Mouth, stand as Supporters. The House empty of Peers. On a Board is written, "Solitudinem faciunt, Pacem appellant". (in English) They (that is, the French) create Solitude, and call it Peace". The Cap of Liberty above the Canopy, below which is painted in capital Letters, "Confusion to all Order". A French Admiral, looking at the Tapestry, which represents the Defeat of y Spanish invincible Armada, & the Portraits of the Immortal English Commanders, says "Me like not de Omen; destroy it". French Soldiers with Swords, Pikes, & screwed Bayonets, attack the Tapestry, on one side of the Room. A Sea Captain, on the Top of a Ladder, tears down y Tapestry from above; his Lieutenant sets fire to it below, & at the same Time pulls the Foot of the Ladder to break his Superior's Neck; saying, "This is 'an easier Way of getting Preferment than de English Way'. Un Commandant en Chef, (in English) The Commander in Chief, in his full Republican Uniform, pointing at the Mace, says, "Here, take away this Bauble; but if there be any Gold, on "it, send is to my Lodging". A French Soldier carries it away on his Shoulder. The Bust of Ræton in the Table, in the Middle between those of Damien & Ravilac.

Sir John Dalrymple, inv.                    Jª Gillray Nº 27. S. James's Street.                    Jª Gillray fecit.

a few miles of water lay in the way of total French victory. 'Let us be masters of the Straits for but six hours, and we shall be masters of the world', he said in July 1804.[13] Within a few months, a vast flotilla of boats and barges was constructed to transport the troops across the Channel. By the spring of 1805, Napoleon had assembled a mighty invasion force of more than 160,000 men. Medals were struck and watches manufactured in anticipation of an imminent French victory.

Invasion fears in Britain reached their zenith. The Whig politician Charles James Fox described 'a picture of a People so terrified as we have been was never before exhibited'. Newspapers referred time and again to the menacing forces in northern France: 'Nothing is spoken of but the premeditated

OPPOSITE ABOVE (TOP) Penny token showing an invasion craft, 1798 (MEC1746) OPPOSITE ABOVE (BOTTOM) French medal commemorating Napoleon's planned invasion of England, 1804 (MEC0830)
OPPOSITE BELOW *Consequences of a Successful French Invasion*, by James Gillray and Sir John Dalrymple, hand-coloured etching, 1 March 1798 (PAG8509)
ABOVE Model of a shutter-telegraph system, c.1795 (MDL0020)
BELOW Swiss watch (with later additions) depicting a French invasion of England, c.1803 (JEW0265)

be strongly opposed. The government took the invasion threat very seriously, withdrawing ships from foreign climes to home waters, particularly the English Channel. As early as 1796, a shutter-telegraph system was in operation, allowing messages to be passed from the south coast to London in a mere fifteen minutes. The county militia was expanded to 116,000 individuals: by 1803, around half a million volunteers were armed and ready to defend the English coast.

Victory at the Battle of the Nile in 1798 temporarily assuaged fears of invasion, though they were resurrected again with Napoleon Bonaparte's seizure of power in France in 1799. The British government's attempts to sue for peace in 1801 were carried forward against a background of anxiety. The Peace of Amiens that resulted from these discussions was settled in France's favour, though it brought only a temporary respite in the conflict. In 1803, war was again declared, and Napoleon committed vast resources to the planned invasion of Britain, including the creation of a new basin at Boulogne, resolute in his belief that only

invasion of this Country, and every day produces fresh proof of the Corsican's determination to attempt our overthrow', wrote one. Rumours and false intelligence abounded. Papers attempted to outdo each other for detail, each publishing 'accurate representations' of the invasion craft. *Lloyd's Evening Post*, a newspaper not normally given to exaggeration, described 'between nine hundred and a thousand vessels of different descriptions' at Boulogne, with troops waiting to embark. They published the account of 'an English Gentleman, lately arrived from Paris', who described the 'undiminished activity' of invasion preparations. The threat became all-consuming: plays were written and produced throughout the summer of 1803 which celebrated patriotic notions and ridiculed Napoleon and his military plans. The French leader was represented as a diminutive, delusional character. The plays promised to place the 'bravery of Britons', and the 'intrepidity of British Tars', against Napoleon, the 'Corsican Fairy'.[14]

Reports of naval activity and attacks on the invasion fleet at Boulogne went some way to calming the public's nerves. Naval officers, confident in their ability to repel any attempt at invasion, reassured those in London. 'I do not say', Admiral St Vincent reportedly stated to the House of Lords, 'that the French will not come. I say only they will not come by sea'. As St Vincent had long known, Napoleon's ambitions were far-fetched and unrealistic. The few miles of water between the two nations proved more of a barrier than he had imagined. Disillusioned with his admirals, and facing a renewed military threat from Austria and Russia, Napoleon was forced to abandon his invasion plans. However, the only true antidote to public alarm was naval victory: the Battle of Trafalgar in October 1805 demolished French sea power and removed the likelihood of a French invasion. Britons would worry about invasion again, for instance in 1809, but the navy had proved itself to be the ultimate guarantor of British safety.

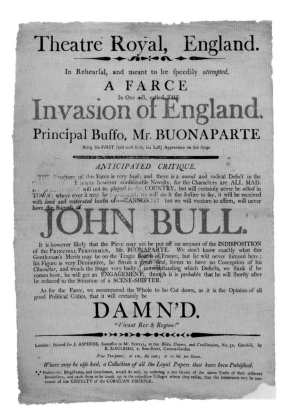

*A Farce...The Invasion of England*, mock playbill, letterpress, c.1803 (PBF5077)

The combined threats of revolution, invasion and mutiny in these years had led many to question the loyalty of the British people; in both 1798 and 1803 the government commissioned surveys to report on the public's disposition. These fears proved to be largely unfounded. Rather than internal dissension, the anxieties prompted by war against revolutionary and Napoleonic France resulted in an outpouring of patriotism, based on an almost unanimous loyalty to crown and constitution. Loyalist associations (sometimes supported by the state) outstripped memberships of radical societies, while volunteer militias sprang up around the country. By the second half of the 1790s, every county had its own volunteer cavalry regiment and every town its own infantry volunteers. Between 1797 and 1804, one in six adult males enrolled in a volunteer corps. At the height of national fears in early 1798, Martha Saumarez, ever the canny observer, described the mass of voluntary contributions that poured in from all quarters, including the fleet that had recently mutinied:

*all descriptions of People have caught the generous flame...it is truly delightful to see Patriotism surmounting avarice & all other selfish Passions. The sailors belonging to the Channel Fleet & the Ships in Port have subscribed a month's Pay but all the Corps in the Kingdom will follow this noble example. The Navy Captains have given also a month's pay in addition to what they may give from their private Fortune. This day's Paper mentions a donation from the Queen of £5000, the Corporation of Bath have subscribed £1000,*

*& the Bankers and Merchants in London have come forward with Contributions suitable to the spirit of Englishmen.*[15]

While news of French invasion plans brought insecurity, reports of naval success proved a welcome tonic, inculcating a sense of national unity and a belief in the navy as Britain's foremost champion. It was in this environment of widespread apprehension and patriotic verve that Horatio Nelson made his mark on the national stage.

*A Correct View of the French Flat-Bottom Boats, intended to convey their Troops, for the Invasion of England...,* published by John Fairburn, hand-coloured etching, 17 August 1803 (PAH7437)

A Correct VIEW of the FRENCH FLAT-BOTTOM BOATS, intended to convey their TROOPS, for the INVASION of ENGLAND, as seen afloat in Charante Bay; in August 1803.— Those Flat-bottom Boats are about 120 feet long, and 40 broad, and will carry 500 Men each, they have on board 4 small Boats, calculated to carry out, or weigh, a kedge-anchor, with which they can heave the vessel a-head, on light, or contrary winds, when they are near the shore.

Destruction of the French Gun-Boats —

, what a glorious sight !
my Bull into a fine pafsion !—
ever leaves me !— I shall now
Thousand French Cut Throats
of !— O my dear Talley, this
isoning hollow ! ———
!— pepper 'em, Johnny !

Pub'. Nov' 22 d. 1803 by H Humphrey
29 S'. James's Street
London

Little Boney & his Friend Talley in high Glee.

# NELSON AND NAVAL WARFARE

## Andrew Lambert

T he log-book of the *Victory* recorded the moment of Nelson's death amid the details of a battle that was then drawing to a close.

*Observed one of the Enemy's Ships blow up and 14 sail of the Enemy's ships standing to the Southward – Partial Firing continued until 3.40 when a Victory having been reported to the Rt. Hon.ble Viscount Lord Nelson KB and Commander in Chief he died of his wounds.*[1]

There was something curiously complete about the juxtaposition of explosion, conclusion and transfiguration. Those events formed a pattern, one that highlighted the nature of Nelson's genius in a striking, artistic manner. Nelson's achievement was not the product of genetic heritage, undaunted courage or lucky accident. He possessed an educated mind, one that never stopped gathering and processing information, assessing ideas, and using the accumulated understanding to achieve his aims. This commitment to career-long education distinguished him from his peers, moulding the genius that enabled him to transform the art of war at sea from the prosaic to the sublime.

There were many reasons why Horatio Nelson was anointed as the secular deity of the British state, ranging from his great victories in

the darkest hour, through popular acclaim and a heroic death in the last and greatest naval battle fought by wooden sailing ships. His effigy stands in majesty, twice life size, far above mere mortals, at the very heart of imperial London in Trafalgar Square, while little more than a mile away his mortal remains slumber in the sepulchral gloom of the crypt of St Paul's, cathedral of the City of London, at the centre of a constellation of British heroism. This one man defined the naval profession and shaped the very identity of the British.

However, Nelson did not invent naval warfare. The system that Nelson operated had been built in the seventeenth century, and refined in the eighteenth by men he had served under. Battles fought by evenly matched fleets of wooden sailing ships armed with heavy cannon were rarely decisive. Linear battle was an exhausting attritional business, the only way to win was to kill or incapacitate so many of the enemy crew that they could not fight or sail the ship. In most cases this took hours, and the losers had ample opportunity to escape before they lost too many ships. Wars between 1688 and 1763 were decided by sustained British economic blockades, naval victories and colonial conquests which wrecked the treasuries of France and Spain. The American

Rear Admiral Sir Horatio Nelson, by Lemuel Francis Abbott, oil on canvas, 1799 (BHC2889)

ABOVE The Rectory, Burnham Thorpe, Norfolk, by Isaac Pocock, oil on canvas, c.1807 (BHC1772)
OPPOSITE Captain Horatio Nelson, by John Francis Rigaud, oil on canvas, 1781 (BHC2901)

War of Independence (1775–83) changed the character of war. The Franco-Spanish alliance posed a very real threat of invasion and catastrophic commercial losses. Britain was saved by allied incompetence and a devastating epidemic. In 1793, the French Revolutionary government occupied modern Belgium, posing an existential threat. So long as the French occupied the Scheldt estuary Britain would be obliged to maintain the navy on a war footing simply to prevent an invasion. Once Adam Duncan had destroyed the Dutch invasion threat at Camperdown on 11 October 1797, the British government moved ten of his ships to the English Channel, releasing ten more powerful ones to reinforce Admiral Sir John Jervis at Lisbon. Jervis then sent his best ships from the blockade of Cadiz to join the flag of Rear Admiral Sir Horatio Nelson, then searching for a French force deep inside the Mediterranean.

While the Victorians were happy to attribute Nelson's success to character and courage, the reality is altogether more compelling. Nelson developed the building blocks of genius through patient study and constant reflection; his transcendent talent was only realised after twenty-eight years of service. Born in the village parsonage of Burnham Thorpe, Norfolk, on 29 September 1758, Horatio was the sixth of the Reverend Edmund and Catherine Nelson's eleven children. While the Nelson line contained successful merchants, the odd mayor and several clerics, it offered no warrior heroes. Instead, Nelson inherited a compassionate concern for his fellow human beings, a dry sense of humour and a predisposition to hypochondria from his father, along with a direct, compelling literary style. Despite her early death when Nelson was only nine, his mother Catherine (*née* Suckling) taught him to 'hate a Frenchman like the devil', and opened the door to a naval career. In March 1771, the twelve-year-old Nelson joined the Royal Navy at Chatham; close by lay the *Victory*, the largest ship in the fleet.

He joined a thoroughly professional organisation. No one could become an officer without six years of sea service, certificates of competence from their captains, and the ability to pass a stiff oral examination in seamanship. Here Nelson was doubly fortunate. Captain Maurice Suckling, a prominent naval officer and a childless widower, took his nephew as a surrogate son. He provided an exemplary naval education and excellent postings, secured his commission as lieutenant, and sent him to the frigate *Lowestoffe* just in time for the outbreak of war against American rebels, and then their French and Spanish allies. The war would fast-track Nelson's career. Suckling died suddenly in July 1778 but Nelson became a captain in July 1779, aged only twenty. Captain William Cornwallis introduced him to the business of fleet battle, and pointed out the best admiral in

the service: Lord Hood. After Rodney's great victory in the Saintes Passage on 12 April 1782, Hood, his second-in-command, complained that Rodney had missed the opportunity to pursue and destroy the shattered enemy fleet, leaving the triumph incomplete. Nelson understood that tactical success was only the beginning: strategic victory would be secured through annihilation, the relentless pursuit of a beaten foe.

The ten years of peace that followed the American War of Independence nearly wrecked Nelson's career. Then, in 1793, Nelson left Burnham to join Hood's Mediterranean Fleet. He learned the art of the admiral by studying Hood's every move. He wanted to know what Hood was thinking – and why. He wanted to match the insight of the most brilliant officer of the age. Hood had uncommon acumen, supreme self-confidence and excellent political connections. In an age when long-distance communications were painfully slow, Hood understood that the man on the spot had to use his own judgement and act on his initiative. Sent to war in 1793 with orders not to occupy any French territory or take sides in the revolution, he knew when to disobey. When offered the chance to occupy the main French naval base at Toulon he grabbed it, and used the opportunity to destroy much of the French fleet. His bold and effective actions were approved. Nelson would show the same political courage, acting in situations where other admirals sent home for orders. Hood led by example, and always briefed his officers: although he had no interest in their opinions, at least he ensured they understood his thinking. Ultimately defeated at Toulon, Hood was undaunted (another key lesson), seizing Corsica despite the army. Nelson lost the sight of his right eye at the siege of Calvi.

However, Revolutionary France would fight to the finish. When Hood went home to winter at Bath, massive French conscript armies attacked and overwhelmed their Austrian opponents, destroying nations and reshaping the map of

Europe. The military revolution in progress on land meant war at sea would have to change; the old system seemed trifling and feeble. Having witnessed French methods of total war in action, Nelson understood that only annihilation would alter the strategic balance, enabling naval power to affect war on land, where the main decisions must be reached.

He learned the mechanics of total war from Admiral Sir John Jervis, who took command in the Mediterranean in early 1796. Jervis kept the fleet at sea, his professional administration and solid logistics providing the final stage of Nelson's command education. In late 1796, Spain changed sides, forcing Jervis to evacuate the Mediterranean. Britain had lost the ability to influence the politics of southern and central Europe or to protect the trade of the Middle East. Disaster loomed. Jervis sent Nelson to evacuate Corsica, and then Elba, Britain's brief Mediterranean empire. Returning from the second mission, Nelson passed through the Spanish fleet and rejoined Jervis off Cape St Vincent on 13 February 1797 with the latest intelligence on the poor state of enemy seamanship and discipline. The next day, Nelson's dramatic contribution secured victory over the larger Spanish fleet. Rather than waiting for orders, he used his understanding of the admiral's methods to anticipate them. Although outnumbered and isolated, Nelson's attack wrecked the Spanish attempt to regroup. Then Nelson drove his crippled ship alongside two enemy vessels, and boarded them sword in hand. While his insight and initiative had turned the battle, Nelson's skilful manipulation of the resulting publicity secured him a national reputation, and he was made a knight of the Bath. The thirty-eight-year-old, now rear admiral had fully justified Maurice Suckling's patronage.

Having reached the heights of glory, Nelson suffered a painful reverse in an amphibious attack on Santa Cruz de Tenerife on 24 July. He learned that bravery and determination were useless in

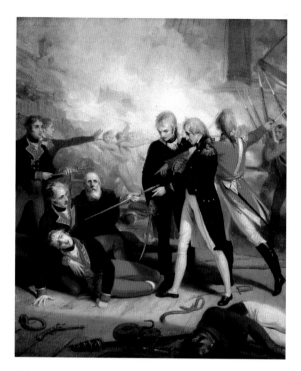

Nelson on board the *San Nicolas* at the Battle of Cape St Vincent, 1797, by Richard Westall, oil on canvas, 1806 (BHC2909)

the face of impossible odds. That night he lost his right arm. He would carry a reminder of that defeat pinned across the front of his coat for the rest of his life. Beneath Nelson's heroic posture lay a powerful streak of self-doubt and hypochondria, nowhere better expressed than in his first left-handed letter.

Once his arm had healed, and his shattered self-belief had been restored by an admiring public and a prominent place in a great national celebration of naval glory at St Paul's, Nelson returned to the Mediterranean. He was given command of a small squadron sent to locate a gathering French invasion armada. When Jervis sent his ten best seventy-four-gun ships to join Nelson he changed the mission to search *and* destroy. Although he missed Napoleon at sea, the final outcome of his agonising pursuit around the Mediterranean exceeded all expectations. Late in the afternoon of 1 August 1798, the French fleet was sighted at anchor in Aboukir Bay, Egypt, and although the light was already fading Nelson did not hesitate and launched his ships into battle. He directed the attack at the head of the French line. With the wind blowing directly down the enemy line he could concentrate on the van ships, achieving an overwhelming concentration of force. He could see there was room between the French line and the shore, and so did Captain Thomas Foley who rounded the French fleet to attack from inshore without orders, because he knew Nelson would back his judgement whatever the result. Nelson's mission-analysis command style set the standard operating procedures, or doctrine, and explained the big picture so that captains could still use their skill and judgement. This approach exploited the advantages of a force possessing superior seamanship and fighting power.

Nelson did not lead the attack: he elected to control its direction. With five British ships attacking the French from the shore side, he opened the second phase of the battle, taking the *Vanguard* to the seaward side of their line, doubling the attack on the enemy ships and hastening the attritional process of grinding down French resistance. Although a nasty head wound sent him below decks for treatment, his captains pressed on. Ben Hallowell and Alexander Ball took up perfect positions to attack the mighty French flagship *L'Orient*, a ship with almost twice the firepower of her smaller British opponents. When the French ship caught fire, Hallowell deliberately directed his cannon into the blaze to prevent the crew putting it out. By the time a bandaged Nelson reached the deck to witness the final catastrophe, both fleets were bracing themselves for the inevitable. At approximately 11:00pm *L'Orient*'s two powder magazines exploded. This stunning *son et lumière* highlighted the defeat of the French fleet, and marked the emergence of a new age of war at sea.

Nelson's first letter written with his left hand, 27 July 1797 (PAR/251)

Nelson's genius transformed the inconclusive attritional naval warfare of the eighteenth century into a compound of startling simplicity and awe-inspiring power. His unerring insight reduced complex problems to clear concepts and simple instructions that could be explained to any captain. This approach to war was unique and special. As a self-conscious hero of the Romantic age, Nelson recognised the new cultural sensibilities – sensibilities that echoed the heightened political passions of the revolutionary era. Early in the eighteenth century, the concept of the 'sublime' had been shaped by Joseph Addison, one of Nelson's favourite authors. Addison's sublime was a fit adjective for Homer's verse dramas, for the actions of heroes in all ages: noble, god-like, heaven-born figures who, by their very existence, could elevate the mental world of mere morals to a higher plane, closer to god than man. These were the models Nelson wished to emulate when he resolved to be a hero. The defining texts of Nelson's sublime were the apocalyptic passages of the Bible, his master text.

The year before Nelson was born, Edmund Burke's *A Philosophical Enquiry into the Origin of our Ideas of the Sublime and Beautiful* argued that the sublime was a suitable description for anything that inspired terror – the strongest of human emotions. In 1790, Burke would establish the philosophical basis of British opposition to the French Revolution. Immanuel Kant took the sublime a stage further as 'the extreme tension experienced by the mind in apprehending the immensity or boundlessness of the grandest conceptions'.

The sublime was equally applicable to the art of war: never more so than on 1 August 1798, when the French flagship *L'Orient* blew up – the dramatic highlight of the Battle of the Nile, and an unprecedented pyrotechnic display and thunderous detonation that briefly turned night into day, leaving all the combatants stunned into silence. This cataclysmic metaphor would recur in Nelson's other battles, with the *Dannebrog* at Copenhagen and *L'Achille* at Trafalgar as later examples of his obsession with annihilation. That his sublime talents could only be encompassed by the art of the apocalyptic sublime was established by Philippe-Jacques de Loutherbourg (see p. 135). It became the standard approach to a critical moment in British history. In 1825, the British Institution paid George Arnald £500 for a Nile picture to hang in the new Naval Gallery at Greenwich Hospital. The artist placed the *Swiftsure* at the centre of his picture, to highlight British heroism. Arnald, previously a landscape painter, recognised the Nile as a sublime subject, in which fire, darkness and drowning men would have called up parallels of biblical judgement to contemporary viewers. After an exhibition in central London in 1827, the picture

hung in the Painted Hall at Greenwich for a century, becoming a great national favourite, and itself featuring within a later painting, Thomas Davidson's 'England's Pride and Glory' of 1894, where it summed up Nelson's life.

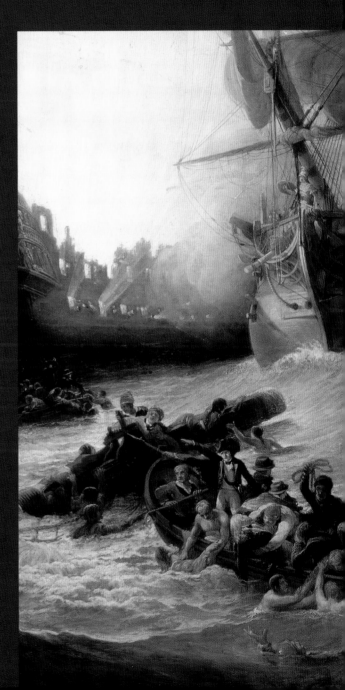

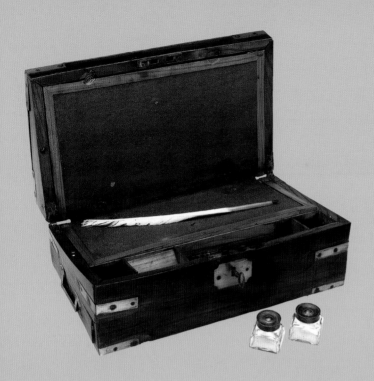

ABOVE Nelson's writing box, c.1798 (AAA3398)

ABOVE RIGHT The 'Turkey Cup' presented to Nelson after the Battle of the Nile by the Levant Company, 1799–1800 (PLT0095)

BELOW RIGHT *Fede* or betrothal ring, one of a pair exchanged by Nelson and Lady Hamilton, 1800–05 (JEW0168)

BELOW Border of a dress embroidered in honour of Nelson and worn by Lady Hamilton, c.1799. 'Bronte' refers to the Sicilian dukedom bestowed on Nelson after the Battle of the Nile (TXT0304)

The following day, Hallowell had his carpenter fashion a pine coffin out of *L'Orient*'s mainmast, and presented it to Nelson. It served as a reminder of his mortality amid the glory and the grandeur of victory, and he would be buried in this simple box. He also had a writing box made from the timber of *L'Orient*. After the battle Nelson, having taken or destroyed eleven of the thirteen French battleships, divided his fleet to exploit British command of the sea, blockading the French army in Egypt, and reviving the Continental alliance against France. The 'Turkey Cup', a gift from the Levant Company, reflected the importance of the Nile for British commerce.

Arriving in Naples soon after the battle, Nelson began a startling relationship with Emma, Lady Hamilton, wife of the British minister at the Neapolitan court and intimate of the Queen of Naples. Among the most beautiful and accomplished women of the age, she was the muse of his later years. Emma worshipped Nelson, whereas his wife Frances cautioned him against taking risks – little wonder the marriage broke down. For all his Christian faith, Nelson had no qualms about the relationship, a point made obvious by the rings they exchanged.

Having secured the Mediterranean, Nelson returned to Britain, and sailed as second-in-command of a fleet sent to break up the Armed Neutrality of northern powers. Tsar Paul I wanted the British to renounce their hard-line economic warfare, which was damaging neutral traders. The British refused. When the fleet reached Copenhagen in April 1801, Nelson was given command of a division. Because the British wanted a negotiated settlement, he used a completely different tactical model. His ships were directed and controlled from the quarterdeck throughout the battle. At its height, Commander-in-Chief Sir Hyde Parker signalled for him to break off the action; Nelson famously refused to acknowledge the signal, dryly putting the telescope to his blind eye. Once the Danish defence line of hulks and batteries had been overpowered, he offered the Danish government an armistice, in highly complimentary terms, and brought the combat to an end. Because he had matched his tactics to the strategic and political needs of the moment, Nelson removed Denmark from the Armed Neutrality without inflicting any lasting injury, enabling the British fleet to sail for Russia. Nelson's importance to Britain was nowhere better understood than at Lloyd's of London, the shipping insurance centre. Unlike the government and the City of London, Lloyd's was quick to reward him for Copenhagen. Nelson also used the wealth he accrued through naval service to purchase the trappings of upper-class domesticity, from plate to dinner services (see pp. 162–63).

Emma Hart, later Lady Hamilton, by George Romney, oil on canvas, 1785–86 (BHC2736)

ABOVE AND BELOW Sauce tureen and ice pail presented to Nelson by the Corporation of Lloyd's after the Battle of Copenhagen, 1801–02 (PLT0101, PLT0096)

On his return to Britain, Nelson commanded the Channel defences. The Peace of Amiens of 1802 established an armed truce but in 1803 the war resumed, with the greatest commanders of the age on opposite sides and opposing elements. Only Nelson had the insight and understanding to match Napoleon, as Napoleon acknowledged by keeping a bust of Nelson in his private quarters.

Sea power allowed Britain to blockade the French economy and restrict the French empire to Europe, while securing British control of global trade. For two years the British rested on the defensive, waiting for the French to show their hand, and expose themselves to a devastating counter-attack. If Napoleon tried to invade England, Ireland, the West Indies or Egypt his ships would be destroyed. Late in 1804, Spain joined the war as an ally of France, giving Napoleon enough ships to challenge British sea power. His plan to invade Britain without a fleet action was countered at every move. When Admiral Villeneuve finally escaped the British blockade, Nelson chased him to the West Indies and, in his most daring campaign, smashed Napoleon's dreams of invasion. By September 1805, Villeneuve's large, Franco-Spanish fleet lay at Cadiz, ideally positioned to attack Britain's allies in the Mediterranean, her Atlantic trade, or the British Isles. It had to be destroyed.

Nelson joined the fleet off Cadiz in late September. His presence electrified the officers and men under his command, while his new battle plan (see p. 164), explained in the great cabin of the *Victory* and followed up in a written memorandum, provided the key to decisive combat. Few of those captains had served with Nelson before; he needed to assess their abilities before he could lead them into battle. If the enemy put to sea, Nelson sought to annihilate them, ending the need for Britain to stand on the defensive.

Napoleon ordered Villeneuve to support an attack on Naples, and Villeneuve, believing Nelson's fleet was a third weaker than his own, put to sea on 19 October. In fact, his thirty-three ships of the line faced twenty-seven British vessels. Nelson shadowed them as they headed east. At dawn on 21 October the fleets were in visual contact. He ordered his fleet into two columns for a novel, risky, head-on approach that exposed the flimsy, unarmed bows of his leading ships to the full weight of enemy broadsides. Knowing that a storm would come that evening, Nelson had no time for tactical finesse, adopting high-risk tactics to secure his strategic objectives. To simplify the task for his captains, he would lead the attack. Locating and destroying the enemy flagship would reduce the

enemy to a confused, leaderless mass that could be defeated by battle-hardened British crews in the remaining hours of daylight. He calculated on taking or destroying twenty enemy ships. Nelson's unique and original battle plan combined great danger with startling speed.

Nelson devoted time and thought to the morale of his people. Having walked around the flagship, talking with the crew, he spread the effect across the entire fleet with the immortal signal: 'England Expects That Every Man Will Do His Duty'. The fleet cheered because Nelson, the embodiment of England and the talisman of victory, had spoken to every man. Such courageous, public leadership made it easier for everyone else to be brave. As the fleets closed, at walking pace, the British sailors had time for breakfast, and lunch. The French and

ABOVE Items from the 'Horatia set' of porcelain purchased by Nelson, c.1802 (AAA4532, AAA4536, AAA4540, AAA4544)
BELOW Coffee pot that belonged to Nelson, 1799–1800 (PLT0120)

Spanish crews may not have had such good appetites; they knew exactly what to expect. While his men dined, Nelson kept his eye on the enemy, waiting for Villeneuve to show his flag. Only then would he know where to strike.

As *Victory* bore down on the enemy fleet she had to endure heavy fire, without being able to reply. Soon round shot were smashing through the ship's bow and the unprotected men on the upper deck. John Scott, Nelson's public secretary, standing on the quarterdeck talking with Captain Hardy, was cut in two. His mangled remains were quickly hove overboard, leaving a pool of blood. Then the ship's wheel was smashed to atoms, and a Spanish bar shot scythed down a file of eight marines on the poop (see p. 175). Nelson quickly ordered the remaining men dispersed to avoid further heavy losses. Yet Nelson and Hardy paced up and down on their chosen ground, the starboard side of the quarterdeck, not a foot from the smashed stump of the wheel, with splinters flying around them. When one hit Hardy's shoe, tearing off the buckle, Nelson observed: 'This is too warm work to last for long.' They had yet to open fire and fifty men had been killed or wounded. Even Nelson was impressed by the cool courage of *Victory*'s crew.

Finally at 12:35pm the concave enemy line allowed *Victory* to open fire, shrouding the ship in smoke, and providing some relief from the torment of waiting. Soon after, she ran under the stern of Villeneuve's flagship, *Bucentaure*, which shuddered under the impact of 100 projectiles from a full double-shotted broadside. More than 200 officers and men were killed or wounded, Villeneuve was the only man left standing on the quarterdeck. However, the *Redoutable* blocked *Victory*'s passage through the enemy line. Immobilised at the epicentre of a savage *mêlée*, Nelson had administered the decisive stroke. The allied fleet had been reduced to a chaotic agglomeration of ships; many fought with remarkable bravery

but they lacked the leadership and skill to meet the impact of the impetuous, irresistible British. Nelson knew that each British ship was a superior force to an enemy of equal size. At close quarters the speed and regularity of British gunnery steadily overwhelmed the allies. Over the next three hours, the Franco-Spanish force collapsed under the weight of unprecedented firepower.

Nelson's attack at Trafalgar broke all the tactical rules: treating a fleet waiting for a fight like one running away, substituting speed for mass, precision for weight, and accepting impossible odds. The real triumph was not of twenty-seven ships against thirty-three, but of twelve against twenty-two. British casualties tell the story: *Victory* had 132

casualties, *Royal Sovereign* 141, *Temeraire* 123, *Neptune* 44, *Mars* 98, *Tonnant* 76, *Bellerophon* 150, *Revenge* 79, *Africa* 62, *Colossus* 200, *Achille* 72 and *Defiance* 70. Yet only one of the men who died that day would be remembered. It was not so much the fact of his death as the manner of it that made the event memorable. Had he been cut in half by a round shot like poor Scott, the final emotional twist of immortality might have slipped from his grasp, his life somehow reduced by the random violence of its end. Instead he died as he had lived, the talisman of the British nation, and the defining genius of the art of war at sea. The fall of Nelson was a truly iconic moment, captured for all eternity by Denis Dighton in his picture of 1825. Walking on

the quarterdeck with Captain Hardy, discussing the way the *Conqueror* had come into the battle, Nelson was hit by a musketball at about 1:15pm. The .69-inch diameter lead ball smashed through his left shoulder blade, punctured his left lung, cut the main artery and lodged in his spine. Knocked to the deck, Nelson landed in Scott's blood, soaking his stockings and breeches (see p. 167).

He knew the wound was mortal. Hardy had him carried below to the cockpit, where surgeon William Beatty was already hard at work. In addition to the cacophonous roar and smoke of the guns and the shuddering motion of the ship as it ground against the enemy, the cockpit possessed a unique horror. The low deckhead, glimmering

ABOVE The Battle of Trafalgar, 21 October 1805, by J.M.W. Turner, oil on canvas, 1822–24 (BHC0565)
OPPOSITE The stockings worn by Nelson when mortally wounded at the Battle of Trafalgar, c.1805 (UNI0067)

lanterns, moaning and screaming men, the stench of blood and the hurried work of amputating shattered limbs made this charnel house as close to hell as any living man could get. Beatty could only confirm Nelson's diagnosis before the admiral insisted that he attend to those who might live. Above them, the battle with the *Redoutable* reached a crescendo when French boarding parties were cut down by the 'Fighting' *Temeraire*'s carronades. At 1:30pm, Captain Jean Lucas surrendered: 490 of his 640-man crew had been killed and eighty-one wounded.

At 3:30pm Hardy was able to tell Nelson that a glorious victory had been won. Despite the terrible injury he had suffered, Nelson lingered for over three hours. After Hardy knelt and kissed him on the cheek, Nelson kept repeating his motto: 'Thank God I have done my duty.' He died slowly, quite literally drowning in his own blood, the ruptured artery filling his lungs. His breathing began to falter and he slipped away without a sound shortly before 4:30pm, just as the fighting died down. Nineteen enemy ships had been taken and the explosion of *L'Achille* provided a suitable coda for the last and greatest fleet battle under sail. The cost had been high on both sides: 1,700 British killed and wounded, 6,000 enemy casualties and nearly 20,000 prisoners. Many of those lives were lost in the storm that followed, along with many prizes, among them Villeneuve's flagship and the mighty Spanish *Santísima Trínidad*. Never again would France or Spain challenge British sea power.

While any competent British admiral would have won off Cape Trafalgar, only Nelson could have done so in a manner that achieved decisive strategic effect. Immanuel Kant's remark that 'genius is the natural ability which gives the rule to art...a talent for producing that for which no definite rule can be given' is both nearly contemporary and of great significance to students of Nelson.[2] In his seminal work *On War*, Prussian general, educator and theorist Carl von Clausewitz developed Kant's concept in an attempt to comprehend the nature of military genius. This 'very highly developed mental aptitude for a particular occupation' was found in those of superior intellect, whose careers had been shaped by a sophisticated and systematic appreciation of their profession.[3] It was the 'harmonious combination of elements', which mastered all the rules and regulations of the profession through study and experience to develop the 'genius' that could transcend rules. Genius enabled men to take quick decisions in complex situations, achieving an instinctive understanding of the situation, the *coup d'oeil* that separated the great commander from the competent. Napoleon argued that the calculation required to solve battlefield problems would have taxed Newton, but,

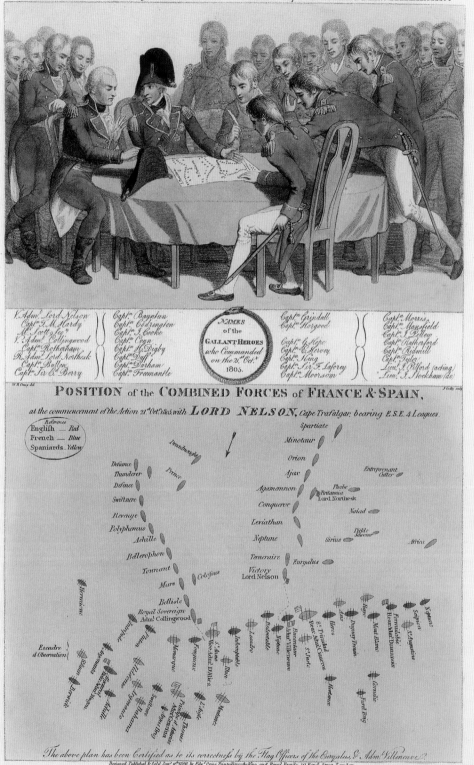

England expects every Man to do his duty.

LORD NELSON explaining to the Officers the PLAN of ATTACK previous to the BATTLE of TRAFALGAR.

NAMES of the GALLANT HEROES who Commanded on the 21.ˢᵗ Oct.ᵗ 1805.

V. Adm.ˡ Lord Nelson
Capt.ⁿ T. M. Hardy
M.ʳ Scott, Sec.ʸ
V. Adm.ˡ Collingwood
Capt.ⁿ Rotheram
R. Adm.ˡ Lord Northesk
Capt.ⁿ Bullen
Capt.ⁿ Sir E. Berry

Capt.ⁿ Bayntun
Capt.ⁿ Codrington
Capt.ⁿ J. Cooke
Capt.ⁿ Cogn
Capt.ⁿ H. Digby
Capt.ⁿ Duff
Capt.ⁿ Durham
Capt.ⁿ Freemantle

Capt.ⁿ Grindall
Capt.ⁿ Hargood
Capt.ⁿ G. Hope
Capt.ⁿ E. Hervey
Capt.ⁿ King
Capt.ⁿ Sir F. Laforey
Capt.ⁿ Moorsom

Capt.ⁿ Morris,
Capt.ⁿ Mansfield
Capt.ⁿ J. Pelley
Capt.ⁿ Rutherford
Capt.ⁿ Redmill
Capt.ⁿ Tyler
Lieu.ᵗ J. Pilford (acting)
Lieu.ᵗ J. Stockham (do)

POSITION of the COMBINED FORCES of FRANCE & SPAIN,

at the commencement of the Action 21.ˢᵗ Oct.ʳ 1805, with LORD NELSON, Cape Trafalgar, bearing E.S.E. 4 Leagues.

Reference
English — Red
French — Blue
Spaniards — Yellow

The above plan has been Certified as to its correctness by the Flag Officers of the Euryalus, & Adm. Villeneuve.

Designed, Published & Sold Jan.ʳ 9.ᵗʰ 1806, by Edw.ᵈ Orme, Printseller to the King, and Royal Family 59 Bond Street London.

SUBSCRIPTIONS for a SPLENDID ENGRAVING of the DEATH of NELSON, SIZE 23 by 17.ᵗʰ are RECEIVED at 59. BOND STREET.

as they had to be solved immediately, only highly educated instinct could hope to meet the need.[4] For Clausewitz, genius was ultimately an intangible quality that could not be taught. In Nelson's case, it was the product of a superior intelligence focused through a lifelong dedication to professional education.[5] Having settled his concept of battle, Nelson brought his captains over to dine on the *Victory* and explained his ideas to them; it was, he noted, like an electric shock. Cuthbert Collingwood understood Nelson's genius:

*He possessed the zeal of an enthusiast, directed by talents which nature had very bountifully bestowed upon him, and everything seemed, as if by enchantment, to prosper under his direction. But it was the effect of system, and nice combination, not of chance. We must endeavour to follow his example, but it is the lot of very few to attain his perfection.*[6]

OPPOSITE *England expects every Man to do his duty. Lord Nelson explaining to the Officers the Plan of Attack previous to the Battle of Trafalgar...*, by James Godby after William Marshall Craig, published by Edward Orme, hand-coloured stipple engraving, 9 January 1806 (PAG9025) BELOW The death of Nelson, 21 October 1805, by Arthur William Devis, oil on canvas, 1807 (BHC2894)

# 9

# THE EXPERIENCES
# AND WEAPONS OF WAR

## Roland Pietsch

Standing before an oil painting depicting majestic sailing ships engaged in battle, the observer is easily captured by a sense of romance. The sailors manoeuvring these ships and firing the guns are, however, often barely visible. In stark contrast to the museum visitor viewing the battle from the gallery's quiet, steady and dry floors, these sailors were in the midst of it, their bare feet on the trembling wooden decks awash with water and blood, shot and splinters flying past their heads, and the horrendous noise of the cannons pounding their ears. How did they experience naval war? What did the men who handled the collection of weapons displayed in the National Maritime Museum actually feel?

Charles Pemberton, pressed into the navy during the war against Napoleon, claimed that he simply fought himself into frenzy:

*I had no time to be frightened during all this, for I was not in my right mind – I was in a whirl: the bustle, hallooing, hurraing, crashing, cracking, rattling, thundering, whizzing, and whistling, made me drunk and delirious; like a fellow in a tavern, who, when he is in the third heaven of jollity, smashes tables and chairs, dishes and glasses – dashes his fist through the door-panels and the windows, all senseless of the scarifying and bruises he inflicts upon himself...and I*

*dare say, if any one had set me the example, I should have ran away and hid myself if I could; only, it happens, that there are no back doors to escape by in these affairs.*[1]

Other sailors were more thoughtful. Samuel Leech remembered from his battle experiences as a fourteen-year-old during the War of 1812:

*We all appeared cheerful, but I know that many a serious thought ran through my mind: still, what could we do but keep up a semblance, at least, of animation? To run from our quarters would have been certain death from the hands of our own officers; to give way to gloom, or to show fear, would do no good, and might brand us with the name of cowards, and ensure certain defeat. Our only true philosophy, therefore, was to make the best of our situation, by fighting bravely and cheerfully.*[2]

A sailor's wartime experiences greatly depended on his ship and what it was engaged in. Taking part in a grand fleet battle in a ship of the line – those floating fortresses, of which the *Victory* is the surviving example, with over 100 guns spread on its multiple decks – was a rare event, something that a sailor would see, if at all, only once or twice in his time in the navy. Sailing

*Sailors in a Fight*, by William Ward after Thomas Stothard, published by John Raphael Smith, mezzotint, 16 April 1798 (PAH7352)

in a smaller, speedy frigate, with guns only on her single upper deck, and being on patrol duty or protecting a convoy, promised a very different experience of war.

The first challenge seamen encountered, however, was the monotony and claustrophobia that could gnaw on their nerves when the enemy was nowhere in sight. This did not mean they were out of danger, though, for their deadliest enemies had already closed in on them: rats and lice, the as-then undiscovered carriers of diseases. Compared to them, the enemy's ships were, for the first part of the eighteenth century, a minor threat. The naval physician James Lind claimed that 'the number of seamen in time of war, who die by shipwreck, capture, famine, fire, or sword, are indeed but inconsiderable, in respect of such as are destroyed by the ship diseases, and by the usual maladies of intemperate climates'.[3] Only in the second half of the eighteenth century, when increased care was taken over diet and hygiene, were the high percentages of disease-related deaths lowered. Even without a battle, then, the combination of limited space, threat of disease, and weeks of waiting and exercising, could create a highly pressured environment, and one in which some sailors may have longed for the day when an engagement would offer a relief valve.

When that day came, the ship had to be transformed from a floating home into a battle station. The order to clear the decks for action was piped: bulkheads, partitions, entire officer's cabins, mess tables, benches, chests and anything superfluous had to be removed. They were not only obstacles for the fighting seamen, but could also produce deadly flying splinters when hit by enemy cannonballs. The decks were sanded – on board the Spanish *Santísima Trinidad*, before the Battle of Trafalgar, one of the novices recounted how: 'My curiosity prompted me to ask a lad who stood next to me what this was for. "For the blood", he said very coolly. "For the blood!" I exclaimed, unable to

repress a shudder.'[4] The sand gave a foothold once the decks were soaked in blood and water.

Fire hoses were rigged to the pumps, water placed in strategic spots to fight fires, weapons distributed to fight boarders, and different types of shot stored near the guns. The carpenters and their mates prepared to undertake any emergency repairs, while the surgeons and their mates warmed their knives and saws, expecting soon to be cutting and sawing their way through flesh and bone in scenes even more gruesome than those on deck. Other non-combatants, such as the chaplain, steward or purser, had to prepare themselves for the prospect of assisting the surgeons, knowing that this was something even hardened seamen dreaded. Time permitting, a meal could be served, alcohol given out to numb fears or letters home could be written and wills exchanged. When the captain ordered 'beat to quarters', everyone had to be at his battle station, silently listening for commands. An eerie stillness set in, as Charles Pemberton noted:

*Every man and boy was mute as he stood at his station...Every thing was now in order...*

*guns cast loose, crow bars for pointing the guns lying at hand on deck, tompions out, all ready for a game of thunder...There was no noise, no laugh...Men, shirtless, with handkerchiefs bandaged tightly round their loins or heads, stood with naked brawny arms folded on their hairy and heaving chests, looking pale and stern, but still...I felt a difficulty in swallowing. Now if we had gone at it at once, without this chilling prelude, why I dare say I should have known very little about the thing which we call fear.*[5]

Depending on the size of cannon, up to seven men made up a gun crew. Unless the ship was fighting on both sides, each gun could be attended by two crews. Guns were classified by the weight of ball they fired and their length, ranging from rare and massive forty-two-pounders, to thirty-two-, twenty-four-, eighteen-, twelve-, nine- and six-pounders. Heading each gun was the captain of its crew. He was responsible for aiming and firing. The other crew members were responsible for sponging the gun (to neutralise any traces of burning cartridge from the previous shot), ramming home the cartridge and wadding, then ramming in the shot and another wad (to prevent the shot from rolling out), and running out the gun. At the bottom of the gun crew's hierarchy was the most junior member, the powder boy. As it was too dangerous to store the powder on deck, it was kept in a magazine below the waterline, and

OPPOSITE French republican banner captured during the Battle of the 'Glorious First of June', 1794 (AAA0564)
BELOW The Battle of the 'Glorious First of June', 1794, by Philippe-Jacques de Loutherbourg, oil on canvas, 1795 (BHC0470)

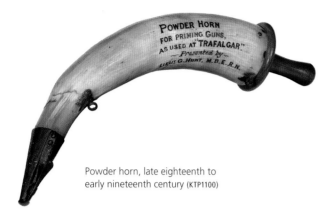

Powder horn, late eighteenth to early nineteenth century (KTP1100)

the job of these boys was to fetch the powder for each round. Being a powder boy gave the young sailors their first experiences of war. Olaudah Equiano, later a famous anti-slavery campaigner, was a fourteen-year-old powder boy during the Battle of Lagos in 1759, when the British and French fleets met during the Seven Years War:

> *My station during the engagement was on the middle deck, where I was quartered with another boy, to bring powder to the aftermost gun; and here I was a witness of the dreadful fate of many of my companions, who, in the twinkling of an eye, were dashed in pieces, and launched into eternity. Happily I escaped unhurt, though the shot and splinters flew thick about me during the whole fight.*[6]

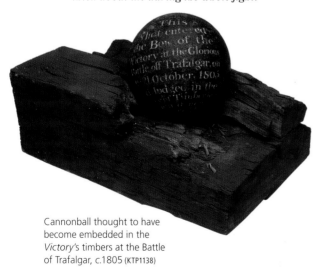

Cannonball thought to have become embedded in the *Victory*'s timbers at the Battle of Trafalgar, c.1805 (KTP1138)

The decision about how much powder to use was made by the gun crew's captain, who would also pour additional powder down the touch hole from his powder horn. The crew's captain had different types of shot at his disposal, each being preferable for specific targets. Round shot – a simple solid iron ball – was the most used, and was designed to penetrate the enemy's hull. When targeting the rigging, chain shot (two balls at each end of a chain, with the chain spreading once fired), and double-headed or bar shot were

Tier shot, late eighteenth to mid-nineteenth century (KTP1144)

more suitable. It is worth remembering that at the receiving end of the gun crew's work were not just wooden structures but also their opposing crews. A direct hit by round shot would blow a man apart and scatter his body parts over his mates. Even when the shot went into the hull, it was likely to unleash a vicious hail of wooden splinters that could be equally deadly. The bar shot opposite shows the effect these weapons could have when they hit men instead of rigging: it killed eight Royal Marines. There was also ammunition aimed specifically at the crews: grape, canister and tier shot, which were small balls confined in containers or canisters, with the balls being scattered by the explosion. Neither round shot nor

ABOVE Spanish bar shot fired at the *Victory* during the Battle of Trafalgar, 1805 (KTP1079) RIGHT Twelve-pounder carronade (the carriage is a later addition), c.1805 (KTP0036)

any of the other shot available to the gun crew contained any explosives. The only naval guns firing explosive shells were mortars, which were carried on specially designed bomb vessels, and were chiefly used to attack towns and fortresses. They required very accurate aiming and timing; consequently, their operation was left to trained artillerymen of the marines or army.

While frequent gun drills were acknowledged to have been the reason for the British navy's more rapid firepower, accuracy in firing was often neglected in training. In fact, during most gun drills the crews did not fire at all, in order to save ammunition. At the same time, the heavy movement of the deck during battle made aiming difficult and also hard to recreate during a drill.

Pair of officers' flintlock pistols, late eighteenth century (AAA2430)

Traversing the gun by applying different pressures to the gun tackles assisted with crowbars or handspikes was possible but far from easy; elevation could be achieved by adjusting the wedge at the breech to lower or raise the muzzle. Having aimed the gun as rapidly as possible, the crew's captain would then fire. The force unleashed was tremendous, and so was the noise, leaving many sailors with long-term hearing damage, the handkerchiefs tied around their heads not giving much protection. One can almost hear the thunder in

the smoke of Philippe-Jacques de Loutherbourg's painting of Lord Howe's victory at the Battle of the 'Glorious First of June' (see p. 173). This battle – in which the British Channel Fleet clashed with the French Atlantic Fleet west of Ushant – was the biggest naval engagement of the eighteenth century. To the left, the sinking French *Vengeur du Peuple* is depicted, its fate witnessed by the twelve-year-old William Parker (later an admiral) and described to his parents as follows:

> *You could plainly perceive the poor wretches climbing over to windward and crying most dreadfully...Oh my dear father! When you consider five or six hundred souls destroyed*

*in that shocking manner, it will make your
very heart relent. Our own men even were a
great many of them in tears and groaning,
they said God bless them.*[7]

Future officers, like Parker, had to learn how
to command their men during battle while simultaneously giving an impression of utter calmness.
Lieutenant Paul Nicholas on board the *Belleisle*
remembered his experience at Trafalgar:

*My eyes were horror struck at the bloody
corpses around me, and my ears rang with
the shrieks of the wounded and the moans
of the dying. At this moment seeing that
almost everyone was lying down, I was half
disposed to follow the example, and several
times stooped for the purpose, but...a certain
monitor seemed to whisper, 'Stand up and
do not shrink from your duty'. Turning
round, my much esteemed and gallant senior
[Captain Hargood] fixed my attention;
the serenity of his countenance and the
composure with which he paced the deck,
drove more than half my terrors away; and
joining him I became somewhat infused with
his spirit, which cheered me on to act the part
it became me.*[8]

Although their experiences of war were different, sailors on board frigates could go through
something very close to the realities of a grand
fleet action when equally matched frigates met
and each was determined to win a decisive
victory. On 25 October 1812, the British frigate
*Macedonian* and the American frigate *United States*
encountered each other near Madeira. Britain
and the United States had been at war since
June that year, so both ships cleared for action.
*Macedonian* carried twenty-eight long eighteen-
pounders, as well as eighteen thirty-two-pounder
carronades, a twelve-pounder carronade, and two

nine-pounders. Carronades had been introduced
in the navy as an addition to the main armament
in 1779. They were shorter, lighter and had a large
bore, delivering heavy firepower at shorter ranges
and requiring fewer men to operate (see p. 175).
Carronades increasingly replaced cannons, particularly on smaller ships, while being less used on
large ships of the line. A first rate like the *Victory*
still carried only two carronades, though these
were capable of firing sixty-eight-pound cannonballs. Serving on board the defeated *Macedonian*,
the lower-deck sailor Samuel Leech left a graphic
description of the firepower of both frigates:

*[T]he whole scene grew indescribably
confused and horrible; it was like some
awfully tremendous thunder-storm, whose
deafening roar is attended by incessant
streaks of lighting, carrying death in every
flash, and strewing the ground with the
victims of its wrath: only, in our case, the
scene was rendered more horrible than that,
by the presence of torrents of blood which
dyed our decks.*[9]

Sailors who were mortally hit were usually
tossed immediately overboard to make space.
There was no Nelsonian funeral procession
for Jack Tar. Badly injured sailors were hastily
brought into the cockpit to the surgeon. If Samuel
Leech thought the scenes on deck already resem-
bled hell, then the sights he encountered here
were equally testing: the operating table, tubs for
amputated limbs, and a surgeon and his mates
smeared with blood. While the battle raged on,
the surgeon went about his work. The threat of
infections – antiseptic practice being unknown
– frequently left him only one solution: amputation. After applying a tourniquet, the surgeon
used an amputation knife to cut through the skin,
tissues and muscles as swiftly as possible until
the bone was exposed. He would then pull back

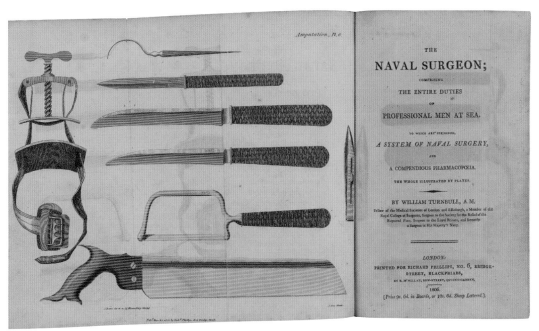

TOP A below-decks sketch showing a man having his leg amputated, graphite, c.1820 (PAD8484)
ABOVE *The Naval Surgeon*, by William Turnbull, 1806 (PBN4879)

the flesh with a retractor, cut through the bone with a saw and then tie off the major blood vessels with silk ligatures. All of this was carried out without anaesthetics and death from shock was not uncommon.

Gunnery frequently decided the outcome of a battle from a distance, yet there was always the possibility that during an engagement the ships could get close enough, either intentionally or accidentally, to prompt boarding attempts. In fact, for a ship being outgunned, forcing a collision and switching to man-to-man combat was potentially a way of turning the tables. In contrast to the well-drilled work of the gun crew, boarding was primeval, tumultuous, often improvised, with no body armour or shields protecting the fighters. Although specific boarding roles were assigned to the gun crews and marines, by the time it came to boarding it was often a case of

hack and run, rather than skill and tactics. After all, those that attempted to board were still primarily sailors, not professional fighters, with many hastily recruited or pressed fishermen, watermen, landsmen and boys among them. Unlike the marines and officers, seamen were not even entrusted with their own weapons, which were locked up and guarded by marines, and only handed out just before the engagement. Small-arms drill was part of the navy's regulations since the middle of the eighteenth century, though it is not clear how often edged weapons and boarding tactics were included. There are few historical documents like Lieutenant William Pringle Green's manuscript containing written training instructions. Dating from the early nineteenth century, they are perhaps an indication that such detailed instruction was a new doctrinal development.

*Instructions for training a ship's crew to the use of arms in attack and defence, by Lieutenant William Pringle Green, early nineteenth century (JOD/48)*

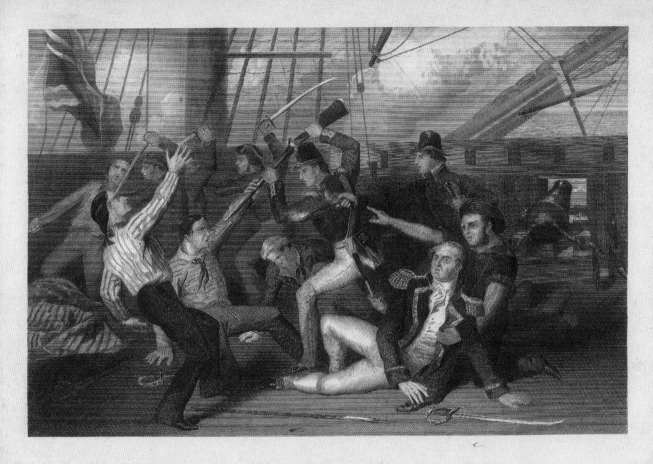

*The Boarding of the Chesape[a]ke by the Crew of the Shannon. Death of Captain Lawrence*, engraving, 1860 (PAD5835)

The War of 1812 provides a notable example of a successful boarding. In May 1813, the British frigate *Shannon*, under the command of Captain Philip Broke, was cruising off Boston to intercept merchant vessels, but also challenging American warships to a duel. As *Chesapeake* left Boston harbour to take up the gauntlet, cheered on by excited spectators on land, preparations were made on board both frigates to arm their crews for the eventuality of a boarding attempt – *Shannon* having a complement of 330 men and *Chesapeake* 379. In addition to muskets and pistols, both crews would have had around seventy-five boarding axes at their disposal, perhaps similar to the tomahawk-style axe depicted overleaf. The axe was both weapon and tool, with a long history of being used at sea. Fire being a constant danger, it was needed to hack free burning rigging and heated shot or for clearing wreckage. The axe was also a terrifying weapon. The drawing below shows considerable use of axes during shipboard fighting, while the central character's musket has been fired and only serves him as an unwieldy cudgel. The same illustration features a sailor fighting with a pike. On board *Shannon* and *Chesapeake* around 100 such pikes were handed out or placed around the ship. Primarily a defensive weapon, pikes were particularly useful in connection with anti-boarding nettings, as used by Captain William Rogers and the crew of the *Windsor Castle* on 1 October 1807, when successfully defending against the boarding attempt of French sailors from the *Jeune Richard* who heavily outnumbered them.

ABOVE RIGHT Pike, nineteenth century (WPN1658)
RIGHT Boarding axe, nineteenth century (XXX2304)
OPPOSITE Captain William Rogers capturing the *Jeune Richard*, by Samuel Drummond, oil on canvas, 1808 (BHC0579)
BELOW A sketch of fighting on deck, graphite, c.1820 (PAD8485)

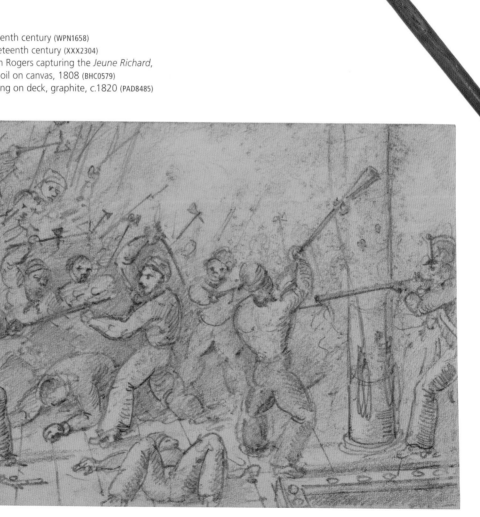

# FLINTLOCK PISTOLS AND MUSKETS, SEVEN-BARRELLED VOLLEY GUN
## LATE EIGHTEENTH TO NINETEENTH CENTURY
### (AAA2440, AAA2446–50, AAA2576, AAA2578, AAA2581, AAA2519)

---

M uskets specifically modified for sea service had appeared during the last quarter of the seventeenth century. Loading was time-consuming, which was one reason why the musket only slowly replaced the crossbow and longbow. Unlike Royal Marines and naval officers, lower-deck sailors were not entrusted with the continuous possession of firearms or other weapons. Instead, these were locked up and guarded by marines, and were only handed out to the crew during preparation for an engagement. Most members of a ship's company would, nonetheless, have received some training in their use. As smoothbore firearms, muskets were not able to deliver accuracy at long range, and were typically only used once combatant ships had come within 100 yards of each other.

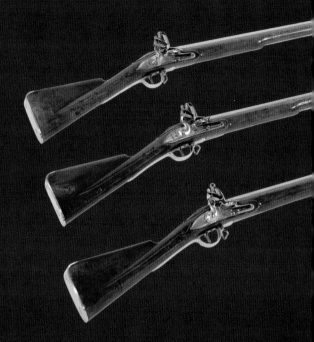

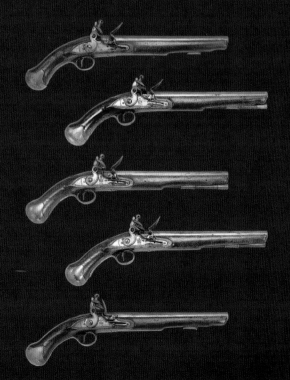

The best shots among the marines were placed high above the deck in the tops. There they were joined by the topmen among the sailors, who not only carried some of the ship's muskets with them, but also tools, spares and buckets of water to deal with any damage or fire in the rigging. Grenades and swivel cannons were also hauled up. Their first targets were usually their counterparts on the opposing ship – once these had been eliminated, they would then have free range to fire down. Muskets were a particular danger to officers who, as the only ones wearing uniform, could be easily picked out, as Nelson's death at Trafalgar exemplified. *Victory* actually had no musketry in her tops, as Nelson had been concerned about small arms setting the sails or rigging on fire. The danger was not far-fetched. In particular, a weapon such as the seven-barrelled volley gun, introduced in the 1780s and firing all of its barrels simultaneously, was a considerable fire hazard.

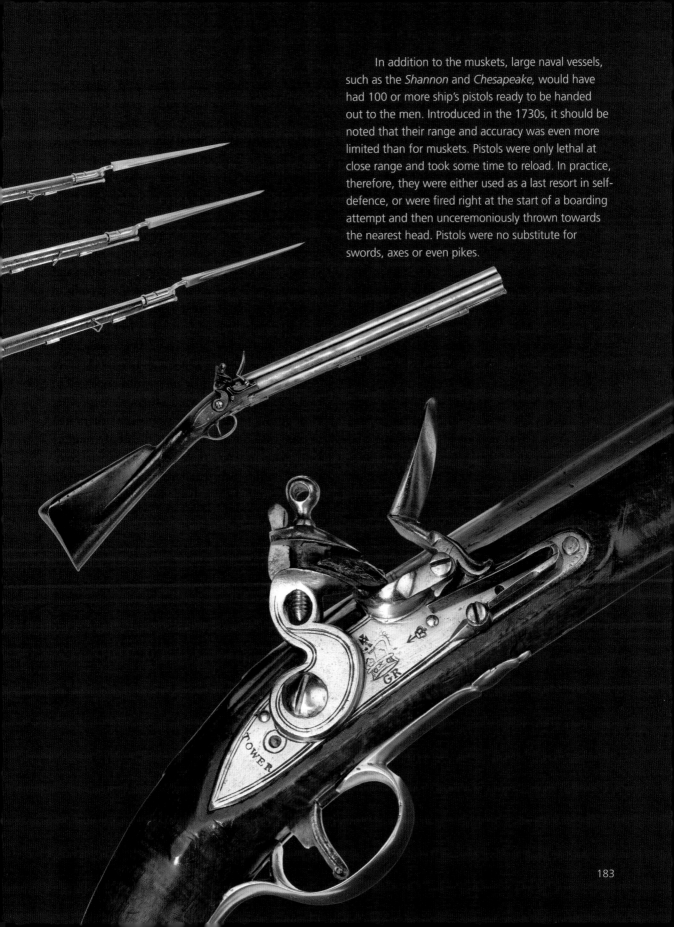

In addition to the muskets, large naval vessels, such as the *Shannon* and *Chesapeake*, would have had 100 or more ship's pistols ready to be handed out to the men. Introduced in the 1730s, it should be noted that their range and accuracy was even more limited than for muskets. Pistols were only lethal at close range and took some time to reload. In practice, therefore, they were either used as a last resort in self-defence, or were fired right at the start of a boarding attempt and then unceremoniously thrown towards the nearest head. Pistols were no substitute for swords, axes or even pikes.

The most important boarding weapons for the crews of *Shannon* and *Chesapeake* would have been cutlasses, swords and sabres – perhaps 150 of which would have been issued. The time for the cutlass came when the fighting parties became intermingled. The often curved and short blades suggest there was no space for sophisticated fencing: it was hacking and slicing instead. The officers also preferred to fight with curved blades, or even dirks, and left the straight blade for ceremony. Most ships had made some plan in advance of combat regarding which men would act as boarders. Some distinguished between 'first boarders' – an attacking force carrying cutlasses and pistols – and 'second boarders', a defensive force with pikes and axes. Behind them, the marines would wait with muskets and bayonets. Fit young lieutenants were meant to lead the boarding party, but it was not unusual for more senior officers like Broke and Nelson to charge ahead – a sign that notions of masculinity and honour could outweigh other considerations, though it certainly guaranteed them the respect of their crews. Tactics aside, the practice often

looked more improvised: when Captain Broke started the successful boarding of *Chesapeake*, shouting 'Follow me who can!', he was reportedly followed by Irish sailor James Bulger, not carrying any weapons at all, but mouthing some Gaelic oaths and looking on board *Chesapeake* for anything with which to club her crew. This was no bar brawl though: 10 per cent of the men lost their lives that day.

Usually a battle did not go all the way to the sinking or violent boarding of a ship. Even in a culture that placed high demands on heroism and masculinity, it was acceptable for the captain to strike the ensign if defeat appeared inevitable. In the aftermath, men on both sides had to come to terms with the loss of some of their mates, with different reactions, as sailor Sam Leech observed: 'some who had lost their messmates appeared to care nothing about it, while others were grieving with all the tenderness of women.'[10] Others had to cope with the loss of a limb, their only comfort being a 'smart ticket' that promised financial compensation for their disability from the Chatham Chest. Naval sailors had contributions to the

OPPOSITE Cutlasses, 1804 pattern (WPN1637–41) RIGHT 'Smart ticket' issued to James Pool, who served at the Battle of Trafalgar, as proof that his injury was sustained at sea, allowing him to draw a pension, 3 November 1805 (ADL/T/16)

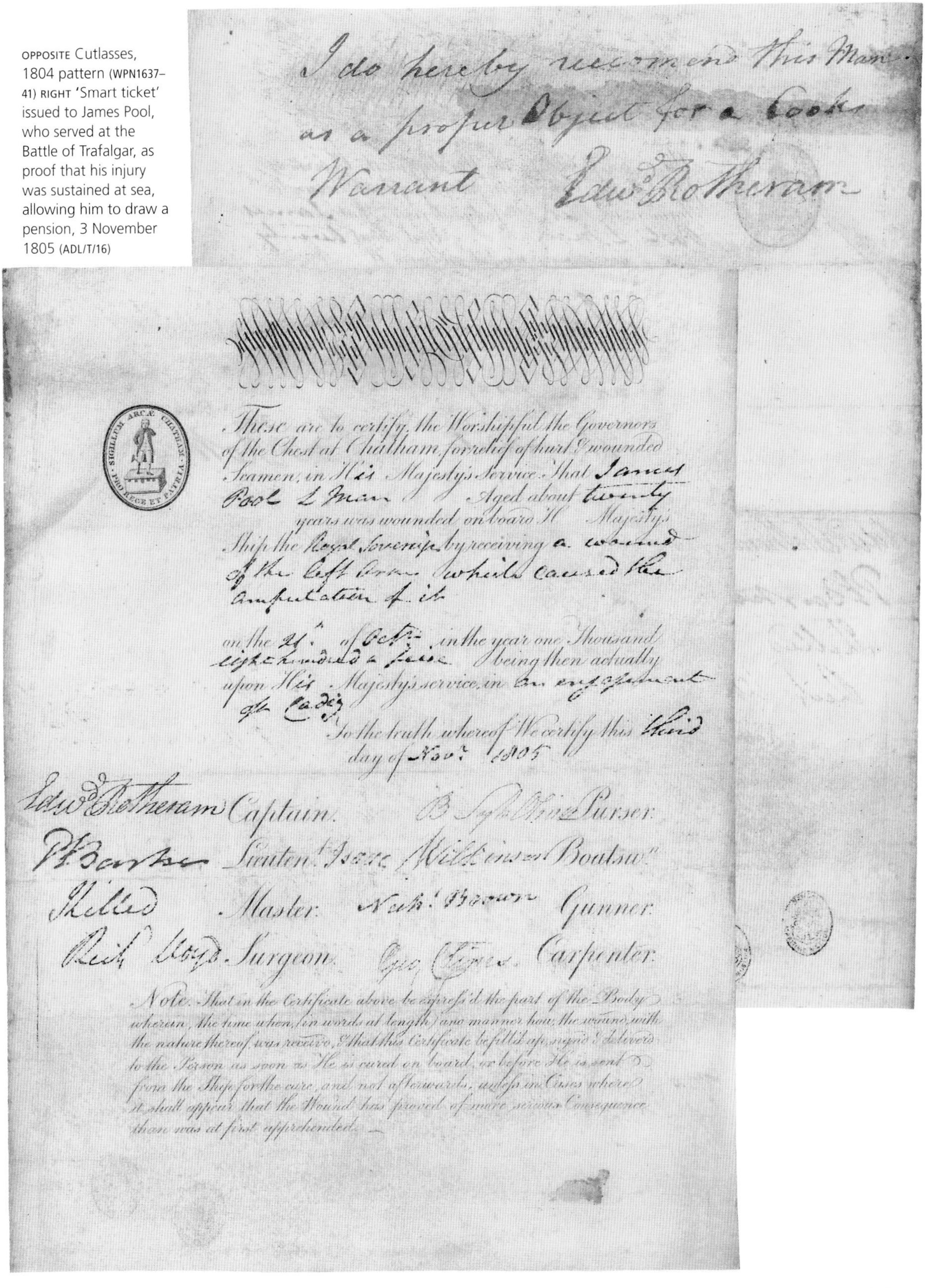

I do hereby recommend this Man
as a proper Object for a Cook
Warrant                    Edwd Rotheram

These are to certify, the Worshipful the Governors of the Chest at Chatham, for relief of hurt & wounded Seamen, in His Majesty's Service. That James Pool L Man Aged about twenty years was wounded on board H Majesty's Ship the Royal Sovereign by receiving a wound of the left arm which caused the amputation of it

on the 21st of Octr in the year one thousand eight hundred & five being then actually upon His Majesty's service in an engagement off Cadiz To the truth whereof We certify this third day of Novr 1805

Edwd Rotheram Captain.              B Sykwing Purser:

Pt Barker Lieutent Isaac Wilkinson Boatsn

Shilled Master: Nath Brown Gunner:

Rich Lloyd Surgeon. Geo Clyfus Carpenter:

Note. That in the Certificate above be exprefs'd the part of the Body wherein, the time when, (in words at length) and manner how the wound, with the nature thereof was receiv'd, & that this Certificate be fill'd up, sign'd & deliver'd to the Person as soon as He is cured on board, or before He is sent from the Ship for the cure, and not afterwards, unless in Cases where it shall appear that the Wound has proved of more serious Consequence than was at first apprehended.

Drawn Etch'd & Pub by Dighton. 12. Charing Cross. March. 1801.

Descriptions of BATTLES by Sea & Land,
in Two Volumes,
From the KINGs Library's at GREENWICH & CHELSEA.

Chatham Chest and Greenwich Hospital deducted from their pay – an occupational health insurance covering injury and retirement. There was a queue of retired seamen waiting to be admitted into Greenwich Hospital, yet also many others who happily took the hospital's so called 'out-pension'.

Some sailors may have sustained battle wounds that were not immediately visible. At the start of the eighteenth century, former seamen began to make up the largest group among the patients in Bethlem Hospital, London's infamous madhouse. During the war against Napoleon, the physician Sir Gilbert Blane was surprised to notice that insanity appeared to be an estimated seven times more common in the Royal Navy than among the general population.[11] Blane's only explanation was that sailors frequently banged their heads against the wooden beams of their ships, often when intoxicated. We might now speculate, though, that sailors struggled to digest their wartime experiences. Facing war without fear, even with intentionally displayed unaffectedness or irony, was the culture the navy fostered. Perhaps this was the only defence mechanism to cope with what was the most dangerous profession of the time. The naval physician Thomas Trotter believed that the young age at which sailors began their seafaring careers helped them adapt to the hardships of naval life: 'the mind, by custom and example, is thus trained to brave the fury of the elements, in their different forms, with a degree of contempt, at danger and death, that is to be met with no where else.'[12] Whether this bravado remained genuine, or whether all negative impressions gathered from a young age were simply locked away uneasily in a sea chest deep down in their souls, we cannot tell. Few sailors published their memoirs. The writers among them were, perhaps, unusual seamen. They frequently marvelled at their shipmates' apparent toughness, looking like lions 'anxious to be at it', as one sailor observed at Trafalgar when Nelson signalled that 'England Expects That Every Man Will Do His Duty'.[13]

In this context, the emerging idea of a nation explains much, but it cannot account for how people conducted themselves in all the numerous conflicts of the eighteenth century. Nor can it illuminate the motivations of everyone on board the *Victory* on that day, not least the almost 10 per cent of her crew who were not British – the Americans, Dutch, Swedes, Germans, even French, and the seamen from the West Indies and Africa. Even when sailors went through similar wartime experiences, each one would have perceived them differently, his feelings dependent on his personal hopes and fears, his belief in the cause and wartime propaganda, his life experience and training. They were opposed by ships containing a similar mix of men, also trapped in their vessels either because they had been forced or had volunteered, with the great majority on both sides losing their lives throughout the century without a grand column or an oil painting to provide a higher meaning to their particular wartime experience and death.

ABOVE Locket commemorating Lieutenant William Harman, who was killed in action, c.1812 (JEW0192)
OPPOSITE *Descriptions of Battles by Sea & Land, in Two Volumes, From the Kings Library's at Greenwich & Chelsea*, by Robert Dighton, hand-coloured etching, March 1801 (PAH3336)

# 10

# NELSON, NAVY AND NATIONAL IDENTITY

## Marianne Czisnik

This chapter examines how one person, Horatio Nelson, stood out in the estimation of the British public. In order to show how and why Nelson, as a man and as a symbol, became part of British popular culture and national identity, what follows is divided into three parts that are arranged in chronological order. The first deals with Nelson's public image in his own lifetime. The second describes his funeral, which was the culminating event in the popular appreciation of Nelson. The last examines how he was commemorated in the years between the Battle of Trafalgar in 1805 and the end of the Napoleonic Wars in 1815.

Nelson's popularity in his lifetime needs to be seen in the context of the French Revolutionary Wars that started in 1792 and continued for almost ten years. This conflict put much of Europe on the defensive against republican France. While continental Europe struggled to form several coalitions against France, Britain appeared to stand apart, thanks to a reliance on its navy that was confirmed in a series of successful fleet actions: the 'Glorious First of June' (1794), Cape St Vincent (1797) and Camperdown (1797). These battles brought fame to admirals Howe, Jervis (who was created Earl St Vincent) and Duncan, respectively. The Battle of Cape St Vincent, fought off the south-western tip of Portugal, had also attracted some attention to Commodore Nelson, who captured two superior Spanish ships during the battle.

When Nelson, as a newly promoted rear admiral, returned to England – following the unsuccessful attack on Santa Cruz de Tenerife in July 1797 that cost him his right arm – he received the freedom of the City of London. One of the aldermen, addressing him in a speech, praised his 'rare heroic modesty...You have given the warmest applause to your Brother Officers, and the Seamen under your command; but your own merit you have not mentioned even in the slightest manner'.[1] Nelson was thus beginning to be perceived as one of the outstanding naval officers of the 1790s and, at the same time, as someone who regarded himself as merely a sailor, who remained indebted to his brother officers and subordinates for his successes.

Nelson's popularity dramatically increased when the news of his great victory at the Battle of the Nile reached Britain. After months of suspense, and ignorance of the French fleet's movements, the news of the victory won by Nelson's squadron caused a highly enthusiastic response back home. Through the *London Gazette Extraordinary* of 2 October 1798, which was copied in newspapers all over Britain, details of Nelson's great success spread quickly throughout the country, and 'a day of Thanksgiving [was] appointed by his Majesty'. Nelson's victory was also celebrated all over the country. Direct responses took a great variety of forms, including

*Extirpation of the Plagues of Egypt; – Destruction of Revolutionary Crocodiles; – or – The British Hero cleansing ye Mouth of ye Nile,*
by James Gillray, published by Hannah Humphrey, hand-coloured etching, 6 October 1798 (PAF3893)

fireworks, a 'Musical Pasticcio', concerts, songs, dances and pantomimes. Plays were quickly written, and enjoyed sufficient popularity to be performed until 1800. Publishers reacted to the immense public interest in the event by producing reports, poems and a huge number of graphic prints, which included depictions of battle-scenes, portraits of Nelson and caricatures. One of these caricatures was entitled *Extirpation of the Plagues of Egypt; – Destruction of Revolutionary Crocodiles; – or – The British Hero cleansing ye Mouth of ye Nile*, and it showed Nelson culling crocodiles,

representations of French warships, in front of an Egyptian shoreline decked with pyramids.

The news of Nelson's victory at the Nile was met by an industry ready to mass produce commemorative pottery. On one cream-ware mug the rush to production meant that an old transfer print of Admiral Rodney was used to portray Nelson. Decorators of other pottery items simply followed their imagination. On Prattware jugs, which were decorated with a moulded portrait, Nelson is hardly recognisable. To make sure that he would be identified, his name was added to the portrait and sometimes potters underlined his appearance by positioning him in a befitting context: for example, with sword in hand and with ships in the background. Only later, when engravings of portraits of Nelson became more available, could commemorative items rely on more authentic likenesses. Potters decorated their ceramics with a variety of motifs to celebrate Nelson and his achievements. Their repertoire can be grouped into the following categories, which were often combined on ceramic pieces: portraits, ships or a battle-scene, a battle plan, trophies (for instance, flags, cannons or swords), symbolic items (such

TOP Prattware scent bottle with a portrait of Nelson, early nineteenth century (AAA5094) ABOVE RIGHT Buttons (converted into a cuff-link at a later date) and pendants commemorating Nelson and the Battle of the Nile, c.1798 (JEW0382, JEW0142, JEW0146) LEFT Prattware jug celebrating Nelson, late eighteenth to nineteenth century (AAA5139)

ABOVE Locket celebrating Nelson's achievements, c.1800 (JEW0202)
BELOW Curtain tie depicting the *Vanguard*, Nelson's flagship at the Battle of the Nile, c.1798 (OBJ0709)

as laurels for victory or, more specifically, crocodiles for the Battle of the Nile) and Nelson's coat of arms. This imagery was sometimes supported by mottoes such as 'Admiral Lord Nelson for ever' or by short pieces of verse.

Lockets and enamelled boxes were equally suitable as mass-produced commemorative items, because it was possible to print patterns on their oval surfaces and lids. These objects conveyed similar imagery as on ceramics, although they mainly focused on one subject at a time, since the surfaces and lids were quite small. Artists consequently also developed imagery particularly suitable for tiny objects. Symbolic items such as anchors, sailors, and allegorical figures such as Britannia, Fame and Hope, were popular. Such motifs were combined on many graphic prints and were produced on a host of commemorative items such as medals, fans, pendants, buttons, watches, curtain ties, ribbons and handkerchiefs. The exotic setting of Nelson's victory seems even to have had an impact on fashion. A caricature showed a couple with 'Dresses a la Nile', with two fashion-conscious individuals wearing clothes inspired by Nelson's Egyptian exploits (see p. 193). Both have crocodiles adorning their absurdist outfits, in recognition of the broader desire of fashionables to dress themselves 'a la Nile'. While Nelson often stood alone on these commemoratives, they could also feature allegorical symbols, honourable historical comparisons, heroic scenes, and also poems and songs that lauded the 'four great naval victories' of the 1790s, and the admirals who commanded at each.

Apart from Nelson's naval and political activities in the Mediterranean after the Battle of the Nile (some of which caused controversy at home), the British public also learned about his involvement with Lady Hamilton, the wife of the British ambassador to Naples, Sir William Hamilton.[2] Later, suspicions of the undue influence that Lady Hamilton appeared to exert on Nelson were

published in several newspapers. Such rumours did not attract much attention at the time and were soon overtaken by gossip about their joint appearances. When Nelson was recalled from his post in the Mediterranean, he chose to travel with the Hamiltons overland to Britain. This enabled central Europeans to show their admiration for the famous admiral. Local newspapers reported that he was followed 'by thousands', and that Nelson pleased them by letting them into his room and by walking among them in Graz 'with the beautiful Lady Hamilton at his arm'. And so it continued in Vienna, Prague, Dresden, along the River Elbe, in Hamburg and across the North Sea, back in England, where 'repeated huzzas of the populace' greeted him. In London, Nelson was followed by cheering crowds wherever he went and it was noted that Lady Hamilton, who often joined him, 'looked charmingly, and is a very fine woman'.[3]

The press recorded his progress meticulously and thus could not fail to notice that Nelson remained in the company of Lady Hamilton. This led to some comments on their scandalous relationship. When Nelson accompanied Sir William and Lady Hamilton on a trip to Wales, during the Peace of Amiens in 1802, he was constantly at the centre of attention. The fact that Nelson was accompanied by his lover and her husband seems not to have disturbed the frenzy about his person. Although the press coverage of Nelson's tour mainly dealt with how he was welcomed and celebrated, there were also reports about him personally. When he was given the freedom of a town or city, the press sometimes informed the public about how he had responded. In all these speeches, Nelson seems to have stressed that 'the merit ascribed to him, however, was more particularly due to the brave men who had been placed under his orders; it was to them the country was indebted'.[4]

When war with France broke out again in 1803, Nelson was given command of the Mediterranean Fleet. His reputation as an effective tool of Britain's defence against France was now settled. He appeared as an experienced and revered admiral whose patriotism, valour and leadership were established. Similarly, these characteristics were complemented by Nelson's acknowledged support for his officers and his noted humanity to his men. His popularity as a fine admiral remained strong even when the French fleet – after two years of blockade – managed to escape and Nelson chased it unsuccessfully through the Mediterranean and across the Atlantic. The public seemed to ignore the fact that Nelson had not brought the combined French and Spanish fleet to battle. Instead, he was praised in the press and on prints for having dared to pursue a fleet of seventeen ships of the line with just ten of his own. He was welcomed back to England 'as enthusiastic[ally] and sincere[ly] as if he had returned crowned with

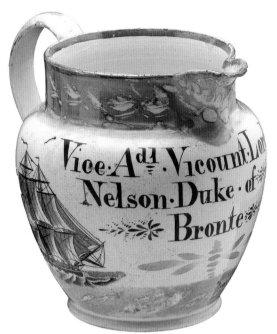

a third great naval victory'.[5] The public seems not to have cared that he now lived openly with the recently widowed Lady Hamilton.

The news of Nelson's death at the Battle of Trafalgar shocked the British public and overshadowed any possible joy about the great victory that he had achieved. Newspapers commented on the 'deep and universal affliction', following the news of his death, which 'is visible to every eye, and is felt in every heart, baffles the efforts of description'. They also observed how 'one universal sentiment of sorrow, and deep regret, pervades the public mind, as it reflects that the nation's "glory and its pride" have fallen!'[6] Nelson's death thus provoked feelings of private, even personal bereavement, as well as public or national loss. The intense public grief is also reflected in a vast production of mourning imagery. Mourning figures produced in immediate response to the

news of Nelson's death became staple features in different media. Prints of varying quality showed mourning female figures or 'Britannia consecrating the Ashes of the Immortal Nelson'.[7] Of the very simple and affordable glass pictures alone, fourteen different designs have survived that represent the public mourning Nelson's death. They all follow the same pattern, which consists of a monument to Nelson (a plinth with a bust or portrait) flanked with mourning figures, often weeping sailors. Similar motifs can be found on an immense number of ceramic items, textiles and other pieces, such as jewellery, glasses and boxes, and even on privately produced pieces of needlework. Cabinetmakers went so far as to produce mourning furniture with an inlaid black line.

The public interest in mourning Nelson's death naturally found its strongest expression in the different stages of the funeral itself. The

# TEXTILE SAMPLER COMMEMORATING ADMIRAL LORD NELSON
## BY MARY GILL, 1808 (TXT0031)

This very private piece, commemorating Nelson, shows that the news of the hero's death affected even a young girl in landlocked Dudley. Designed for private use, an object of this kind reflects the urge to remember Nelson more than two years after his death at the Battle of Trafalgar even in places that were relatively far away from any coast. Moreover, this teenage admirer of Nelson not only wished to consume what others had produced, but also made a point by contributing in her own individual way to the commemoration of the hero, 'Slain 21$^{st}$ Oct$^r$ 1805'. In order to do so, Gill chose stitching – a format with which many girls were familiar – and used staple elements of stitching convention, such as the name of the artist, Nelson's death, the date the sampler was made and a decorative fringe. The young maker transferred to this particularly female means of artistic expression a monumental tribute to Nelson. At the time, this was one of the most popular visual elements used in designs marking his sacrifice.

The sampler thus also reflects the aesthetic impact of mass-produced imagery. The image of a monument to Nelson that the thirteen- or fourteen-year-old Mary Gill used for her decorative stitching was particularly popular on small and cheap commemorative pieces – for example, the relatively inexpensive glass pictures and enamelled boxes that were particularly directed towards the female consumer. Monuments on patch-boxes and glass pictures usually had a plinth with an inscription, and figures in mourning were often shown standing under a weeping willow. The similarities with Mary Gill's private commemoration include even the wording 'Sacred to the Memory of Nelson'. The design is, therefore, an eloquent testimony of the degree to which Nelsonian imagery had entered the imaginations and domestic lives of people across Britain.

The fact that Mary Gill represented a monument on her private piece of commemoration, rather than the similarly popular death scene, may have been for the simple practical reason that a death scene would have been much more difficult to stitch. Her choice of motif may also, however, be attributed to the idea that silent grief and mourning seemed more appropriate to a sensitive young female than a brutal scene of battle and death. In any case, this private piece indicates that British females were as much affected by his death as their male compatriots, and that in order to express their grief they readily absorbed and reapplied those forms of mourning imagery that were produced in great amounts in reaction to the death of Nelson.

MARY GILL
Born 7th August.
17 94

SACRED
to the Memory of
NELSON
Slain 21st Octr
1805.

Dudley. 1808.

solemnities consisted of three major stages: the lying in state in the Painted Hall of Greenwich Hospital; a procession by water to Whitehall; and a procession by land to St Paul's Cathedral in the City of London, where Nelson was to be interred. Newspapers requested fuller details of the funeral, and suggested that the procession should include members of *Victory*'s crew who had fought next to the fallen hero. These promptings were quickly addressed with an appeasing official declaration ordering a detachment of able seamen of the *Victory* to take part in the procession. This appeared appropriate, as *The Times* observed, because of the 'uncommon interest in the obsequies of the Hero' among 'the lower classes'.[8]

The event attracted people from many parts of the country. The rush to see the coffin in the Painted Hall at Greenwich surpassed all expectations. *The Times* reported that so many people pressed to see the lying in state that those who got into the hall were 'pushed onward with such rapidity, as to afford none of them the opportunity of having more than a short and transient glance of the solemn object of their curiosity'.[9]

Nelson's funeral procession on the Thames, 8 January 1806 (detail), by Daniel Turner, oil on canvas, 1807 (BHC0569)

The procession by water was the first occasion for the wider public to see the coffin, and large numbers seized this opportunity. The *Gentleman's Magazine* described how the 'decks, yards, rigging, and masts of the numerous ships on the river, were all crowded with spectators; and the number of ladies was immense'. An eyewitness who had mingled with the crowds wrote to a friend about those assembled: 'every post of vantage wherever the procession could be seen was swarming with living beings, all wearing mourning, the very beggars having a bit of crape on their arms.'[10] The event thus allowed very different social groups to join in what could be described as a nation's mourning.

Nelson's body remained overnight in Admiralty House. From 6:00am the following morning, crowds began to assemble along the route of the funeral procession to St Paul's Cathedral. According to one eyewitness, 'while it was still dark hundreds more than what are usually seen at mid-day, were assembled...It would be impossible to convey an adequate idea of the multitude of persons who crowded from all quarters of town

A Correct Representation of the Funeral Barge which conveyed the Body of the late Lord Nelson from Greenwich to Whitehall. Jan.y 8.th 1806

ABOVE *A Correct Representation of the Funeral Barge which conveyed the Body of the late Lord Nelson from Greenwich to Whitehall, Jany. 8 1806*, published by W.B. Walker, hand-coloured mezzotint, 1 March 1806 (PAF4376)
OPPOSITE Figurehead of Nelson's funeral carriage, 1805 (FHD0093)

and country to witness this interesting spec-tacle'.[11] Even those who had found places at the beginning of the processional route had to wait until noon for it to begin, and even longer for the funeral car to appear. Only the figurehead of the ship-shaped carriage survives to this day, and the effect that it produced on the avidly waiting crowds is famously described in Lady Bessbor-ough's words:

> Amongst many touching things the silence of that immense Mob was not the least striking; they had been very noisy. I was in a House in Charing Cross, which look'd over a mass of heads. The moment the Car appear'd which

bore the body, you might have heard a pin fall, and without any order to do so, they all took off their hats. I cannot tell you the effect this simple action produc'd; it seem'd one general impulse of respect beyond any thing that could have been said or contriv'd.[12]

Less known is the account of someone who witnessed the same event from within the crowd, and thus could also report on what was said: 'as [the funeral car] passed, all uncovered, and many wept. I heard a great deal said among the people about "poor Emma" [Lady Hamilton], and some wonder whether she will get a pension or not'.[13] It appears that Nelson had an appeal

ABOVE *Interment of the Remains of the late Lord Viscount Nelson in the Cathedral of St Paul…*, by Frederick Christian Lewis after Augustus Charles Pugin, published by James Cundee, hand-coloured aquatint, 1 April 1806 (PAH7332)
BELOW Ticket to admit the painter, John Hoppner RA, into the funeral procession from the Admiralty to St Paul's Cathedral, 9 January 1806 (REL0788)

among the wider public not only as a hero but also as a lover.

The actual interment was celebrated with a grand service at St Paul's. The cathedral had filled shortly after it opened at 7:00am, but 'the interest was so deep, that no uneasiness whatever appeared to be produced by the time which it became necessary to wait, exposed to a great severity of cold'. The impressively staged service included music by Handel and Purcell, as well as scores specially composed for the occasion. It also used new techniques to illuminate the cathedral, and to admit the coffin into the tomb by a mechanism invisible to the spectators. When the coffin was to be lowered into the crypt, the men from the *Victory* gave the scene a final personal touch. They were supposed to lay flags of the *Victory* to descend into the grave, but 'desirous of retaining some mementoes of their great and favourite commander, [they] tore off a considerable part of the largest flag, of which most, if not all, of them, obtained a small portion'.[14]

The funeral prompted a boom in the printing business. The printed output about the funeral consisted not only of newspaper accounts of the event, many filling several columns, but also complete publications dedicated solely to the funeral. Other printed works on offer to the mourning public included prints of the coffin, the armorial bearings, the funeral barge and car, as well as of different stages of the funeral. Glass pictures were produced in great numbers for less well-off customers. Nelson's funeral, therefore, afforded an outlet for the nation's genuine grief at the death of the great hero. It was a means of coming to terms with a traumatic national shock and of paying public tribute. This strong emotional response was subsequently exploited and

Snuff handkerchief showing Nelson's funeral carriage, c.1806 (TXT0267)

The immortality of Nelson, by Benjamin West, oil on canvas, 1807 (BHC2905)

transformed thereafter to form the basis of Nelson's image after his death.

The reaction to the news of Nelson's death triggered a wave of visual representations of him in the years that followed. These representations took various forms, including pictures, material artefacts and monuments. Foremost among the Nelson imagery produced in immediate reaction to the Battle of Trafalgar were depictions of the death of Nelson. Since details about how he had actually died emerged slowly, the early and often relatively cheap visual representations of the event relied more on the vivid imagination of their creators, who idealised the event. Many of these idealisations show Nelson falling into or lying in the arms of Neptune, Britannia or the goddess of Victory. This way of depicting the scene was used in Gillray's caricature, *Death of Admiral Lord Nelson*, published about ten days before the funeral. Nelson, with a sword in his hand and his hat in front of him on the deck, lies in the arms of a weeping Britannia; Captain Hardy is at his side and a kneeling sailor brings a French flag; above, Fame with her trumpet proclaims 'Immortality'. For the amusement of his customers, Gillray gave Captain Hardy the appearance of George III and the sailor that of the Duke of Clarence (the king's son, and later William IV), with whom Nelson had served as a young captain in the West Indies. Well-informed purchasers might have recognised the features of Emma Hamilton on the figure of Britannia.

Although it became known that Nelson died, like an ordinary sailor, on the dark orlop deck, the idealisation of his death was taken even further. While some artists now strived to represent the scene as it actually happened, Benjamin West created a thoroughly allegorical piece on the death of Nelson. His image of 'The Immortality of Nelson' is arranged as an apotheosis, using the easily recognisable personifications of Victory, Britannia and Neptune, thus linking Nelson to

*The Death of Admiral Lord Nelson – in the moment of Victory*, by James Gillray, published by Hannah Humphrey, hand-coloured etching, 29 December 1805 (PAF3866)

British naval superiority. In this apotheosis, not only is the body of Nelson lifted in a physical sense; his death is elevated at the same time, in a figurative sense, to sublime significance.

The visual commemoration of Nelson went beyond paintings and engravings and found expression in a variety of material artefacts. Most of these commemorated Nelson himself, rather than mourning his death, and the first that poured onto the market were quickly produced ceramic items, reusing earlier motifs. In general, however, the visual representation of the Battle of Trafalgar resulted in artefacts that were less attractive than those produced after the Battle of the Nile. They did not contain motifs that could be developed into fanciful decorations. There was no colourful blowing up of a French flagship, and the grey Atlantic did not conjure up any exotic imagery, such as pyramids or crocodiles. In order to represent the sombre subject of the Battle of Trafalgar, producers of commemorative wares therefore reverted in part to traditional elements of decoration, such as a plan of the battle, but they generally focused directly on the hero of the day.

The most common portraits of Nelson were transfer-printed ceramic items, taken either directly from portrait prints or developed out of them. Nelson is recognisable by the empty sleeve, his decorations and his white hair. Additional inscriptions give his name, and often a short reference to his achievements, a verse or the words of his famous signal, usually wrongly rendered as 'England Expects Every Man To Do His Duty'. The correct version is: 'England Expects That Every Man Will Do His Duty.' Nelson's conclusive victory at Trafalgar was sometimes summarised by varying the quotation from Julius Caesar, '*veni, vidi, vici*': for example, 'He saw – he faught – he conquered – and he died.' Most telling, however, are the verses that often accompany the portraits of Nelson. Without exception they express grief at the hero's death. In addition to the different inscriptions, the portraits were surrounded by common maritime and naval imagery, such as anchors, flags and naval trophies. A striking omission on such pottery is the actual death scene that figured so prominently in prints and paintings that were produced in response to the Battle of Trafalgar. The reason for this omission may lie in the fact that potters tended to reuse earlier prints in varying combinations, and simply adapted the wording of their products to the new occasion. Nelson was also the subject of moulded and hand-painted ceramics. The simplest versions of commemorative ceramics were those which merely bore a hand-painted inscription, such as 'To the Memory of Lord Nelson', or simply his title and name.

Although ceramics dominated the commemorative market, the immense interest in Nelson after Trafalgar

Box of circular prints commemorating the victories of Nelson and other British admirals, c. 1820s
(OBJ0201)

LEFT AND ABOVE Earthenware mug and patch-box commemorating Nelson, c.1806
(AAA4892, OBJ0014)

also found expression in other media. Medallions of different sizes, medals, glasses, bottles, wax pictures, patch-boxes, fans and even handkerchiefs bore his portrait. Patch-boxes, as after the Nile, often included short verses or phrases to commemorate Nelson, such as: 'Trafalgar the Battle was Fought – Nelson's Life the Victory bought.' More elaborate items took longer to produce, but still found a market, years after Trafalgar. Ceramic busts of Nelson, wine coolers with his portrait moulded onto them, and boxes with pictures of naval victories (prominently figuring Nelson) were produced towards the end of the Napoleonic Wars.

A more enduring response to the death of Nelson than such material artefacts and prints was the building of monuments to his memory. In that respect, his death had happened at an apposite moment, because public monuments became extremely widespread across Britain at the beginning of the nineteenth century. Monumental representations ranged from columns and obelisks to statues. The controversy regarding whether to represent Nelson idealised with two arms and in a dress from antiquity was soon settled in favour of a more authentic representation. The popularity of this kind of portrayal on monuments had been indicated in mourning imagery, and was also reflected in commemorative items moulded after monuments, some modelled on the shape of Nelson's monument in Birmingham.

In the remaining years of the Napoleonic Wars, there were no other battles fought at sea that matched Trafalgar's scale and importance. Nelson was consequently regarded as the prime representative of the naval profession. At the same time he was perceived as the hero whose final victory at Trafalgar paved the way for the victory over France on land. Nelson had thus become part of British national identity. Elements of his image, not least his personal injuries and sacrifices, and his kinship with ordinary sailors, ensured that his popularity lasted well beyond the period discussed here. His affair with Lady Hamilton kept threatening to damage his image, but it also offered additional layers of interest in his person. Nelson continued to influence popular perceptions of the navy, and remained a central part of the national self-image.

# BEYOND TRAFALGAR

Roger Knight

Trafalgar was the last of the great set-piece battles of the French Revolutionary and Napoleonic Wars, completing the process of eliminating enemy battle fleets which had begun eight years earlier. In 1797 the Spanish fleet had been all but destroyed at Cape St Vincent. Later in the year the same had happened to the Dutch at Camperdown, completed when the remainder of their fleet had been captured during the Den Helder expedition of 1799. In 1798 the French navy had suffered a major blow at the Battle of the Nile from which, psychologically, it had never recovered. After 1805 Napoleon all but ignored his navy for the next two years, except for an initial period when he decided to use the remnants of his fleet to make up powerful raiding squadrons. But for the most part during this war, French warships were in port, to be harried by blockading British ships if they attempted to sail.

From 1805 onwards, Britain possessed a much larger navy than in the French Revolutionary Wars. Before Trafalgar, Britain possessed 330,000 warship tons, the equivalent of France, Spain and the Netherlands combined. During and after the battle, France and Spain lost twenty-three ships of the line, some sunk or wrecked, and others captured. Hence the balance of tonnage swung even further in Britain's favour: by the end of 1805, the margin was over 200,000 tons.[1] However, after 1807, Britain had to face other hostile powers for

long periods: the Russians, Danes, Norwegians and Swedes. The climax of the European naval war came in 1809, when the British fleet reached its maximum size of 709 commissioned warships, measuring 469,227 tons, although the number of seamen borne on warships did not peak until 1813, at over 147,000 men.

Britain kept 100 ships of the line in commission, though for long periods they had little to do. The real work was done by sixth rates and frigates, and also hundreds of even smaller warships, carrying fewer than twenty guns. This small-ship navy was created rapidly by contracting with private shipyards all over Britain, many of which up to this point had built only merchant ships and had had nothing to do with the navy. No private shipyards in Devon and Cornwall, for instance, had ever built a warship before 1803, but between that year and 1815 they produced sixty-eight small ones, totalling just over 27,000 tons. The Navy Board signed contracts for more than 300 small warships, brig sloops, gun brigs or gunboats, while a number of fast cutters and luggers were also built. Brig sloops, for instance, approximately eighty-feet long and measuring 380 tons, were armed with perhaps sixteen guns and manned by 120 men. During the Napoleonic Wars, 174 brig sloops were ordered by the Navy Board, and eighty-seven of the smaller gun brigs, while fifty similar captured vessels also joined the British

*Britannia in tribulation for the loss of her Allies or John Bulls advice,* published by Walker, hand-coloured etching, August 1807 (PAF4001)

fleet.² In total, the private sector built far more warships than the state dockyards. If the output of the large private yards on the Thames and in the Solent are also included – concerns which had long built large warships by contract – merchant yards built 84 per cent of all warships, or 72 per cent by tonnage in these years. The royal dockyards could therefore concentrate upon repairs and refits. The construction and maintenance of a much-enlarged fleet was a convincing demonstration of Britain's industrial muscle.

These new, small warships were useful in many ways, although gun brigs were particularly designed for invasion defence. Warships from frigates to luggers performed reconnaissance missions, intercepted enemy coastal shipping or watched, raided and bombarded foreign ports. Above all, they convoyed trade in coastal and near-European waters, so important for keeping Britain's economy buoyant and expanding. These small vessels were constantly at sea and much was demanded of them, and consequently they suffered considerable losses. In the month of June 1805, for instance, three gun brigs foundered without trace in the English Channel, with the loss of 350 men. With a smaller draft, these ships could operate in the shallow waters of the North Sea and the Baltic, where their role was to confront the new and formidable enemy, the Danes, who were confined to small ships, their main fleet having been seized by the British in 1807. The Danes scored some remarkable successes. In July 1810, for instance, five Danish brigs captured an entire convoy of forty-seven British merchant vessels off the Skaw in Norway, not far from the entrance to the Baltic.[3] On windless days in the Sound and the Great Belt, swarms of Danish boats would attack and attempt to board larger British warships.

Whatever the considerable long-term effects of the overwhelming victory at Trafalgar, the battle itself had no immediate impact at all on the conflict in Europe. In August 1805 Napoleon had marched his army away from the Channel at Boulogne towards central Europe, lifting the threat of invasion. Successive British governments used this lull to build Martello towers and other fortifications. For the next two years the French emperor and his army were fully occupied in attacking and defeating Austria and Russia at Austerlitz, Prussia at Jena and Auerstadt, and in June 1807 Russia again at Friedland. In July Napoleon signed the Treaty of Tilsit with the tsar, at which time he was

at the apex of his strength, with the major powers of Russia, Austria and Prussia subjugated. At this point, he again turned his attention to the invasion of Britain.

After Nelson's dash across the Atlantic in pursuit of Admiral Villeneuve in 1805, no French battle fleet ventured out of European waters again during the age of sail. The British were, therefore, able to consolidate their control on distant stations. In the West Indies Admiral Sir John Duckworth scored a considerable squadron success in a worthy postscript to Trafalgar. Duckworth was a wrongheaded and tactless admiral who was to be court martialled almost as many times as he was to be in action. As commander-in-chief in Jamaica during the Peace of Amiens, he had captured a good many prizes when the news of the resumption of war arrived, which prompted the merchants at Kingston to mark his command with some handsome plate. In late 1805 Duckworth returned to the West Indies, chasing French warships of which he had no real intelligence, and luckily his ships ran into a powerful French raiding squadron at San Domingo. The competence and experience of the captains and crews of the British ships were more telling than Duckworth's leadership: all five French ships of the line were destroyed on 6 February 1806, the last big-ship action of the war. It was a prequel to the systematic British conquest of all the French West Indian possessions.

Operations on other distant stations had mixed success. The Cape of Good Hope was taken from the Dutch in January 1806, but the naval commander of the expedition, Admiral Sir Home Popham, added to his reputation for originality laced with egocentricity by heading

LEFT Silver tea kettle presented by the merchants of Kingston, Jamaica, to Vice-Admiral Duckworth, c.1804 (PLT0040)
OPPOSITE ABOVE Duckworth's action off San Domingo, 6 February 1806, by Nicholas Pocock, oil on canvas, 1808 (BHC0571)
OPPOSITE BELOW Presentation sword given by the City of London to Admiral Sir John Duckworth, 1806 (WPN1121)

westwards from the Cape to attack the Spanish colonies in South America, without orders to do so. With the acquiescence of the army commander, General Baird, Popham took his ships and troops west across the South Atlantic. Initial success at Buenos Aires soon led to military disaster and withdrawal. The government had to accept Popham's decision, but he was fortunate to escape with no more than a rebuke in the subsequent court martial. The Indian Ocean was the other area of weakness, where the French island of Mauritius acted as a base for enemy frigates,

and losses of merchant ships, particularly East Indiamen, were damaging trade. Embarrassment increased when a squadron of four British frigates was destroyed while attacking French ships in Grand Port, Mauritius, in August 1810 (see p. 212). However, by December of that year enough troops and ships had been gathered with the help of the East India Company to capture Mauritius. Soon after, Java was acquired. The French and the Dutch no longer possessed any overseas territory.

From the evening of the Battle of Trafalgar, Nelson's second-in-command, Admiral Cuthbert

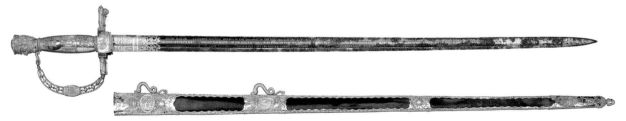

Collingwood, had taken command of the Mediterranean Fleet. Collingwood's great achievement was to maintain a sound defensive strategy which enabled British trade to flow, using the island of Malta both as a place to gather convoys for escort home, and a base from which merchant ships could venture to Napoleonic Europe to break the Continental blockade. Toulon was blockaded, although contested to the end, as the action under Sir Edward Pellew in 1813 proved, when the French fleet was forced back to port (see p. 214). Collingwood had considerable resources: in 1807 he commanded seventy-four warships and over 25,000 seamen, but there were never enough for all his tasks and he suffered long periods of lack of direction and intelligence from London, caused by disrupted communications. Collingwood's diplomacy was masterly, especially in his relations with the North African states, upon which he was dependent for food and water.

He had considerable operational success. He seized the Ionian Islands from the French, and dispatched frigates to disrupt enemy trade at the top of the Adriatic. Collingwood patched up relations with the Turks, after a fleet under the energetic but hapless Duckworth was repelled from the Dardanelles. When the revolt in Spain against French domination broke out in 1808, Collingwood established good relations with Spanish admirals and his ships caused havoc along the coast disrupting French supplies and communications. Ministers had such confidence in Collingwood that he was kept out in the Mediterranean for far too long, becoming worn out with the responsibility, and he

BELOW *Combat du Grand Port...*, a celebration of the defeat of British ships at Mauritius, 24 August 1810, by E. Chavane after Pierre Julien Gilbert, published by Gavard, engraving, 1843 (PAF4778)
OPPOSITE Cuthbert Collingwood painted posthumously as a rear admiral, by Henry Howard, oil on canvas, 1827 (BHC2625)

Pellew's action of 5 November 1813 during the blockade of Toulon (1810–14), by Thomas Luny, oil on canvas, 1830 (BHC0604)

pleaded to be sent home. Ministers wanted to block the attempts by the Duke of Clarence, a younger son of George III and by now a senior admiral, to obtain the Mediterranean command: a more unsuitable appointment could hardly be imagined. The easiest way out of this tricky situation was to continue to refuse Collingwood's requests to strike his flag. Finally, in early 1810, ministers relented and the admiral sailed for England, but died, very probably of stomach cancer, two days out from Port Mahon in Minorca.

More than anything, the conflict at sea during the war against France was marked by aggressive commercial blockades by both Britain and France. Napoleon tried to destabilise the English economy by trying to block British goods, or goods which had come via Britain, from entering ports within

France or those under his control. The most comprehensive orders were the Berlin Decrees of November 1806. Britain matched his every move by declaring all European ports to be under a state of blockade from the sea. As each side raised the stakes, the operation of neutral shipping in European waters, particularly American shipping, became impossible. Napoleon, however, was unable to make all the countries that he controlled proof against smuggling. For instance, Britain captured Heligoland, a small island off the German coast, from which a vast amount of British manufactured goods and sugar, coffee and tea were smuggled into German ports. Customs officers in subject countries would turn a blind eye for a consideration from merchants, to supplement their poor salaries. Napoleon failed to crack

Britain's credit and financial structures, partly because of the smuggling and partly because markets were found elsewhere in the world to compensate.[4] Keeping British trade flowing, however, was an underlying objective for British sea power in any war, but never more so than in the long struggle against Napoleon's power in Europe.

In the weeks after the Treaty of Tilsit in July 1807, Napoleon looked likely to seize the Danish and Portuguese fleets, but the British government, led by the young foreign secretary, George Canning, forestalled the French. Ignoring the legality of attacking a neutral nation without provocation, warships and transports, many already gathered at Great Yarmouth, soon effected a landing north of Copenhagen. The naval commander, James Gambier, successfully combined with the army commander, General Lord Cathcart. The city refused to capitulate and was bombarded, and the Danes were forced to surrender (see pp. 216–17). The Danish warships, together with naval stores worth £320,000, were sailed to England. Half-finished ships on the stocks in Copenhagen dockyard were destroyed. It was a swift and ruthlessly efficient operation, completely catching Napoleon off his guard. Privately, he was said to have admired it. Publicly, of course, he protested at the illegality of the proceedings, as did most of the countries of Europe.

ABOVE Mourning ring commemorating Vice-Admiral Lord Collingwood, c.1810 (JEW0155)
BELOW Le dernier Exploit des Anglois a Copenhague 1807 ou le Triomphe de Gambier, Cathcart, Popham &c, showing the removal of naval stores from Copenhagen, etching, c.1807 (PAF4762)

Engelhændernes sidste Daad i Kiøbenhavn 1807
som en varig Triumph for Gambier, Cathcart, Popham &c.

Le dernier Exploit des Anglois à Copenhague 1807
ou le Triomphe de Gambier, Cathcart, Popham &c.

1807 was a bad naval year for the French emperor, having started with the prospect of securing 100 ships of the line from subjugated states, all of which escaped his clutches. He sent an army to Lisbon to impose his will, using Portugal's refusal to implement his Berlin Decrees as an excuse. As the French army marched into the city, the Portuguese royal family, its treasury, much of its civil service and its fleet left the Tagus, escorted by a powerful British squadron. Napoleon had lost the fleet of yet another country. In addition, when Spain rose up against French rule in 1808, Spanish ships eluded him as well. Sweden and Russia were the other two errant states. A squadron of Russian ships at Lisbon, where the naval commander-in-chief, Admiral Sir Charles Cotton, skilfully negotiated with the Russian admiral, was escorted by British ships of the line to Spithead. There they lay rotting at their anchors until Russia again changed sides after Napoleon's invasion in 1812.

If the naval war was to be won or lost, it was no longer to be in the traditional areas of conflict – the Western Approaches, the Mediterranean or the West Indies. The number of ships in the Channel Fleet was dramatically reduced. In the 1790s, seventy-five ships manned by 38,000 men had blockaded Brest and the other French Atlantic bases; by September 1809 only thirty ships remained, manned by 7,000 seamen. A brief flurry of activity took place in April 1809 in Aix Roads when French ships at anchor were attacked by a squadron commanded by James Gambier, with reasonable success, though the aftermath descended into a welter of accusations and a court martial when Captain Thomas Cochrane attacked Gambier in the press for excessive caution. The reduced blockade of the French Atlantic ports still continued, and the fierce weather and tidal

*Bombardement de Copenhague, du 2 au 5 Septembr. 1807*, by Jean Laurent Rugendas, hand-coloured aquatint, early nineteenth century (PAH8055)

B

*Une considérable Flotte angloise commendée p.* *Général Lord Cathcard qui, non obstant de la re[...]* *refusant de rendre la place, elle fu[...]*

# BARDEMENT DE COPENHAGUE,

*Du 2 au 5 Septembr. 1807.*

*Admiral Gambier étant paru devant l'île Zeelande le 15 Aout de bargua un corps d'armée sous les ordres du*
*ce rigoureuse des Danois, avança jusqu'à Copenhague et somma cette place. Le Commendant danois Général Peyman*
*bardée par les Anglois du 2 jusqu'au 5 Septembre, où le Commendant se vit forcé de capituler.*

*Se vend à Augsbourg chez I. Laurent Rugendas.*

conditions were the real enemy rather than French naval aggression. An epic escape in a gale off Basque Roads in 1812 by the *Magnificent* (seventy-four guns) was justly celebrated. Her anchor dragged, and when she was only 500 yards from rocks, her captain, John Hayes, cut his cables and 'club-hauled' the ship to safety. Hayes was thereafter known as 'Magnificent Hayes'.[5]

The Spanish uprising in Madrid in May 1808 led to the British army, supported by the navy and transports, establishing a bridgehead in Portugal, which slowly opened up the major strategic threat

to Napoleon in southern Europe. But the French naval situation was weak, as outlined in October 1811 by Lord Liverpool, at that time secretary of state for war. He wrote to Wellington in the Iberian Peninsula: 'The only stations in which the French have any fleet from which danger could be apprehended to any quarter are the Scheldt and Toulon... As to the other French ports in the Channel and the Bay of Biscay, they have only one ship of the line at Brest, one at Rochefort, not ready for sea, and four at L'Orient, of which, two only can be said to be ready for sea, and those wretchedly manned.'[6]

*This representation of His Majesty's Ship Magnificent, 74 Guns, John Hayes, Esq Captain...*, by C. Hunt after Pierre Julien Gilbert, published by Ackermann & Co., hand-coloured aquatint, c.1830s (PAH9217)

*Painted by Gilbert.*                                                                                           *Eng.d by C. Hunt*

*This Representation of His Majesty's Ship* **Magnificent** *, 74 Guns, JOHN HAYES, ESQ. CAPTAIN,*
*Shewing (after cutting the Cables in a S.W. Gale) the manner of making Sail under reefed Courses and close reefed Top sails,*
*with Yards and Topmasts struck, and saving the Ship from destruction on a Lee Shore on the 17th Dec.r 1812*
*Is by Gracious Permission dedicated to HIS MOST EXCELLENT MAJESTY WILLIAM IVth by His Majesty's faithful Subject & Servant*        *John Hayes, Capt. R.N. C.B.*

*The Empress's wish – or Boney Puzzled!!,* by Isaac Cruikshank, published by J. Johnstone, hand-coloured etching, 9 August 1810. Napoleon had crowned himself 'Emperor of the French' on 2 December 1804 (PAD4784)

The new naval battleground became the southern North Sea and the Baltic. The main British target was the port of Antwerp, forty-five miles up the River Scheldt, where Napoleon had gathered shipwrights from all over Europe in an attempt to build a fleet that could give him sufficient advantage to invade England. The British government's fear of the resources available to Napoleon led it in 1809 to undertake an enormous, unwieldy, badly led and late amphibious expedition of more than 600 sail, transports and warships to attack Antwerp after landing at Walcheren. The French brought up troops and the expedition became bogged down, though Flushing, at the mouth of the Scheldt, was taken. By September, more than 8,000 soldiers had been struck down by the virulent marsh fever, and were dying at the rate of 250

a week. The withdrawal was protracted and military failure brought about a political crisis within the government of the Duke of Portland. For the rest of the war the British concentrated upon a year-round blockade off the Scheldt to ensure that any French ships that were built and manned did not escape. This remained the situation until the end of hostilities, despite many schemes to dislodge the French fleet, which every summer sailed down to the mouth of the Scheldt where it anchored.

The great naval success of the later years of the war was the presence of a considerable British fleet in the Baltic between 1808 and 1812, commanded by a relatively junior admiral, Sir James Saumarez. With Napoleon dominating the countries around the coasts of the Baltic, it was a task that involved

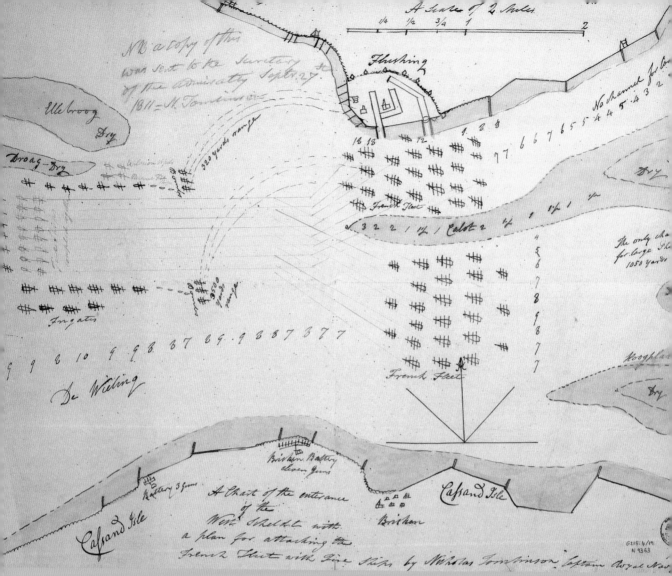

ABOVE Chart of the entrance of the West Scheldt with a plan for attacking the French fleet with fire ships, by Nicholas Tomlinson, ink and wash, 1811 (G218:4/19)

OPPOSITE *Admiral Sir James Saumarez...*, by Charles Turner after Casimir Carbonnier, mezzotint, 1 November 1823 (PAD3477)

delicate diplomacy, to which the thoughtful Saumarez was equal. His relations with Sweden, for instance, could have been particularly difficult since, for a long period, that country was technically at war with Britain. He established trust with the Swedes who responded by helping in all sorts of ways, and none more important than providing fresh water and what fresh food they could. In return, the presence of the British fleet ensured that Napoleon could not directly intervene in the country.[7] Saumarez commanded between forty and eighty ships, though the majority of the ships of the line sailed with the admiral to England at the start of each winter to avoid the ice-bound Baltic. Supplying his fleet and provisioning the crews, which more than outnumbered the inhabitants of every town in Sweden except Stockholm, was a notable achievement of the Victualling Board in London, for locally available supplies were limited. The major strategic and economic achievement, however, was to keep trade flowing, and every year thousands of merchant ships laden with timber, hemp and other naval stores sailed through the Great Belt, escorted by British warships. Naval protection for this vital trade continued until 1812, when the entire strategic situation was dramatically changed by Napoleon's retreat from Moscow and the destruction of the greater part of the *Grande Armée*.

This pivotal and unexpected French military defeat affected the balance of the war in every theatre, and nowhere more so than across the Atlantic where the United States had finally lost patience with Britain over constraints on neutral trade and a number of other issues, including the impressment of American seamen. President James Madison declared war in June 1812. One of the calculations of the 'war-hawks' was that the conquest of Canada should be easy, given that Britain was so locked into mortal combat with Napoleonic France. In the event, Napoleon's defeat at the hands of Russia eventually enabled Britain to deploy ships in great number. In July 1814, seventy-seven British warships were on the North American station, nine of them ships of the line, two-and-a-half times the number at the beginning of the war, many of them freed from service in the Baltic.

British strategy in 1812 was to impose a commercial blockade on American ports, in order to exhaust the United States treasury, for taxes on imports and exports provided the bulk of government revenue. Admiral Sir John Borlase Warren succeeded in disrupting American trade before a dissatisfied government replaced him in early 1814. Warren's time in command had become unpopular in Britain because of the failure of several single-ship actions in 1812, when three frigates, the *Macedonian*, *Java* and *Guerriere*, were defeated by the *United States* and *Constitution*. These were not the only single-ship defeats, and they caused shock and embarrassment to a British government and a public accustomed to naval success. A general feeling that the navy had become complacent was offset by the action between the British

frigate *Shannon* and the *Chesapeake* off Boston in June 1813, in which the accurate British fire created havoc on the American ship, causing it to strike its flag after only twelve minutes (see pp. 222–23). This turning of the tables was followed by several other successful British actions, before superior British numbers finally told. The Americans were powerless to stop a British raid on Washington, DC, during which ships in the navy yard and government buildings were burned, including the presidential mansion. The naval officer who had most claim on the success of this operation was Rear Admiral George Cockburn (see p. 225). The burning of Washington was a symbolic act, but the British would have done better to remain at sea, for they did not need to put troops ashore to

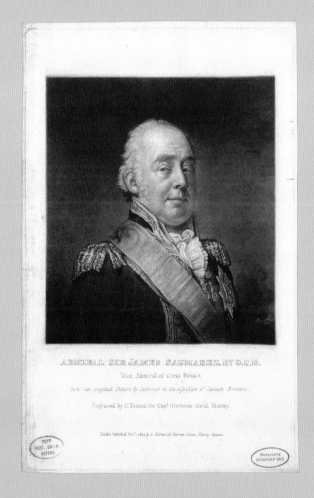

ADMIRAL SIR JAMES SAUMAREZ, BT G.C.B.

Vice-Admiral of Great Britain

From an original Picture by Carbonier in the possession of Captain Brenton

Engraved by C. Turner for Capt Brenton's Naval History.

London, Published Nov. 1 1823 by C. Turner 50 Warren Street, Fitzroy Square.

*The Brilliant Achievement of the Shannon Frigate, Captn. Broke in boarding and capturing the United States Frigate Chesapeake off Boston, June 1st 1813 in Fifteen Minutes*, by William Elmes, hand-coloured aquatint, August 1813 (PAH8127)

oblige the Americans to sue for peace: the defeat of a British force at New Orleans underlined this unnecessary strategy. It was an American victory that came too late to affect the Treaty of Ghent, which brought the war to an end on 24 December 1814. By then, thirty-two American warships, from sloops to large frigates, had been destroyed, captured or were blockaded in American ports. Over 1,400 American merchant vessels had been captured.[8]

Although Napoleon's power on the Continent had been weakened, he still fought on against allies that were beginning to act effectively together. In mid-October 1813, he was badly beaten in the 'Battle of the Nations' at Leipzig, and eventually accepted that France had run out of resources and the will to continue the struggle. He abdicated and was sent to Elba, landing on the island in May 1814. Nine months later, however, while the allies were

negotiating at Vienna, Napoleon escaped in a desperate gamble to recover power. He was soon in Paris at the head of a considerable army. The allied forces were dispersed and had to be rapidly reconstituted. Only a few thousand British troops were still on the Continent: garrisons were stripped of regular troops from all across the nation, including Ireland. The navy and the transport service did well in bringing soldiers at the rate of 10,000 a month to the Belgian coast, usually landing men and horses on a beach because of the lack of sufficient port facilities. The transports could hardly have done so well without twenty years of wartime experience. By the end of May, Wellington's forces numbered 36,000. In June, when operations started, his field force was 90,000 men including allies.[9] As in Portugal and Spain, the navy was there in case Wellington needed to retreat. In fact, after the decisive allied victory over Napoleon at the Battle of Waterloo in 1815, the ships only had to evacuate the wounded and French prisoners of war, of whom there were several thousand.

The ten years of war against Napoleonic France that followed Trafalgar were complex and gritty, requiring stamina and perseverance. Apart from the armed forces, large swathes of the civilian population were involved: shipbuilders, farmers, merchants, industrialists and, above all, taxpayers. With no large-scale actions, warfare did not favour dashing naval commanders. Those who had administrative ability and diplomatic skills succeeded, such as Collingwood and Saumarez, alongside the efforts of Lord Keith, who took years of heavy responsibility as commander-in-chief of the North Sea Fleet when the invasion threats were at their most alarming. Additionally, Gambier and Cotton performed solidly, while Sir John Borlase Warren deserves a better press for his actions in North America. Keats and Samuel Hood were the most promising of the more junior admirals, while Pellew and Cockburn demonstrated by their subsequent careers that they were more than dashing risk-takers. The showy egotists, such as Sir Home Popham or Thomas Cochrane, Lord Dundonald, made fools of themselves.

The Congress of Vienna in 1815 left an overwhelmingly dominant Royal Navy, a result that was not welcomed by the other nations of Europe, which would have preferred France to retain some power. Napoleon, however, by his extreme conduct, demonstrated that the only safe course for Europe was the complete destruction of his power, a process that allowed British influence and wealth to flourish and overwhelm all other nations.[10] So it came to be in 1815 that the British ended up with 50 per cent of world naval tonnage. It was the only time in the history of wooden navies that a single country possessed half the world's battle fleet.

ABOVE Rear Admiral Sir George Cockburn, by John James Halls, oil on canvas, c.1817 (BHC2619)
BELOW Gold chain said to have been given to a British sailor by Napoleon Bonaparte, c.1814 (JEW0210)

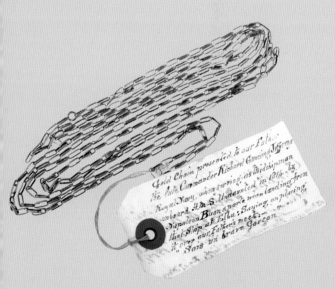

# THE *BELLEROPHON* IN PLYMOUTH SOUND IN 1815
JOHN JAMES CHALON, OIL ON CANVAS, 1816 (BHC3227)

## NAPOLEON BONAPARTE ON BOARD THE *BELLEROPHON* IN PLYMOUTH SOUND
SIR CHARLES LOCK EASTLAKE, OIL ON CANVAS, 1815 (BHC2876)

---

Complex circumstances after the Battle of Waterloo in mid-June 1815 led to the surrender of Napoleon to Captain Maitland of the *Bellerophon,* one of the many British warships off the French coast looking out for the defeated emperor. Negotiations between Napoleon and Maitland started on 10 July. Five days later, Napoleon boarded the *Bellerophon* under conditions that were later disputed, the emperor claiming that he was to be allowed to live in England, and that Maitland had given his word.

The ship anchored in Plymouth Sound on 24 July, throwing the responsibility for Napoleon's treatment and security on the shoulders of the seventy-year-old Admiral Lord Keith, commander-in-chief of the Channel Fleet. The cabinet decided that General Bonaparte (for the British government had never recognised his status as emperor) should be sent as a prisoner to St Helena. After Napoleon's dramatic escape from Elba earlier in the year, ministers wanted him out of the way. He was to be transported by the *Northumberland,* commanded by Rear Admiral Sir George Cockburn, and the provisioning and readying of this ship and her escorts began immediately and at top speed.

In the meantime, in Plymouth Sound, Napoleon quickly attracted attention. Between 5:00pm and 6:00pm every evening – when he walked the *Bellerophon*'s quarterdeck for fresh air – in launches, gigs and any vessel that could be hired, the public came to see the man who had kept Europe at war for over two decades. Lord Keith stationed guard-boats to keep people at least 300 yards away. No

one except the crew was allowed on the *Bellerophon* and security was tight, as can be seen from the close proximity of the marine sentry to Napoleon in Eastlake's portrait. Nevertheless, as Chalon's picture conveys, the sight of 'Boney' created great excitement. Keith wrote to his daughter: 'I wish he was sent away, for I am plagued to death; the women go near the ship and the guard boats have been desired to fire.'

On 2 August, the *Bellerophon* sailed without warning. An attempt had been made by Admiral Sir Alexander Cochrane to bring Napoleon before the Court of the King's Bench through a writ of *habeas corpus*, to appear as a witness in a libel case. The first lord of the Admiralty said of Cochrane that, 'the most charitable opinion which can be formed

respecting him is that his intellects are not altogether sound'. Had the writ been served on Lord Keith, legally Napoleon would have had to attend. The Admiralty ordered the *Bellerophon* to anchor off Start Point, twenty miles to the east, where the public in general, and the bailiff with the writ in particular, could not reach them. Two hundred years later it seems a comical episode, but it certainly worried the government then.

On 9 August 1815, the *Northumberland* sailed for St Helena. The Admiralty chose wisely in sending the tough Rear Admiral Cockburn to take the emperor and his retinue to exile. Cockburn was a fluent French speaker and stood no nonsense: even in captivity Napoleon was a formidable character. After a passage of sixty-seven days he reached his final destination

# AUTHOR BIOGRAPHIES

DR QUINTIN COLVILLE is Curator of Naval History at the National Maritime Museum, London. After studying Modern History at Magdalen College, Oxford, he completed his MA and PhD at the V&A and the Royal College of Art. He has held research fellowships at the University of Oxford, the Institute of Historical Research and the National Maritime Museum, and lectureships at the universities of Kent and Warwick. His research was awarded the Julian Corbett Memorial Prize in Modern Naval History, and his article 'Jack Tar and the Gentleman Officer' received the Royal Historical Society's Alexander Prize. He is lead curator of the NMM's 'Nelson, Navy, Nation' gallery.

DR MARIANNE CZISNIK studied law in Germany and practised environmental administration in the state of Brandenburg. She then researched Nelson's life, image and iconography at the University of Edinburgh, where she was awarded her PhD. A leading Nelson scholar, she has published on a wide range of subjects related to Nelson. Her book *Horatio Nelson: A Controversial Hero* was published in 2005. She is currently head of finance of the State Office of Environment, Health and Consumer Protection of Brandenburg, but also continues researching Nelson. She is preparing an edition of his letters to Lady Hamilton for the Navy Records Society.

DR JAMES DAVEY is Curator of Naval History at the National Maritime Museum, London, and a Visiting Lecturer at the University of Greenwich. After completing his PhD he held a Caird Research Fellowship before joining the curatorial team at the NMM, where he is co-curator of the 'Nelson, Navy, Nation' gallery. He is the author of *The Transformation of British Naval Strategy: Seapower and Supply in Northern Europe, 1808–1812* (2012) and co-author, with Richard Johns, of *Broadsides: Caricature and the Navy, 1756–1815* (2012). James is a Reviews Editor of the *Journal for Maritime Research* and a Council member of the Society for Nautical Research.

ROGER KNIGHT spent most of his career in the National Maritime Museum, starting as Deputy Custodian of Manuscripts in 1974 and leaving as Deputy Director in 2000. He then taught at the Greenwich Maritime Institute, University of Greenwich, as Visiting Professor of Naval History. In 2005 he published *The Pursuit of Victory: The Life and Achievement of Horatio Nelson.* He has written numerous books and articles on eighteenth-century naval politics and administration, the last being a study of victualling (with Martin Wilcox), *Sustaining the Fleet, 1793–1815: War, the Navy and the Contractor State* (2010). His latest book is *Britain against Napoleon: The Organization of Victory, 1793–1815* (2013).

ANDREW LAMBERT is Laughton Professor of Naval History in the Department of War Studies at King's College, London. He is a Fellow of the Royal Historical Society and Director of the Laughton Naval History Unit in the War Studies Department. His books include: *The Crimean War: British Grand Strategy against Russia, 1853–1856* (1991); *The Last Sailing Battlefleet: Maintaining Naval Mastery, 1815–1850* (1991); *'The Foundations of Naval History': Sir John Laughton, the Royal Navy and the Historical Profession* (1997); *Nelson: Britannia's God of War* (2005); *Franklin: Tragic Hero of Polar Navigation* (2009); and *The Challenge: Britain against America in the Naval War of 1812* (2012).

BRIAN LAVERY has written more than thirty books, mainly on maritime history, including *Ship of the Line* (1983) and *Nelson's Navy* (1989). He is Curator Emeritus at the National Maritime Museum, and served for more than twenty years on the advisory committee of HMS *Victory*. He was historical adviser for the film *Master and Commander*, and the BBC series *Empire of the Seas*. He has sailed in many vessels, from a dinghy to a square-rigger, and lectures regularly on cruise ships. Recent works include a three-volume history of the lower deck of the Royal Navy, and a manual for the SS *Great Britain* in Bristol.

DR MARGARETTE LINCOLN is Deputy Director and Director of Research and Collections at the National Maritime Museum in London. She has published widely in eighteenth-century studies. Her books include *Representing the Navy: British Sea Power, 1750–1815* (2002), *Naval Wives and Mistresses, 1745–1815* (2007), and the catalogue for the Museum's special exhibition, *Nelson & Napoléon*, edited in 2005. She is currently working on British pirates and the media, 1680–1730.

DR ROLAND PIETSCH MA (TU Berlin), PhD (Queen Mary, University of London) is the author of *The Real Jim Hawkins: Ships' Boys in the Georgian Navy* (2010), and currently holds a Caird Fellowship at the National Maritime Museum to explore the connection between masculine ideals and mental health among sailors in Nelson's time. Next to his academic pursuits he has, like a roving sailor, tried his hand at various other professions, from being a historian for television documentaries, to running a music venue in London. He recently returned to his hometown to take up a position at New York University (NYU), Berlin.

NICHOLAS RODGER was educated at University College, Oxford. Following seventeen years as Assistant Keeper in the Public Record Office, he became the Anderson Senior Research Fellow of the National Maritime Museum, and subsequently Professor of Naval History at Exeter University. He is a Senior Research Fellow of All Souls College, Oxford, and a Fellow of the British Academy, and has won the Duke of Westminster's Medal for Military Literature, the British Academy Book Prize, and the

Hattendorf Prize for Naval History. His many publications include *The Safeguard of the Sea: A Naval History of Britain, 660-1649* (1997), and *The Command of the Ocean: A Naval History of Britain, 1649-1815* (2004).

DAN SNOW is a historian, broadcaster and author. He has a particular interest in the eighteenth century, and his book *Death or Victory: The Battle of Quebec and the Birth of Empire* (2009) focused on the fall of Quebec in 1759. The same year he made *Empire of the Seas* for the BBC, a series charting the rise of British naval hegemony from the late sixteenth to the early twentieth century. He is also the co-author of *Battlefield Britain: From Boudicca to the Battle of Britain* (2004); *Twentieth-Century Battlefields* (2008); and *The Confusion of Command: The Memoirs of Lieutenant-General Sir Thomas D'Oyly 'Snowball' Snow, 1914-1918* (2011).

DR TED VALLANCE is Reader in Early Modern History at the University of Roehampton, and has previously taught at the universities of Sheffield, Manchester and Liverpool. He is the author of *A Radical History of Britain: Visionaries, Rebels and Revolutionaries – The Men and Women Who Fought for Our Freedoms* (2009); *The Glorious Revolution: 1688, Britain's Fight for Liberty* (2006); and *Revolutionary England and the National Covenant: State Oaths, Protestantism and the Political Nation, 1553-1682* (2005). With Harald Braun he has edited two volumes on conscience and casuistry in early modern Europe: *Contexts of Conscience in the Early Modern World: 1500-1800* (2004), and *The Renaissance Conscience* (2011).

KATHLEEN WILSON is Professor of History and Cultural Analysis and Theory at the State University of New York, Stony Brook. She publishes on British culture and empire, including: *The Sense of the People: Politics, Culture and Imperialism in England, 1715-1785* (1995); *The Island Race: Englishness, Empire and Gender in the Eighteenth Century* (2003); and *A New Imperial History: Culture, Identity and Modernity in Britain and the Empire, 1660-1840* (2004). She is currently finishing a book entitled *Strolling Players of Empire: Theatre, Culture and Modernity in the English Provinces*, and her next project will be *Admirals as Heroes: Naval and Military Adventuring and the Making of British Masculinity from Drake to Nelson*.

# NOTES

**INTRODUCTION: N.A.M. RODGER**

1 N.A.M. Rodger, 'Queen Elizabeth and the Myth of Sea-power in English History', in *Transactions of the Royal Historical Society*, sixth series, vol. 14 (2004), pp. 153-74.

2 Philip Woodfine, 'The Anglo-Spanish War of 1739', in Jeremy Black (ed.), *The Origins of War in Early Modern Europe* (Edinburgh, 1987), pp. 185-86.

3 Philip Woodfine, *Britannia's Glories: The Walpole Ministry and the 1739 War with Spain* (Woodbridge, 1998), quoting at p. 235 the diplomat Sir Everard Fawkener; Philip Woodfine, 'Ideas of Naval Power and the Conflict with Spain, 1737-1742', in Jeremy Black and Philip Woodfine (eds), *The British Navy and the Use of Naval Power in the Eighteenth Century* (Leicester, 1988), pp. 71-90.

4 Nicholas Rogers, *Crowds, Culture and Politics* (Oxford, 1998), pp. 122-51; Kathleen Wilson, *The Sense of the People: Politics, Culture and Imperialism in England, 1715-1785* (Cambridge, 1995), pp. 256-58.

5 Quoted by Margarette Lincoln, *Representing the Royal Navy: British Sea Power, 1750-1815* (Aldershot, 2002), p. 99.

6 John Ehrman, *The Younger Pitt: The Years of Acclaim* (London, 1969), p. 313.

7 Alison Yarrington, *The Commemoration of the Hero, 1800-1864: Monuments to the British Victors of the Napoleonic Wars* (London, 1988), p. 7; Holger Hoock (ed.), *History, Commemoration, and National Preoccupation: Trafalgar, 1805-2005* (Oxford, 2007); Lynda Pratt, 'Naval Contemplation: Poetry, Patriotism and the Navy 1797-1799', in *Journal for Maritime Research* (December 2000), p. 4.

8 Pratt, 'Naval Contemplation'.

9 Charles Robinson, *The British Tar in Fact and Fiction* (London, 1911), p. 274, quoting a correspondent to *The Connoisseur* in 1755.

10 F. McKno. Bladon (ed.), *The Diaries of Colonel the Hon. Robert Fulke Greville, Equerry to His Majesty King George III* (London, 1930), p. 40.

11 Sir Nicholas Harris Nicolas (ed.), *The Dispatches and Letters of Vice Admiral Lord Viscount Nelson* (London, 1844-46, 7 vols), vol. 7, Nelson to Charles Connor, 1803 addenda p. ccxiv.

12 Michael Lewis, *A Social History of the Navy, 1793-1815* (London, 1960), p. 44; N.A.M. Rodger, *The Wooden World: An Anatomy of the Georgian Navy* (London, 1986), p. 272; Sir John Ross, *Memoirs and Correspondence of Admiral Lord de Saumarez* (London, 1838, 2 vols), vol. 2, p. 72.

13 Nicolas, *Dispatches and Letters of Vice Admiral Lord Viscount Nelson*, vol. 1, to the Admiralty, 21 September 1787, p. 257.

14 Nina Kynynmound, Countess of Minto, *Life and Letters of Sir Gilbert Elliot, First Earl of Minto* (London, 1874, 3 vols), vol. 2, p. 235.

15 Matthew Anderson, *War and Society in Europe of the Old Regime, 1618–1789* (Leicester, 1988), p. 202.

16 Jeremiah R. Dancy, 'British Naval Manpower during the French Revolutionary Wars, 1793–1802' (Oxford D.Phil. thesis, 2012).


## CHAPTER 1: EDWARD VALLANCE

1 George Savile Halifax, *A Rough Draft of a New Model at Sea* (London, 1694), pp. 4–5; N.A.M. Rodger, 'The Military Revolution at Sea', in his *Essays in Naval History, from Medieval to Modern* (reprinted papers, Farnham, 2009), chpt. 5, pp. 62–63.

2 Jonathan Israel, *The Dutch Republic, its Rise, Greatness and Fall, 1477–1806* (Oxford, 1995), p. 849.

3 N.A.M. Rodger, *The Command of the Ocean: A Naval History of Britain, 1649–1815* (London, 2004), p. 138.

4 Edward Vallance, *The Glorious Revolution: 1688, Britain's Fight for Liberty* (London, 2006), p. 125.

5 Rodger, *Command of the Ocean*, p. 150.

6 Edward Powely, *The Naval Side of King William's War* (London, 1972), p. 141.

7 Steven Pincus, *1688: The First Modern Revolution* (New Haven, 2009), p. 275.

8 Rodger, *Command of the Ocean*, p. 147.

9 Rodger, 'Form and Function in European Navies, 1660–1815', in his *Essays in Naval History*, chpt. 13, p. 11.

10 W.T. Morgan, 'The British West Indies during King William's War, 1689–1697', in *The Journal of Modern History*, vol. 2, (1930), p. 394.

11 Morgan, 'The British West Indies', p. 381.

12 See John Ehrman, 'William III and the Emergence of a Mediterranean Naval Policy, 1692–1694', in *Cambridge Historical Journal*, vol. 9, (1949), pp. 269–92.

13 Morgan, 'The British West Indies', p. 406.

14 Ehrman, 'William III', p. 282.

15 Following the argument of Robert D. McJimsey, 'A Country Divided? English Politics and the Nine Years' War', in *Albion*, vol. 23 (1991), pp. 61–74.


## CHAPTER 2: KATHLEEN WILSON

1 Jonathan Scott, *When the Waves Ruled Britannia: Geography and Political Identities, 1500–1800* (Cambridge, 2011); J.G.A. Pocock, *Virtue, Commerce and History* (Cambridge, 1983); Wilson, *The Sense of the People*.

2 *The Craftsman*, quoted in *London Evening Post*, 17–18 August 1738.

3 Bryan McLean Ranft, *The Vernon Papers* (London, 1958), p. 194.

4 *Gentleman's Magazine*, vol. 10 (1740), March, April and November; vol. 11 (1741), May and November; *London Evening Post*, 13–15 November 1740; *Salisbury Journal*, 18 November 1740; for further documentation, see Wilson, *The Sense of the People*, pp. 137–65.

5 At this election the parliamentary opposition made an electoral recovery in the large boroughs, a significant improvement on their performance in 1734.

6 *Newcastle Courant*, 2 May 1741.

7 *The Champion*, 17 February 1739.

8 Timothy Breen, *The Marketplace of Revolution: How Consumer Politics Shaped American Independence* (New York, 2004), p. 15.

9 National Maritime Museum (NMM), Vernon Papers, VER1/4, 26 March, 11 April 1746.


## CHAPTER 3: BRIAN LAVERY

1 It is very difficult to establish exactly how much was spent. N.A.M. Rodger explains some of the difficulties with eighteenth-century finance in *The Insatiable Earl: A Life of John Montagu, 4th Earl of Sandwich* (London, 1993), pp. 134–35.

2 Roger Morriss, *The Royal Dockyards during the Revolutionary and Napoleonic Wars* (Leicester, 1983), p. 14.

3 Morriss, *Royal Dockyards*, p. 16.

4 Morriss, *Royal Dockyards*, p. 109.

5 James Stanier Clarke (ed.), *The Naval Chronicle*, vol. 32 (July to December 1814) (Cambridge, 2010), pp. 110–11.

6 The National Archives (TNA), ADM 106/1163/364.

7 NMM, SAN/V/5, dockyard visitations.

8 Nicolas, *Dispatches and Letters of Vice Admiral Lord Viscount Nelson*, vol. 1, p. 4.

9 Edmund Bushnell, *The Compleat Ship-Wright* (London, 1664).

10 Mary Lacy, *The Female Shipwright* (Greenwich, 2008), p. 81.

11 Lacy, *Shipwright*, p. 151.

12 Daniel Baugh (ed.), *Naval Administration, 1715–1750* (London, 1977), pp. 300–02.

13 TNA, ADM354/177/21.


## CHAPTER 4: QUINTIN COLVILLE

1 Vincent McInerey (ed.), *Landsman Hay: The Memoirs of Robert Hay* (Barnsley, 2010), p. 170.

2 I am indebted for this information to Dancy, 'British Naval Manpower'.

3 William Spavens, *The Narrative of William Spavens, a Chatham Pensioner* (London, 1998; first published 1796), p. 1.

4 Samuel Leech, *A Voice from the Main Deck: Being a Record of the Thirty Years Adventures of Samuel Leech* (London, 1999) p. 10.

5 John Nicol, *The Life and Adventures of John Nicol, Mariner* (London, 1822), p. 7.

6 William Lovett, *The Life and Struggles of William Lovett in his Pursuit of Bread, Knowledge and Freedom* (London, 1876), pp. 2–3.

7 Quoted in Brian Lavery, *Royal Tars: The Lower Deck of the Royal Navy, 875–1850* (London, 2010), p. 149.

8 Rodger, *The Wooden World*, p. 256.

9 Hay, *Landsman Hay*, pp. 52–53.

10 NMM, JON/11, 'Account of the heights, ages, country and trades of the crew of HMS *Caledonia*', 1811.

11 Joseph Tanner (ed.), *Samuel Pepys's Naval Minutes* (London, 1926), p. 250.

12 Daniel Goodall, *Salt Water Sketches; Being Incidents in the Life of Daniel Goodall* (Inverness, 1860), pp. 25–26.


**CHAPTER 5: DAN SNOW**

1 Historical Manuscripts Commission *Various*, vol. 6, to G.B. Doddington, 16 March 1757, pp. 38–39.

2 Peter Padfield, *Maritime Supremacy and the Opening of the Western Mind: Naval Campaigns that Shaped the Modern World, 1588–1782* (London, 2003), p. 199.

3 Richard Middleton, *The Bells of Victory: The Pitt-Newcastle Ministry and the Conduct of the Seven Years' War, 1757–1762* (Cambridge, 1985), pp. 109–10.

4 Peter Kemp (ed.), 'Boscawen's letters to his wife, 1755–56', in Christopher Lloyd (ed.), *Naval Miscellany* (London, 1953), vol. 4, p. 248.

5 Richard Middleton, 'British Naval Strategy, 1755–1762: The Western Squadron' in *Mariner's Mirror*, vol. 75, no. 4 (November 1989), p. 350.

6 TNA, CO5/51, Townshend to Pitt, 18 September 1759.

7 Middleton, *Bells of Victory*, p. 121.

8 *Memoirs of the Siege of Quebec...from the Journal of a French officer* (London, 1761), pp. 3–4, Richard Gardiner to George Hobart, 18 February 1761.

9 Michael Duffy, 'The Foundations of British Naval Power', in Duffy (ed.), *The Military Revolution of the State, 1500–1800* (Exeter, 1980), pp. 49–85.


**CHAPTER 6: MARGARETTE LINCOLN**

1 *The Citizen*, 21 September 1756, in *A Collection of Several Pamphlets, very little known...relative to the Case of Admiral Byng* (London, 1756), p. 42.

2 See Margarette Lincoln, 'Naval Ship Launches as Public Spectacle, 1773–1854', in *Mariner's Mirror*, vol. 83, no. 4 (November, 1997), pp. 466–72.

3 *Morning Chronicle*, 16 January 1798, quoted by Timothy Jenks, *Naval Engagements: Patriotism, Cultural Politics and the Royal Navy, 1793–1815* (Oxford, 2006), p. 129.

4 Charles Fletcher, *The Naval Guardian* (London, 1805), p. 157.

5 Samuel Leech, *Thirty Years from Home, or A Voice from the Main Deck* (Boston, 1843), p. 73.

6 Thomas Dibdin, *Songs by Charles Dibdin* (London, 1881), p. xxviii.

7 Terence Lockett and Pat Halfpenny (eds), *Creamware & Pearlware* (Stoke-on-Trent, 1986), p. 22.

8 Linda Colley, *Britons: Forging the Nation, 1707–1837* (New Haven, 1992), especially pp. 86–87; Kathleen Wilson, '"Empire of Virtue": The Imperial Project and Hanoverian Culture, *c.* 1720–1785', in Lawrence Stone (ed.), *An Imperial State at War: Britain from 1689 to 1815* (London, 1993), pp. 128–64.

9 David Hancock, *Citizens of the World: London Merchants and the Integration of the British Atlantic Community, 1735–1785* (Cambridge, 1995), pp. 354, 357.

10 Thomas Trotter, *A Practicable Plan for Manning the Royal Navy and Preserving our Maritime Ascendancy without Impressment* (Newcastle, 1819), pp. viii, 30.


**CHAPTER 7: JAMES DAVEY**

1 Jane Austen, *Northanger Abbey* (Oxford, 2003), p. 145.

2 Anon, *Objections to the War Examined and Refuted by a Friend of Peace* (London, 1793), p. 3.

3 Jane Henrietta Adeane (ed.), *The Girlhood of Maria Josepha Holroyd (Lady Stanley of Alderley). Recorded in Letters of a Hundred Years Ago: from 1776 to 1796* (London, 1896), Maria Josepha Holroyd Stanley to Ann Firth, 18 February 1794, p. 399.

4 N.A.M. Rodger, 'Mutiny or Subversion? Spithead and the Nore', in Thomas Bartlett *et al.* (eds), *1798: A Bicentenary Perspective* (Dublin, 2003), pp. 551–52; NMM, MKH/15, 'An Address to Alexander Hood, Esq. and his Officers Commanding on Board HMS *Mars*', 25 June 1797.

5 Suffolk Record Office (SRO), SA3/1/2/1, Martha Saumarez to Sir James Saumarez, 18 May 1797.

6 *Memoirs of Richard Parker, The Mutineer; Together With...A Narrative of the Mutiny at The Nore and Sheerness From its Commencement to Its Final Termination* (London, 1797), p. 15.

7 NMM, Markham Archive, 'Court Martial of George Shave'.

8 *Letters from Mrs Elizabeth Carter to Mrs Montagu Between the Years 1755 and 1800 Chiefly on Literary and Moral Subjects*, vol. 3 (London, 1817), Elizabeth Carter to Elizabeth Robinson Montagu, 23 June 1797, p. 358.

9 *An Account of the Present English Conspiracy...* (London, 1798).

10 NMM, AGC/24/5, Sir Charles Grey to Dundas, 25 June 1797.

11 NMM, PRV/49/5, Admiralty to Captain Purvis, 7 July 1797.

12 *The Star*, 10 February 1798; *True Briton*, 12 February 1798.

13 *Correspondence de Napoléon Premier* (Paris, 1858–69, 32 vols), vol. 11, p. 514.

14 Leslie Mitchell, *Charles James Fox* (Oxford, 1992), p. 205; *The British Gazette and Sunday Monitor*, 9 October 1803; *Lloyd's Evening Post*, 22–24 February 1804; *The British Gazette and Sunday Monitor*, 31 July 1803.

15 SRO, SA3/1/2/1, Martha Saumarez to Sir James Saumarez, 14 February 1798.

## CHAPTER 8: ANDREW LAMBERT

1 TNA, ADM51/4514, part 3, the *Victory* log-book, 21 October 1805.
2 Translation taken from Beatrice Heuser, *Reading Clausewitz* (London, 2002), p. 72.
3 Carl von Clausewitz, *On War* (New Jersey, 1984), p. 100.
4 I am indebted to my friend Professor Heuser's discussion of this subject in her *Reading Clausewitz*, pp. 72–74.
5 Clausewitz, *On War*, p. 112.
6 Edward Hughes (ed.), *The Private Correspondence of Admiral Lord Collingwood* (London, 1957), Collingwood to Dr Carlyle, 24 August 1801, p. 130; Nicolas, *Dispatches and Letters of Vice Admiral Lord Viscount Nelson*, vol. 7, Collingwood to Pasley, 16 December 1805, p. 241.


## CHAPTER 9: ROLAND PIETSCH

1 Charles Pemberton, *The Autobiography of Pel. Verjuice* (London, 1929), p. 202.
2 Leech, *Main Deck*, p. 76.
3 James Lind, *An Essay on the Most Effectual Means of Preserving the Health of Seamen in the Royal Navy* (London, 1757), p. xvii.
4 Quoted in Peter Warwick (ed.), *Voices from the Battle of Trafalgar* (Newton Abbot, 2005), pp. 116–18.
5 Pemberton, *Pel. Verjuice*, pp. 39, 219.
6 Olaudah Equiano, *The Interesting Narrative of the Life of Olaudah Equiano* (Boston, 1791; reprinted 1995), pp. 76–77.
7 Letter in Augustus Phillimore, *The Last of Nelson's Captains* (London, 1891), p. 34.
8 Taken from Warwick, *Voices*, pp. 168–69.
9 Leech, *Main Deck*, pp. 73–74.
10 Leech, *Main Deck*, pp. 81–82.
11 Gilbert Blane, 'Statements of the Comparative Health of the British Navy, from the Year 1779 to the Year 1814, with Proposals for its Farther Improvement', in *Medico-Chirurgical Transactions*, vol. 6 (1815), pp. 564–65.
12 Thomas Trotter, *Medicina Nautica: an essay on the diseases of seamen, comprehending the history of health in His Majesty's fleet under the command of Richard Earl Howe* (London, 1797), p. 38.
13 Warwick, *Voices*, p. 109.


## CHAPTER 10: MARIANNE CZISNIK

1 *The Times*, 29 November 1797.
2 See Marianne Czisnik, 'Nelson and the Nile: The Creation of Admiral Nelson's Public Image', in *Mariner's Mirror*, vol. 88 (February 2002), pp. 41–60; Czisnik, 'Nelson at Naples: A Review of Events and Arguments', in *Trafalgar Chronicle*, vol. 12 (2002), pp. 84–121.
3 Gitta Deutsch and Rudolf Klein, *Otto Erich Deutsch, Admiral Nelson und Joseph Haydn. Ein britisch-österreichisches Gipfeltreffen* (Vienna, 1982), pp. 78, 81; *The Morning Chronicle*, 8 November 1800; James Stanier Clarke (ed.), *The Naval Chronicle*, vol. 4 (July to December 1800) (Cambridge, 2010), pp. 429–30.
4 *Berrow's Worcester Journal*, 2 September 1802.
5 *The Times*, 20 August 1805.
6 *The Times*, 7, 9 and 14 November 1805; *Naval Chronicle*, vol. 14 (July to December 1805), p. 386.
7 Lily Lambert McCarthy, *Remembering Nelson* (Portsmouth, 1995), pp. xix, 89, 95.
8 *Bell's Weekly Messenger*, 1 December 1805; *The Times*, 13 December 1805, quoted in Timothy Jenks, 'Contesting the Hero: The Funeral of Admiral Lord Nelson', in *Journal of British Studies*, vol. 39 (2000), p. 436.
9 *The Times*, 6 and 7 January 1806; *Naval Chronicle*, vol. 15 (January to July 1806), pp. 49–50, 52.
10 *Gentleman's Magazine*, vol. 76 (1806), p. 66, quoted in Richard Davey, *A History of Mourning* (London, no date), p. 75.
11 Joshua White, *Memoirs of the Professional Life of the late Most Noble Lord Horatio Nelson* (London, 1806), supplement pp. 39–40.
12 Castalia, Countess Granville (ed.), *Lord Granville Leveson Gower (First Earl Granville). Private Correspondence, 1781–1821* (London, 1916), vol. 2, p. 155.
13 Quoted in Davey, *Mourning*, p. 77.
14 *Naval Chronicle*, vol. 15, p. 225; White, *Professional Life*, supplement p. 65.


## CHAPTER 11: ROGER KNIGHT

1 Jan Glete, *Navies and Nations: Warships, Navies, and State Building in Europe and America, 1500–1860* (Stockholm, 1993), vol. 1, p. 378.
2 Rif Winfield, *British Warships in the Age of Sail, 1793–1817* (London, 2005), pp. xiv, 291.
3 Rodger, *Command of the Ocean*, p. 558.
4 Silvia Marzagalli, 'Napoleon's Continental Blockade: An Effective Substitute to Naval Weakness?', in Bruce A. Elleman and Sarah Paine (eds), *Naval Blockades and Seapower: Strategies and Counter-Strategies, 1805–2005* (London, 2006), pp. 32–33.
5 Richard Woodman, *The Victory of Seapower: Winning the Napoleonic War, 1806–1814* (London, 1998), p. 58.
6 Paul Krajeski, *In the Shadow of Nelson: The Naval Leadership of Admiral Sir Charles Cotton, 1753–1812* (Westport, Connecticut, 2000), p. 183, quoting British Library, Add. Mss. 38246, Liverpool Papers, 3 October 1811.
7 Tim Voelcker, *Admiral Saumarez versus Napoleon: The Baltic, 1807–1812* (Woodbridge, 2008), pp. 155–76.
8 Brian Arthur, *How Britain Won the War of 1812: The Royal Navy's Blockades of the United States, 1812–1815* (Woodbridge, 2011), pp. 106, 199, 221–26.
9 Rory Muir, *Britain and the Defeat of Napoleon, 1807–1815* (New Haven, 1996), p. 353.
10 Rodger, *Command of the Ocean*, p. 574.

# FURTHER READING

## Introduction

Stephen Conway, *The British Isles and the War of American Independence* (Oxford, 2000)

J.E. Cookson, *The British Armed Nation, 1793–1815* (Oxford, 1997)

Gerald Jordan and Nicholas Rogers, 'Admirals as Heroes: Patriotism and Liberty in Hanoverian England', *Journal of British Studies*, vol. 28 (1989)

Paul Langford, *Public Life and the Propertied Englishman 1689–1798* (Oxford, 1991)

Margarette Lincoln, *Representing the Royal Navy: British Sea Power, 1750–1815* (Aldershot, 2002)

Gerald Newman, *The Rise of English Nationalism: A Cultural History, 1740–1830* (London, 1987)

Nicholas Rogers, *Crowds, Culture and Politics in Georgian Britain* (Oxford, 1998)

Alison Yarrington, *The Commemoration of the Hero, 1800–1864: Monuments to the British Victors of the Napoleonic Wars* (London, 1988)

## Chapter 1: *Invasion and Threat*

John Ehrman, *The Navy in the War of William III, 1689–1697: Its State and Direction* (Cambridge, 1953)

Steven Pincus, *1688: The First Modern Revolution* (New Haven, 2009)

N.A.M. Rodger, *The Command of the Ocean: A Naval History of Britain, 1649–1815* (London, 2005)

Edward Vallance, *The Glorious Revolution: 1688, Britain's Fight for Liberty* (London, 2006)

## Chapter 2: *Patriotism, Trade and Empire*

Gerald Jordan and Nicholas Rogers, 'Admirals as Heroes: Patriotism and Liberty in Hanoverian England', *Journal of British Studies*, vol. 28, (1989)

Kathleen Wilson, 'Empire, Trade and Popular Politics in Mid-Hanoverian Britain: The Case of Admiral Vernon', *Past and Present*, no. 121 (November 1988)

Kathleen Wilson, *The Sense of the People: Politics, Culture and Imperialism in England, 1715–1785* (Cambridge, 1995)

## Chapter 3: *Dockyards and Industry*

Daniel Baugh (ed.), *Naval Administration, 1715–1750*, (London, 1977)

Jonathan Coad, *The Royal Dockyards, 1690–1850* (Aldershot, 1989)

Roger Knight (ed.), *Portsmouth Dockyard Papers, 1774–1783* (Portsmouth, 1987)

Mary Lacy, *The Female Shipwright* (republished Greenwich, 2008)

Roger Morriss, *The Royal Dockyards during the Revolutionary and Napoleonic Wars* (Leicester, 1983)

## Chapter 4: *Life Afloat*

Roy Adkins and Lesley Adkins, *Jack Tar: The Extraordinary Lives of Ordinary Seamen in Nelson's Navy* (London, 2009)

Brian Lavery, *Nelson's Navy: The Ships, Men and Organisation, 1793–1815* (London, 1989)

Brian Lavery, *Royal Tars: The Lower Deck of the Royal Navy, 875–1850* (London, 2010)

Janet Macdonald, *Feeding Nelson's Navy: The True Story of Food at Sea in the Georgian Era* (London, 2006)

N.A.M. Rodger, *The Wooden World: An Anatomy of the Georgian Navy* (London, 1996)

## Chapter 5: *Expansion and Victory*

Fred Anderson, *The Crucible of War: The Seven Years War in North America, 1754–1766* (New York, 2001)

Jeremy Black and Philip Woodfine (eds), *The British Navy and the Use of Naval Power in the Eighteenth Century* (Leicester, 1988)

R. Dull, *The French Navy and the Seven Years War* (Lincoln, 2005)

Richard Middleton, *The Bells of Victory: The Pitt-Newcastle Ministry and the Conduct of the Seven Years' War, 1757–1762* (Cambridge, 1985)

Peter Padfield, *Maritime Supremacy and the Opening of the Western Mind: Naval Campaigns that Shaped the Modern World, 1588–1782* (London, 1999)

## Chapter 6: *Naval Personnel in Popular Culture*

David Drakard, *Printed English Pottery: History and Humour in the Reign of George III, 1760–1820* (London, 1992)

Francis Haskell, *History and its Images. Art and the Interpretation of the Past* (London and New Haven, 1993)

Geoffrey L. Hudson (ed.), *British Military and Naval Medicine 1600–1830* (Amsterdam and New York, 2007)

Emma Vincent Macleod, *A War of Ideas: British Attitudes to the Wars Against Revolutionary France, 1792–1802* (Aldershot, 1998)

Alison Yarrington, *The Commemoration of the Hero: Monuments to the British Victors of the Napoleonic Wars* (New York, 1988)

## Chapter 7: *Mutiny and Insecurity*

Linda Colley, *Britons: Forging the Nation, 1707–1837* (London, 1992)

John Cookson, *The British Armed Nation: 1793–1815* (Oxford, 1997)

James Davey and Richard Johns, *Broadsides: Caricature and the Navy, 1756–1815* (London, 2012)

Mark Philp (ed.), *The French Revolution and British Popular*

*Politics* (Cambridge, 1991)

Mark Philp (ed.), *Resisting Napoleon: The British Response to the Threat of Invasion, 1797–1815* (Aldershot, 2006)

N.A.M. Rodger, 'Mutiny or subversion? Spithead and the Nore', in Thomas Bartlett (ed.), *1798: A Bicentenary Perspective* (Dublin, 2003)

**Chapter 8: *Nelson and Naval Warfare***

Linda Colley, *Britons: Forging the Nation, 1707–1837* (London, 1992)

Julian Corbett, *The Campaign of Trafalgar* (London, 1910)

Andrew Lambert, *Nelson: Britannia's God of War* (London, 2004)

Sir H.N. Nicolas, *The Dispatches and Letters of Vice-Admiral Lord Viscount* Nelson (London, 1844–46; reprinted 1998), 7 vols

M.D. Paley, *The Apocalyptic Sublime* (New Haven, 1986)

Colin White (ed.), *Nelson: the New Letters* (Woodbridge, 2005)

**Chapter 9: *The Experiences and Weapons of War***

William Gilkerson, *Boarders Away: With Steel – The Edged Weapons and Polearms of the Classical Age of Fighting Sail, 1626–1826* (Providence, 1991)

William Gilkerson, *Boarders Away II: With Fire – The Small Firearms and Combustibles of the Classical Age of Fighting Sail, 1626–1826* (Providence, 1993)

Samuel Leech, *A Voice from the Main Deck: Being the Record of the Thirty Years Adventures of Samuel Leech* (London, 1857)

Roland Pietsch, *The Real Jim Hawkins: Ships' Boys in the Georgian Navy* (Barnsley, 2010)

Liza Verity, *Naval Weapons* (Greenwich, 1992)

Peter Warwick (ed.), *Voices from the Battle of Trafalgar* (Newton Abbot, 2005)

**Chapter 10: *Nelson, Navy and National Identity***

Marianne Czisnik, 'Nelson and the Nile: The Creation of Admiral Nelson's Public Image', *Mariner's Mirror*, vol. 88 (February 2002)

L.P. Le Quesne, *Nelson Commemorated in Glass Pictures* (Woodbridge, 2001)

Margarette Lincoln (ed.), *Nelson & Napoléon* (London, 2005)

Lily Lambert McCarthy, *Remembering Nelson* (Portsmouth, 1995)

Richard Walker, *The Nelson Portraits: An Iconography of Horatio Viscount Nelson, K.B., Vice Admiral of the White* (Portsmouth, 1998)

Colin White (ed.), *The Nelson Companion* (Annapolis, 1995)

**Chapter 11: *Beyond Trafalgar***

Christopher D. Hall, *British Strategy in the Napoleonic War, 1803–1815* (Manchester, 1992)

Christopher D. Hall, *Wellington's Navy: Sea Power and the Peninsular War, 1807–1814* (London, 2004)

Kevin D. McCranie, *Admiral Lord Keith and the Naval War against Napoleon* (Florida, 2006)

Roger Morriss, *Cockburn and the British Navy in Transition: Admiral Sir George Cockburn, 1772–1853* (Exeter, 1997)

# ACKNOWLEDGEMENTS

Many debts of gratitude have been accrued in the process of writing and editing this book. We have been supported from the very beginning by Kevin Fewster, Margarette Lincoln and Nigel Rigby. The broader Museum team engaged with the accompanying gallery project have also been understanding when the publication took us away from other curatorial work: our thanks go to Lucinda Blaser, Hannah Kay, Anna Salaman and Megan Thomas. During both the writing and the proofing stages we have received assistance from many of our curatorial colleagues, but particular mention must go to Richard Johns, John McAleer, Rory McEvoy, Jeremy Michell, Amy Miller, Simon Stephens and Barbara Tomlinson for their help and advice.

Special thanks are owed to Robert Blyth, whose good humour and wisdom have been familiar and calming influences, and who commented on the book in its entirety. Similarly, we are most grateful to Pieter van der Merwe for his painstaking editorial work. In the Museum's Caird Library, Mike Bevan, Martin Salmon and Richard Wragg offered archival counsel on more than one occasion. In addition, many of the objects shown in this book have been newly photographed. The quality of the images is testament to the organisation of Will Punter, the dedicated work of Tina Warner and David Westwood, and the skills of many specialists within the Conservation Department. We also offer thanks to John Lee, our publisher at Conway, Karin Fremer, Georgina Hewitt and Christopher Westhorp. Lastly, we would like to single out two members of the Museum's commercial team without whom this book could not have been completed. Rebecca Nuotio's encouragement and guidance were invaluable from early discussions through to the completed publication. Kara Green's perseverance, eye for detail and mastery of schedule have at all points been exceptional.

# PICTURE CREDITS

# INDEX

Illustrations in *italics*

PREVIOUS INDEX PAGES: Panorama of the Battle of Trafalgar,
by William Heath, watercolour, *c.*1820 (PAJ3938)